SCEPTICISM AND
REASONABLE DOUBT

Scepticism and Reasonable Doubt

THE BRITISH NATURALIST TRADITION
IN WILKINS, HUME, REID
AND NEWMAN

M. JAMIE FERREIRA

CLARENDON PRESS · OXFORD
1986

Oxford University Press, Walton Street, Oxford OX2 6DP

Oxford New York Toronto
Delhi Bombay Calcutta Madras Karachi
Kuala Lumpur Singapore Hong Kong Tokyo
Nairobi Dar es Salaam Cape Town
Melbourne Auckland

and associated companies in
Beirut Berlin Ibadan Nicosia

Oxford is a trade mark of Oxford University Press

Published in the United States
by Oxford University Press, New York

British Library Cataloguing in Publication Data

Ferreira, M. Jamie
Scepticism and reasonable doubt: the
British naturalist tradition in Wilkins,
Hume, Reid and Newman.
1. Skepticism
I. Title
121'.5   BD201
ISBN 0-19-824912-8

Library of Congress Cataloging in Publication Data

Ferreira, M. Jamie.
Scepticism and reasonable doubt.
Bibliography: p.
Includes index.
1. Skepticism—Controversial literature—History.
2. Belief and doubt—History.   3. Naturalism—History.
4. Great Britain—Intellectual life.   I. Title.
II. Title: Skepticism and reasonable doubt.
B837.F47   1986   146'.0941   86-18023
ISBN 0-19-824912-8

Printed and bound in Great Britain by
Butler & Tanner Ltd
Frome and London

TO MY PARENTS

Preface

HISTORICALLY one of the ways in which people have attempted to counter scepticism has been by appeal to 'the make and temper of human nature', 'the laws of the mind', or 'the common voice of mankind'. These are all appeals to 'the natural'—to how we are constituted, to what we, as human beings, are and do in the arena of believing. My interest lies both in the variety of forms such responses to scepticism, which I will term 'naturalist' responses, can assume, and in the status of such responses. In this study I will focus on a variety of such responses to scepticism, offered in Britain between the seventeenth and nineteenth century. One is by David Hume (1711-76), often considered a paradigm sceptic—here I will be highlighting the 'naturalist' strand in his thought in terms of its potential challenge to scepticism. Although this strand has received increasing attention from Hume scholars, estimates of its status and implications vary considerably. The other responses I will consider are by three other British figures—the Protestant Bishop and founder of the Royal Society, John Wilkins (1614-72), the Protestant Common Sense philosopher Thomas Reid (1710-96), and the Roman Catholic John Henry Newman (1801-90).

The choice of Hume, Reid, and Newman for analysis in light of each other may seem surprising at first glance, and so deserves at least a brief justification. First, an attack on scepticism was an overriding concern of both Reid and Newman, with Hume and Locke as explicit targets. Although neither Reid nor Newman gave attention to the 'naturalist' elements in Hume's thought, the analysis of 'naturalist' elements in their work points the way to a reassessment of Hume and opens up the possibility of a continuity of 'naturalist' elements from the seventeenth century through Hume and Reid, to the Victorians who were influenced by them. Secondly, Reid's work (which has only relatively recently begun to receive some of the philosophical attention it deserves) was in his own day and for a great part of the nineteenth century widely accepted as a significant, perhaps even decisive, attempt to refute Hume; thus it constituted a crucial part of the intellectual inheritance on which

Victorian thinkers drew, and it could be expected that Newman's anti-sceptical proposals would be illuminated by reference to it. Thirdly, the historical connection between Reid and Newman can be documented: Newman studied Reid seriously and commented on him at length. Apart from this, however, the result of looking at them in light of each other is mutual illumination—Newman's queries and comments on Reid occasion new questions about Reid's account; focusing on issues and problems in Reid's account leads to asking new questions of Newman's proposal, which in turn leads to further useful comparative analyses of Reid's account. In particular, for example, the comparison with Newman leads one to examine more carefully Reid's thought on 'reasoning', and thus to complement what has become a one-sided preoccupation with Reid's views on 'first principles' and the intuitive faculty of 'common sense' which picks them out. It therefore facilitates an understanding of Reid's view of the relation between reasoning and 'common sense', and thus of the role of reasoning in his general response to scepticism.

The determination of the character and development of such 'naturalist' responses to scepticism will contribute to a broader appreciation of that segment of British intellectual history from the seventeenth through the nineteenth century. It will thereby correct misleading generalizations like the following made in a recent study of scepticism: 'After receiving short shrift from the philosophical community during the interval from David Hume to the present century, scepticism regained the focus of attention after World War II, when it found a series of important opponents.'[1] But my aim is constructive as well as historical, for I hope by analysis of a variety of appeals to 'the natural' to contribute as well to the continuing question of the implication of 'naturalist' replies to scepticism in general, as a philosophical issue in its own right.

[1] Nicholas Rescher, *Scepticism: A Critical Appraisal* (Totowa, NJ, 1980), pp. 5–6.

Acknowledgements

M Y foremost debt of gratitude is due to the American Council of Learned Societies for two grants: the first, a Fellowship for Recent Recipients of the Ph.D. (1979), allowed me to explore the potential for this project; the second, a Study Fellowship for 1983-4, allowed me to complete a rough draft, using resources in the United Kingdom, especially in Oxford. Among those resources were Basil Mitchell, John Kenyon, Peter Strawson, and Rom Harré; Tim Sutton and Ian Ker deserve very special thanks for hours and hours of sharing Reid and Newman, respectively. Basil Mitchell, D. D. Raphael, Cora Diamond, and George Mavrodes generously offered comments on versions of the manuscript.

I am grateful to Gerard Tracey, archivist of the Birmingham Oratory, for much patient help during the summer of 1981 and during a visit in 1984, not least of all for his indispensable aid in deciphering Newman's handwriting. Dorothy Johnston, of King's College Library, Aberdeen, kindly assisted me with the Birkwood Collection of Reid manuscripts in 1984. Charles Marsh provided patient hours of proof-reading and bibliographical assistance.

I want to acknowledge, finally, the kind permission of the editors of the following journals for allowing me to draw on materials initially published with them: *The Philosophical Quarterly* ('Hume's Naturalism: Proof and Practice', January 1985), and *The Journal of the History of Philosophy* ('Locke's Constructive Scepticism—A Reappraisal', April 1986).

Charlottesville, 1985

Contents

Contents

I

Proof and Practice

A. PROOF AND UNREASONABLE DOUBT

CONSIDERED by many to be a paradigm of intellectual ruthlessness and austerity, David Hume none the less twice challenged in print the severity of the dichotomy made in the century preceding him between 'knowledge' (or 'demonstration') and 'probability'. First with an abstract reference to philosophy,[1] and then later specifying Locke as the exponent of the inadequate dichotomy, he proposed as a corrective the intermediate category of 'proof'—namely, 'such arguments from experience as leave no room for doubt or opposition'.[2] Hume's suggestion is that Locke failed to recognize that category of 'proof' and consequently accepted a dichotomy which leads to conclusions which are, at the very least, at variance with common usage (a usage to which Hume himself adheres). Whether or not Hume was correct in attributing this failure to Locke, it is clear and important that Hume saw his reading of Locke as an unproblematic reading, one for which he need not argue. The category of 'proof', then—whatever its character and implications in Hume's account—is at the very least seen by him as a necessary corrective and not simply a repetition or reinforcement of a category commonly assumed in philosophical circles.

Hume's reading of Locke, however, becomes problematic in the light of well-documented analyses of a tradition of 'constructive scepticism' expressed and developed in the works of William Chillingworth, John Tillotson, John Wilkins, and Joseph Glanvill in the fifty years preceding Locke's *Essay*, in which the category of 'moral certainty'—constituted by the absence of 'reasonable' ground for doubt—provided a bridge between 'knowledge' and

---

[1] A Treatise of Human Nature, ed. L. A. Selby-Bigge (Oxford, 1978), p. 124.
[2] *Enquiries Concerning the Human Understanding and Concerning the Principles of Morals*, ed. L. A. Selby-Bigge (Oxford, 1975), p. 56 n.

'probability'.[3] Henry Van Leeuwen claims in his study, *The Problem of Certainty in English Thought, 1630-1690*, that Locke's view in the *Essay* should be seen as the 'culmination' of that fifty-year development—in particular, that the *Essay* provided a 'generalized' version and 'application' of the 'major themes' of those predecessors, and offered a doctrine which was in fact 'in its fundamental features identical with those of his predecessors [although] there are terminological differences'.[4] Van Leeuwen is not alone in that assessment, for his claim has been reiterated in the suggestion in a recent review of Locke's thought that 'it is plain that Locke belongs to this tradition of constructive scepticism'.[5] If these claims are correct, then Hume was simply wrong to think that Locke failed to do justice to the category of 'proof' he was proposing as a corrective, for Locke was the culmination of a tradition which was centrally concerned to provide just such a bridge-category— namely, 'moral certainty'—in which there was, as Hume phrased it, 'no room for doubt'.

Moreover, other later critics of Locke would also have been guilty of failing to give Locke sufficient credit on this and, consequently, on related matters. For this criticism of Locke as failing to appreciate the category of 'proof' was not confined to Hume, but was, I shall be arguing, implicit in the criticisms of Locke offered by figures following Hume—in particular, by Thomas Reid and John Henry Newman. In addition, the 'appeal to common sense' and 'the deep interest in the psychological aspects of knowledge' are themes which it has been suggested were 'undoubtedly inspired in large part by Locke's *Essay*'.[6] But these were some of the very issues which Locke was criticized as failing to do justice to by both Reid and Newman in their shared charge that Locke's account (contrary to his own stated intentions and self-understanding) depends on a priori speculation rather than an accurate *descriptive* appeal to human nature.

Such criticisms may simply have been misguided, the result of misunderstanding Locke. They could, however, have been instead (as I shall argue in Chapter 2 that they were) a recognition, more

[3] See the ground-breaking work done by Richard H. Popkin, particularly in *The History of Scepticism from Erasmus to Spinoza* (Berkeley, 1979), esp. pp. 1-171, and that done by his student Henry G. Van Leeuwen (see n. 4 below).

[4] The Hague, 1963, pp. 121, 124.

[5] R. S. Woolhouse, *Locke* (Brighton, Sussex, 1983), p. 14.

[6] Van Leeuwen, p. 142.

or less implicit, of elements in Locke's thought which support an understanding of him as departing in a significant way from (rather than culminating) the tradition preceding him, which emphasized a category of non-demonstrative or 'moral' certainty equal to that of demonstration. In other words, I shall argue that Locke can be seen as departing from the tradition of an anti-sceptical appeal to our human 'constitution', which was informed by a doctrine that only 'reasonable' doubt precluded certainty and that not all doubt that was 'possible' was thereby 'reasonable', in so far as he departs from its position on the philosophical status of such unreasonable doubt. These criticisms of Locke might effectively signal (as I will argue throughout this study that they do) the resumption of the tradition preceding Locke, which I call a 'naturalist' tradition because of its appeal to human nature, in which variations on the theme of 'reasonable doubt' and a category like that of 'proof' were central, and in which that category generated legitimate certainty. The theme of 'reasonable doubt' and the category of 'proof' are obvious ingredients in the seventeenth-century accounts and in Newman's, but I suggest that they were present, more or less explicitly and in varying degrees, in Hume and Reid as well. In other words, these criticisms of Locke, whether just or not, as alien to or unappreciative of concerns which were in fact the concerns of the 'naturalist' tradition preceding him, suggest what this study will document and analyse—namely, that in and through these critics this 'naturalist' anti-sceptical tradition was being taken up again and further developed.

Van Leeuwen's study of the responses to scepticism offered in the seventeenth century by Chillingworth, Tillotson, Wilkins, and Glanvill serves as a starting-point for my study in two ways. First, in so far as my study highlights the doctrine of reasonable doubt as an element in a 'naturalist' response to scepticism, it expresses agreement at a general level with many of his conclusions about the character of the tradition preceding Locke. In that sense I will begin where he leaves off, for he concludes his study by raising the question 'What became of it [the theory of certainty developed in England between 1630-90] in subsequent European and British thought'.[7] Though he gives enticing hints, referring in passing to Hume and the Scottish Common Sense response to Hume, it was

---

[7] Ibid., pp. 144-5.

beyond the scope of his project to explore that subsequent history—the present study can be seen as an attempt to answer his question at least in part.

His work, however, serves as a starting-point in an opposite way as well since I will, as noted above, be taking issue with at least part of his characterization of the response to scepticism preceding Locke, and, taking issue, therefore, with a conclusion he shares with others concerning Locke's relation to that earlier tradition. My analysis in Chapter 2 of one of the significant figures of that earlier tradition, John Wilkins, thus challenges in a crucial respect his monolithic characterization of that tradition. If there is warrant in Locke's thought for considering him a departure from, rather than a culmination of, a significant part of the tradition preceding him, this would help to explain how Locke could have been interpreted by those after him who witnessed (whether knowingly or not) to the earlier 'naturalist' tradition as alien to its overriding concerns. Such warrant provides ground for a revision of Hume as calling Locke back to an earlier tradition, and for seeing later critics of Locke, like Reid and Newman, as similarly harking back to that tradition.

Although Hume's intentions concerning the philosophical relevance of his references to 'the natural' are debatable, Reid clearly affirms a positive relation between 'the natural' and 'the justified' (or at least 'the not unjustified'). Newman shares this crucial affirmation with Reid. I will be contending in this study that (1) the doctrine of 'reasonable doubt' referred to earlier—namely, the doctrine that only 'reasonable' doubt precludes certainty, and that not all doubt that is 'possible' is thereby 'reasonable' in a given case— was a significant, although at times only implicit, ingredient in a continuing line of British 'naturalist' responses to scepticism from the seventeenth century to the nineteenth. I will be contending, moreover, that (2) such a doctrine is one way in which a 'naturalist' account might support a positive relation between 'natural' and 'justified' (or 'not unjustified') and thus go beyond merely a particular kind of 'practical' reply to the sceptic.

Throughout the study I will be attempting to clarify the character of the appeal to 'the natural' made in the three accounts by focusing on the following three themes: (*a*) 'proof' (as opposed to demonstration and probability), (*b*) practice (in terms of 'practical' certitude as well as the role of a 'practice'), and (*c*) the role and status of 'common sense'. These themes are leverage points, or points of entry, through which the salient aspects and various forms of such 'naturalism' can be picked out. Appeals to 'the natural' can in principle have two separate foci: first, beliefs which are immediate or non-inferential (e.g. intuitive truths); second, beliefs which are the conclusions of processes of reasoning. The distinction between reasoned and non-reasoned will therefore underlie the analysis of all three themes. The two foci, although separate, are related in the sense that analysis of the category of proof in reasoning, for example, can shed light on the character of the 'naturalist' response as a whole (including the understanding of the non-reasoned or immediate beliefs) since the understanding of proof in reasoning can be seen as a specification or application of an immediate or unreasoned first principle or of a more general position underlying first principles as such. By thus illustrating and analysing a variety of ways in which anti-sceptical accounts can appeal to 'the natural', this study can contribute to the broader question of the philosophical implications of 'naturalist' accounts in general.

B. NATURALISM, DESCRIPTION, AND PRACTICE

'Naturalist' accounts have generally been put under the rubric of 'descriptive', 'practical', or 'psychological' responses to scepticism—as opposed, for example, to what are termed 'cognitive', 'philosophical' or 'epistemological' responses. And the question whether an appeal to 'the natural' can succeed in offering more than an acceptance of the sceptic's critique mitigated by the counter-description of the unavoidability of the beliefs in question has thereby been answered in the negative. I suggest, however, that the question is not that easily settled—in part because the crucial terms 'practical' and 'descriptive' can cover a variety of claims which need to be distinguished.

The question of what can be achieved by a 'naturalist' account is raised by those who argue that an appeal to unavoidable instincts and beliefs does not address the sceptic's challenge at the relevant philosophical level. A 'naturalist' response, on this view, is tantamount to an acceptance of the sceptic's philosophical thesis, coupled with the counter-description of the necessity or unavoidability of the challenged beliefs. But such an interpretation of a 'naturalist' appeal trades on an important vagueness in the phrase 'acceptance of the sceptic's philosophical thesis'. I am not referring here to what is no doubt true—namely, that there are many varieties of scepticism, some more restricted than others.[8] Rather I am pointing out that a crucial element in any definition of a sceptic's 'philosophical thesis' is omitted if one simply stops with the claim that we do not have a particular kind of warrant for a particular kind of claim, since in itself this may merely indicate a sensitivity to differences in subject-matter, with no sceptical intent or implication. The thesis that matters of fact cannot be demonstrated is not necessarily a sceptical thesis. More importantly, even the thesis that there is no 'argument' at all justifying the beliefs in question (for example, external world, other minds, induction) is not necessarily as such a sceptical thesis either. What is distinctively sceptical about the sceptic's challenge is the claim that *because* there is no 'argument', something essential is lacking—something which should be there, is not there. It is not at all clear, without begging the question, whether an acceptance of the view that there is and can be no 'argument' for the relevant beliefs is an acceptance of the sceptic's 'philosophical thesis', since that view does not necessarily commit one either way on the question whether the lack of such argument is to be lamented in any way. To refuse to see the absence of argument as a lack is to fail to accept precisely what is sceptical about the sceptic's claims. Thus, the acceptance of the view that no 'argument' justifies the beliefs in question does not necessarily preclude an appeal to 'the natural' from offering a response to the sceptic in which the category of 'proof', for example, carries with it implications which critically comment on, and thereby mitigate, the sceptic's philosophical thesis.

The strictly 'practical' response to scepticism, therefore, is one which mitigates the sceptic's challenge *only* in the sense of offering, with bowed 'philosophical' head, a counter-description of the unavoidability of beliefs. The strictly 'practical' mitigation is the response: 'admittedly, no argument, therefore not just or certain or true, because not fulfilling a legitimate requirement—but nevertheless unavoidable'. It is crucial in any study of responses to scepticism, therefore, to determine whether a response is limited to the

---

[8] For a discussion of 'globality' and 'strength' as they are exemplified in the contemporary debate about scepticism, see 'Some Forms of Epistemological Scepticism', by George S. Pappas, in *Essays on Knowledge and Justification*, eds. George S. Pappas and Marshall Swain (Ithaca, NY, 1978), pp. 309-16.

practical in that way, and it is important to point out that much of interest is liable to be ignored by facile characterizations of responses as 'practical and psychological'.

Moreover, 'naturalist' accounts are underdetermined in principle in an important respect concerning the 'description' attributed to them—in other words, appeals to 'the natural' and 'description' can hide an important ambiguity. In one sense all such appeals can be located under the rubric 'what we, as human beings, are or do'. They can, that is, be considered appeals to 'description'. Appeals to description of what human beings are or do, however, can in principle support two very different models of response to the sceptic. Consider, for example, how Richard Rorty's suggestive reading of the history of philosophy illustrates this.[9] He offers a contrast between two models of knowing, and hence of response to the sceptic—a 'confrontation' model and a 'conversation' model. The 'confrontation' model uses an ocular paradigm and sees justification in terms of individual causal explanation. A wrong turn was taken in philosophy, Rorty claims, by Locke's use of this model which confuses 'explanation and justification'.[10] Justification is not, as Locke seemed to think, a function of causal psychological explanatory entities; rather, Rorty claims, it is based on linguistic relations between persons and propositions (or between propositions themselves) rather than on relations between persons and objects. The appropriate model of justification, therefore, is a 'conversation' model which sees justification in terms of socio-linguistic relations and placement in a 'logical space of reasons'.[11]

This contrast between individual causal explanation and socio-linguistic relations is obviously an important one. What is equally important, however, is that appeal to 'the natural' or to 'human nature' can, in principle, be understood in terms of either model. Conversely, both models are actually appeals to description of what we as human beings are or do. What is implied in Rorty's view is that only in the case of the 'conversation' model does description have a bearing on justification (i.e. since it is description of norms embedded in social relations). But precisely because both models are appeals to description of some sort, the traditional contrast between 'description' and 'prescription' is not adequate

---

[9] *Philosophy and the Mirror of Nature* (Princeton, 1979), esp. Pt. II.

[10] Ibid., pp. 139-48.

[11] Ibid., pp. 157, 141, and *passim* Pt. III.

for determining the status of a given naturalist account. The causal explanation/socio-linguistic relations distinction cuts across the 'descriptive/prescriptive' distinction because an appeal to human nature (or naturalist description) does not, as such, dictate on which side of the causal explanation/socio-linguistic relations contrast it falls.

Matters are even more complicated. On Rorty's view 'explanation' is equated with 'causal description' and both are contrasted with 'justification'. Others, however, would claim that the request for 'explanation' *and* 'justification' must be rejected—all that is left is something different, namely 'description'.[12] In other words, what some see as the appropriate locus of justification is seen by others as the realm of description *rather than* of justification. At the very least it should be clear that an appeal to description or rejection of description needs to be spelled out in each case by reference to its alternatives, if we are to determine whether differences between accounts are terminological or substantive. For both reasons, then, the usual contrasts between 'descriptive/prescriptive' and by extension, between 'psychological/philosophical' are not precise enough as they stand to be a useful tool for illuminating the status of a given anti-sceptical account.

One of the significant consequences of the influence of Locke's account was, I suggest, the historical neglect of accounts after his which used naturalist descriptive language, because the use of such language seemed automatically to imply that they belonged, like Locke's, in the causal explanation tradition of justification. This obscured the possibility of recognizing their distinctive contributions to the problem of the justification of belief. When discussing his philosophical task, Reid calls it, as we shall see, an 'anatomy of the human mind'. Newman, on the other hand, describes his comparable project as a 'grammar of assent'. Both, however, emphasize naturalist description as the appropriate corrective to previous inadequate accounts. It is important then to reconsider the anti-sceptical tradition after Locke to assess whether these 'naturalist' appeals to description were necessarily subject to the confusion attributed to Locke, or effectively distinguished between justification by causal explanation and justification by socio-linguistic relations, or offered yet another alternative. Consideration of the

---

[12] This, I take it, is the position, for example, of the later Wittgenstein.

focal points mentioned earlier—proof, practice, and common sense—will constitute the mechanism for answering that question.

It should be obvious, I think, that the presence (much more, the centrality) of a doctrine of 'reasonable doubt' in a given account, whether explicitly emphasized or not, will contour the ways in which causal explanation can be conceived by that account to be relevant to the sceptic's challenge. Such a doctrine will, moreover, contour the ways in which empirical generalizations about the socio-linguistic context are conceived by that account as relevant to the question of justification. To the extent then that such a doctrine figures in a given account, the character and implications of its 'naturalist' description will be affected.

The following chapter will initiate the examination of the naturalist tradition of anti-scepticism as it was developed after Locke by introducing a seventeenth-century form of 'constructive scepticism', analysing its position on doubt and certainty, and re-evaluating Locke's relation to it.

2

Unreasonable Doubt: The Seventeenth-Century Tradition—Wilkins and Locke

MEDIEVAL thinkers worked with a dichotomy between *scientia* (knowledge based on intuition and demonstration) and *opinio* (probability based on testimony). In the seventeenth century there developed, however, a new concept of probability based on 'internal evidence' or the statistical witness of the 'signs' of nature.[1] This new concept mediated the medieval dichotomy, establishing an epistemological continuum. At the same time in England, a response to scepticism was emerging, occasioned by theological disputes over 'the rule of faith'. In *The Problem of Certainty in British Thought, 1630–1690*, Van Leeuwen documents the development of this response to scepticism, at first theologically motivated but then secularized and assimilated by the Royal Society, in which a category of 'moral certainty' was constituted by the absence of 'reasonable' doubt.[2] This response has been termed 'constructive scepticism'— 'constructive' because it argues that we have 'sufficient' certainty for everyday needs or practical purposes, but 'scepticism' because it denies the dogmatism which seems to be the only alternative to conceding the sceptic's main point.[3] Such 'constructive sceptics' used the category of 'moral certainty' to forge a continuum between knowledge and probable belief. The two traditions—one bringing in the new concept of probability and the other arguing for 'moral certainty'—can be said to have coincided in particular individuals. One such individual was John Wilkins (1614–72), Bishop of Chester and a founding father of the Royal Society. In what follows I will concentrate on his response to scepticism, augmenting it with

[1] Ian Hacking, *The Emergence of Probability* (Cambridge, 1975), esp. Chaps. 2–5.
[2] The Hague, 1963.
[3] Popkin, *History of Scepticism*, esp. pp. 1–171.

reference to other seventeenth-century figures, and complementing it with a brief look at Locke's position.

The task of this chapter is twofold. First, by illustrating the claim that the category of 'unreasonable' doubt, in terms of which 'moral certainty' was understood, was the heart of a naturalist appeal which informed the constructive scepticism that developed in the seventeenth century, I hope to substantiate the further claim that such an appeal was a crucial element in the intellectual inheritance on which later anti-sceptical thinkers could—and did—draw.[4] In other words, despite developments which deflected attention from it, a consensus on several critical issues bequeathed both an intellectual agenda and a framework of response (in terms of both rationale and examples) to later generations. Secondly, I will re-evaluate the claim made by Van Leeuwen and others that Locke was the 'culmination' of or 'clearly belongs to' this seventeenth-century tradition of constructive scepticism preceding him. At the very least Van Leeuwen's claim that in spite of 'terminological' differences Locke's view in the *Essay* was 'in its fundamental features identical with those of his predecessors', appealing like them to 'the certainty of ordinary life and the doctrine of levels of certainty',[5] needs qualification. In particular, claims about '*the*' seventeenth-century tradition of constructive scepticism need to be qualified in the light of possible differences within that tradition itself. I will be arguing that putatively terminological differences signal substantive differences between Locke's position and at least one major representative of the tradition preceding him—in other words, that Locke's restrictions on the word 'certainty' fit with and reinforce a more substantive restriction in his doctrine which serves to distinguish it importantly from that tradition as exemplified, at the very least, in Wilkins. This will render plausible how Locke could have been interpreted by Hume and others (whether self-consciously or not) as alien to the concerns of the earlier naturalistic tradition. The grounds for that interpretation are worth exploring because whether or not it is correct it focuses attention on issues which provide the possibility of a better understanding of

---

[4] Two works of special importance in assessing these claims are Wilbur Samuel Howell's *Logic and Rhetoric in England, 1500–1700* (Princeton, 1956), and Barbara J. Shapiro's *Probability and Certainty in Seventeenth-Century England* (Princeton, 1983).

[5] Van Leeuwen, pp. 124, 121.

Locke's place in the historical progression of British thought and the basis for a more informed appreciation of later accounts which responded to his.

A. WILKINS AND MORAL CERTAINTY: CONSTRUCTIVE SCEPTICISM AND UNREASONABLE DOUBT

The son of a reputedly ingenious and mechanically-minded Oxford goldsmith, John Wilkins cultivated his inherited talent in mathematical and scientific pursuits.[6] First in London while a chaplain and then in Oxford as Warden of Wadham, he participated in the gatherings which were the nucleus of what would become the 'Royal Society'. 'Of this brilliant group', it is said, 'Wilkins was the centre; and he deserves, more than any other man, to be esteemed the founder of the Royal Society.' In 1662, when the charter of the Society was passed, he became its first secretary. Though his importance to the founding of the Royal Society is beyond question, first and foremost Wilkins was the Right Reverend The Lord Bishop of Chester. Consecrated in 1668, one of his most marked characteristics as bishop was a sympathetic leniency toward dissenters. That leniency was seen by some as an expression of a praiseworthy tendency to moderation and flexibility, but it was seen by others as a rather questionable tendency, revealed throughout his life, to political shrewdness at the cost of principle. It is, at any rate, safe to say that he was both ambitious and generally well loved. His writings expressed the two poles of his life's interest—ranging from works on the habitability of the moon, the planetary character of the earth, and modes of rapid communication, to discourses on providence and prayer. *An Essay towards a real Character and a Philosophical Language* (1668) is generally considered his most important work,[7] but for our purposes his most significant contribution is his response to scepticism, embedded in his thought about religion.

It is primarily in his posthumously published *Of The Principles and Duties of Natural Religion* (1675)[8] that one finds his views on

[6] *Dictionary of National Biography* XXI, pp. 264-7.

[7] Thomas Reid refers explicitly to this work by Wilkins in his *Essays on the Intellectual Powers*.

[8] Further references to Wilkins will be to this work in the 7th edition (London, 1715), which differs from the 1675 edition in the Bodleian Library, Oxford, only in terms of minor changes in spelling, punctuation, or capitalization.

evidence and justification of belief, with the opening chapters providing very explicit attention to basic definitions and distinctions. Assent is divided into two kinds—'Knowledge or Certainty' is contrasted with 'Opinion or Probability', the former being 'That kind of *Assent* which doth arise from such plain and clear Evidence as doth not admit of any reasonable Cause of doubting' (4), while the latter is 'That kind of Assent which doth arise from such Evidence as is less plain and clear' and so is 'not so weighty and perspicuous as to exclude all reasonable doubt and fear of the contrary' (9). Knowledge (Certainty) is subdivided into three 'kinds': Physical certainty (from the evidence of sense), Mathematical (or logical) certainty, and Moral certainty (4). The last category is the crucial one for any mitigation or rejection of scepticism and the hallmark of this particular seventeenth-century development is the way in which it understood such moral certainty.

Since no one, Wilkins writes, can 'pretend to such a perfect unerring Judgment on which the Divine Power it self could not impose' (8), the highest certainty possible to humans is 'conditionally infallible' certainty. On the 'supposition' that our faculties are true, and that 'we do not neglect the exerting of them', conditionally infallible certainty is the assurance of a 'necessity that some things must be so as we apprehend them, and ... cannot possibly be otherwise' (8). Such certainty is possible only in physical and mathematical (logical) cases. Except in those cases, there is 'no natural Necessity, that such Things must be so, and that they cannot possibly be otherwise, without implying a Contradiction' (7). Nevertheless, in company with cases of conditionally infallible certainty, and in contrast to cases of probability, some conclusions which lack that necessity 'may ... be so certain as not to admit of any reasonable Doubt concerning them' (7). Such certainty, 'which is the only certainty of which most Things are capable' is 'moral' or 'indubitable' certainty and arises from the evidence of 'the Nature of Things', 'Testimony', or 'Experience' (8). It is on the basis of the unreasonableness of doubt in such cases that principles which are '*morally certain*' are not '*merely* probable' (27).

The division Wilkins makes is one between conditionally infallible certainty (or knowledge), indubitable or moral certainty (or knowledge), and mere probability. The distinction on which this division rests is that between doubt which is impossible, doubt which is possible but unreasonable, and doubt which is reasonable

in a given case. Moral certainty constitutes a bridge-category between doubt which is impossible and doubt which is reasonable,
and establishes a continuum because it shares characteristics with
both the other kinds of knowledge and with probability.

What constitutes 'physical' certainty, based on sense (the *'highest
kind of Evidence'* — 5), is that doubt is impossible because there is
nothing more certain on the basis of which one could put the
conclusion in jeopardy. Concerning sense perception, he writes:

He that would go about to confute me in any of these Apprehensions,
ought to bring a *Medium* that is better known, and to derive his Argument
from somewhat that is more evident and certain than these Things are,
unless he can think to overthrow and confute that which is more plain and
certain, by that which is less plain and certain. (5)

To count as a reasonable ground for doubting the evidence of
sense, the challenging claim would have to be more certain—and
the implication is that such a condition is impossible to fulfil in
such cases.

In cases of 'mathematical' or 'logical' certainty, doubt is impossible for a different reason—namely, that (assuming the premisses
and the reliability of our faculties) denial of the conclusion is a
contradiction. He writes:

There is such a kind of Connexion betwixt the Terms of some Propositions,
and some Deductions are so necessary as must unavoidably enforce our
Assent ... supposing our Faculties to be true, they cannot possibly be
otherwise, without implying a Contradiction. (6)

In other cases, however, even when doubt is possible, it may be
unreasonable, for 'when we have for the proof of any thing, some
of the highest kinds of Evidence, in this case it is not the suggestion
of a mere possibility, that the thing may be otherwise, that ought
to be any sufficient cause of doubting' (23). This is the warrant for
his earlier claim that experience generates moral certainty 'of the
succession of Night and Day, Winter and Summer' and leaves no
'reason to doubt, whether the House wherein now I am, shall this
next Minute fall upon me, or the Earth open and swallow it up'
(9). 'A Man may make no doubt', he writes, 'whether he himself
were baptized, whether such persons were his Parents' (23-4), or
whether the sun will rise, simply on the ground that 'the contrary
is not impossible, and doth not imply any Contradiction' (24).

Those who entertain 'actual hopes' or 'actual fears' of something 'merely upon account of the possibility of it' would 'be generally accounted out of their Wits', and '*Doubt* is a kind of *fear* ... and 'tis the same kind of Madness for a Man to *doubt* of any thing, as to *hope for*, or *fear* it, upon a mere Possibility' (25-6). His conclusion is quite simply that

> He that will raise to himself, and cherish in his mind, any real doubts, according to the mere possibility of things, shall not be able to determine himself to the belief or practice of any thing. (25)

Such a person 'must not stay within Doors, for fear the House should fall upon him, for that is possible: Nor must he go out, lest the next Man that meets him should kill him, for that also is possible'—and similarly for 'any other Action' (25).

It is worth noting that the kinds of examples used to express the unreasonableness of doubt, as noted above, have been repeated in succeeding generations of responses to scepticism up to and including the present day. Other paradigmatic examples come into play as well. Wilkins writes concerning the evidence of testimony 'which depends upon the Credit and Authority of the Witnesses', that

> these may be so qualified as to their *ability* and *fidelity*, that a Man must be a fantastical incredulous Fool to make any doubt of them. And by this it is that I am sufficiently assured, That there was such a Person as Queen *Elizabeth*; That there is such a Place as *Spain*. (9)

Similarly,

> *That there was such a Man as King* Henry *the Eighth, that there are such Places as* America, *or* China ... may in themselves be equally true and certain with those other Matters, *That we now see and are awake, That the three Angles in a Triangle are equal to two right ones*. (19)

Wilkins's emphasis on the distinction within the realm of 'possible' doubt between doubt that is reasonable and doubt that is unreasonable is found in the writings of others of the period. Both John Tillotson and Joseph Glanvill, for example, refuse to equate unreasonable doubt with impossible doubt. Tillotson (who introduced and edited the work of Wilkins to which I have been referring) distinguishes between an 'infallible Assurance [which] excludes all possibility of error and mistake' and an 'undoubted Certainty [which] doth not exclude all possibility of Mistake, but only all just and reasonable cause why a prudent and considerate

Man should doubt'.[9] His explanation: even where the assumed falsehood of a putative fact 'implies no Contradiction', we can be 'very well assured ... nor hath any prudent Man any just Cause to make the least Doubt of it' *because* 'a bare Possibility that a Thing may be, or not be, is no just Cause of doubting whether a Thing be or not'.[10] His example: 'It is possible all the People of *France* may die this Night. ... It is possible the Sun may not rise to Morrow Morning; and yet, for all this, I suppose that no Man hath the least Doubt but that it will.'[11] Elsewhere he suggests the unreasonableness of doubting 'whether there was such a Man [as William the Conqueror], or not; and whether there be such a place as *Spain*, or not' because 'it is fond for any Man to alledge a bare possibility of the contrary, as a reasonable cause of doubting concerning any thing, for which we have as good evidence as the thing is capable of'.[12] Moreover, 'he is not a rational Doubter that desires more [evidence]' in order to be certain.[13] Like Wilkins and Tillotson, Glanvill contrasts '*Infallible* Certainty [which is] an absolute Assurance, that things are as we conceive and affirm, and not possible to be otherwise' with '*Indubitable* Certainty', a 'firm Assent to any thing, of which there is no reason of doubt' (more precisely, 'not the least reason to doubt').[14] His rationale is the same: 'the bare possibility [that a thing may be otherwise than it appears to our senses] doth not move us'.[15] Evidence from testimony can also be 'indubitable', 'no more doubted than the first Principles of Reason or Sense. Thus we believe, without the least scruple about it, That there are such places as *Rome*, and *Constantinople*, and such Countries as *Italy* and *Greece*, though we never saw them.'[16] William Chillingworth illustrates a similar position by reference to belief 'that there is such a city as Constantinople' or belief in 'Caesar's Commentaries'.[17]

[9] Tillotson, 'Of the Faith or Persuasion of a Divine Revelation', *Works*, 4th ed., Vol. III (London, 1728), p. 429.

[10] Tillotson, *The Rule of Faith, Works*, 9th ed. (London, 1728), p. 559.

[11] Ibid.

[12] Tillotson, *Works*, 4th ed., Vol. III, p. 431. Cf. 9th ed., *Rule of Faith*, p. 558 and the sermon 'The Wisdom of Being Religious', p. 16.

[13] Tillotson, *Rule of Faith*, p. 558.

[14] 'Of Scepticism and Certainty', *Essays on Several Important Subjects in Philosophy and Religion* (London, 1676), p. 47 (see also pp. 47–8).

[15] Ibid., p. 49 (cf. p. 50).

[16] Ibid.

[17] *The Works of William Chillingworth*, 12th ed. (Philadelphia, 1841), p. 431.

Whereas Chillingworth and Tillotson put moral certainty under the rubric of probability, Wilkins makes knowledge and certainty synonymous, or at least coextensive. But all of them see the distinctive characteristic of moral certainty as the unreasonableness of doubt in such cases. They not only share a rationale, they also share a penchant for similar kinds of illustrations. And all of them see moral certainty as a kind of intermediate category establishing a continuum between knowledge and probability. Although Chillingworth and Tillotson separate moral certainty from knowledge, they show by this that certainty is possible even when knowledge is not obtainable. Thus a continuum between knowledge and probability is generated because certainty overlaps the two distinct categories—moral certainty is thus a bridge-category. Though Wilkins does not allow certainty to overlap the two categories of knowledge and probability, but radically separates certainty from probability, moral certainty effectively provides a similar bridge-category between knowledge and probability and generates a similar continuum because it shares some characteristics with each of the two main categories.

Before considering the status of such moral certainty in Wilkins's account, I want to look briefly at his attempt to distinguish conditionally infallible certainty from indubitable certainty qualitatively either in terms of the impossibility of doubt or the necessity of assent. If the reasonableness or unreasonableness of doubt is genuinely used as the criterion, all evidence is put on a continuum—there are no longer objects suitable only for belief, or only for knowledge. The impossibility of doubt in the abstract becomes an idle category. And although Wilkins attempts to argue for a qualitative distinction between conditionally infallible certainty and indubitable certainty, by arguing that in the latter case doubt is possible while in the former it is impossible, this is ruled out by his inclusion of physical certainty under the rubric of conditionally infallible certainty. In such cases the 'impossibility' of doubt is a quite different impossibility from that in mathematical and logical cases. The defence of such impossibility in cases of sense evidence depends on his notion of requiring that the challenging evidence be more certain than the challenged—and this makes such physical certainty more akin to moral than to mathematical. The case of physical certainty illustrates the relevance of context in the way that moral certainty does, and explains why the unreasonableness of doubt is the hallmark at the same time of certainty or knowledge in general, and of moral certainty in particular.

But not only is it true that the impossibility of doubt in physical cases is more like the situation in cases of moral certainty than mathematical certainty, the impossibility of doubt in the latter case is a more complex issue even on his own terms than he seems to recognize. Consider his attempt to distinguish conditionally infallible from indubitable certainty in terms of the necessity of assent. In cases of mathematical (logical) certainty, 'every Man's Judgment (though never so much prejudiced) must necessarily assent to them' (6). In the case of indubitable or moral certainty, however, the evidence does not 'necessitate every man's Assent, though his Judgment be never so much prejudiced against them' (6)—that is, prejudice can hinder assent in such cases (although 'every Man whose Judgment is free from prejudice will assent'—8). At the very least his recognition that we must not 'neglect the exerting' of our faculties in cases of conditionally infallible certainty (8) implies that even in cases of mathematical or logical evidence assent is not necessitated against our will, despite anything we do or fail to do. Moreover, he emphasizes the influence of character and will on the appropriation of evidence when he notes that the 'true cause' for the sceptical refusal to assent without the highest possible evidence is *not* 'because they have no *reason* for it [such assent], but because they have no mind to it' (22–3). Again, he points out that

There are some Men, who have sufficient Abilities to discern betwixt the true differences of things; but what through their vicious Affections and voluntary Prejudices, making them unwilling that some things should be true; what through their inadvertancy or neglect to consider and compare things together, they are not to be convinced by plain Arguments; not through any insufficiency in the *Evidence*. (31)

Note that the influence of personal appropriation is not limited by him to lack of moral uprightness or love of truth, but also includes presumably non-vicious and non-voluntary 'inadvertancy or neglect' to consider particular pieces of evidence or relations between them. The latter failures can obviously infect even the plainest of 'plain Arguments'—i.e. demonstrations in mathematics and logic— and shows that his initial presentation of the force of mathematical and logical evidence assumes more than merely the supposition of the reliability of our faculties.

Thus, in spite of the claim that prejudice cannot hinder assent in cases of mathematical (logical) evidence, the implication is that no case is exempt from the possibility that assent can be hindered. Conversely, his claim that even in cases where the evidence is not that of sense, mathematics, or logic, 'every Man whose Judgment is free from prejudice *will* consent unto them' (6, ital. mine) allows that all cases of freedom from prejudice (construed broadly) leave open the possibility that assent is as constrained as in cases of sense, mathematical or logical evidence. This implied possibility is in fact just what he does express explicitly in his claim that

The Mind of Man *may and must* give a firm assent to some things, without any kind of hesitation or doubt of the contrary; where yet the Evidences for such things are not so infallible, but that there is a possibility, that the things may be otherwise. (23, reverse emphasis mine)[18]

The radical break between necessitated and non-necessitated assent is, therefore, implicitly and sometimes explicitly qualified by the recognition (admittedly obscured when he deals with demonstrative evidence) of the need for personal appropriation of any and all evidence.

Wilkins's sensitivity to the influence of subjective appropriation of evidence is often expressed in a negative fashion, emphasizing the ill effects of prejudice, but his sensitivity to the relevance of contextual appropriation of evidence—the suiting of evidence-requirements to subject-matter—is a positive one. A guiding principle of his thought is that '*Things of several kinds may admit and require several sorts of proofs, all which may be good in their kind*' (20). Reinforcing his position by explicit reference to Aristotle,[19] and using Aristotle's example, he writes:

How incongruence would it be for a Mathematician to persuade with Eloquence, to use all imaginable insinuations and intreaties that he might prevail with his hearers to believe that *three and three make six*? It would be altogether as vain and improper in matters belonging to an Orator to pretend to strict Demonstration. All things are not capable of the same kind of Evidence. (20-1)

Thus, it is 'not rational', he says, to expect demonstration 'in such

[18] Van Leeuwen ignores this complexity in Wilkins's account when he writes that Locke's position was stronger than the earlier tradition's since Locke did not see assent in such cases as voluntary (p. 135).

[19] See the note on Wilkins, Van Leeuwen, p. 67 n. 57.

other matters as are not of the like Nature' (21). It is not merely impractical to require the in-principle highest possible evidence—it is 'not rational'.

But the recognition of the legitimacy of a contextual suiting of proof requirements to subject-matter does not lead him to allow any arbitrary adoption of belief, for 'it is not, ought not to be, any prejudice to the Truth or Certainty of any thing, that it is not made out by such kind of Proofs of which the nature of that thing is not capable, *provided* it be capable of satisfactory Proofs of another kind' (21-2, ital. mine). In fact, the relevance of contextual (and personal) appropriation of evidence highlights the need for guidelines which he sets forth in principles six and seven in Chapter III. The 'Rule', which a man would 'be generally accounted a Fool' not to follow, is 'to incline to that which is most probable and likely, when they cannot attain to any clear unquestionable certainty' (30).

This suggests an 'ethic of belief'—a view of the relevance of obligation with respect to evidence and belief. If 'ought implies can', this seems out of place given his claims that 'the Judgments of Men must by a natural Necessity, preponderate on that side where the greatest Evidence lies' (30-1). Moreover, when evidence is equally balanced 'an impartial Judgment cannot be obliged to incline to one side rather than to the other, because our *Assent* to things must by a Necessity of Nature, be proportioned to our *Evidence* for them' (32). But this 'necessity' is not incompatible with his 'rule' because the meaning of a duty to believe or to proportion our assent to evidence is

That Men should be careful to preserve their Minds free from any wilful prejudice and partiality, that they should seriously attend to, and consider the Evidence proposed to them, so as to take a just Estimate of it. (30)

That is, it is a duty to *indirectly* affect believing, by adopting practices which lead to unprejudiced appropriation of evidence. Only the prescription of direct volitional governance of beliefs would be incompatible with the claim that we *necessarily* assent to the side with most evidence. What is prescribed rather is the adoption of a policy of approaching and treating evidence in a particular frame of mind—attempting, for example, to avoid selective attention to or disproportionate emphasis on some aspects of the evidence as opposed to others.

This is clear too in his view that religious belief cannot have 'such cogent Evidence, as to necessitate Assent' because that would not leave 'any place for the virtue of *Believing*, or the freedom of our Obedience; nor any ground for Reward and Punishment' (26). But the need for freedom is satisfied for him as long as 'that which is necessary to beget this certainty in the Mind, namely, *impartial Consideration*, is in a Man's power' (27). Thus, constraint imposed by the unreasonableness of doubt in particular cases is not incompatible with the need for freedom because the locus of freedom is in the indirect or preliminary action of the agent. This explains his conclusion that religious principles need not be 'merely *probable*' to guarantee sufficient religious freedom (27). The point is not only that the prescription to proportion our assent to evidence is compatible with the descriptive necessity of our response to evidence, but, moreover, that in this way the constraint of moral certainty can in principle be as powerful as that of demonstration, without prejudice to the need for non-compelled believing.

To return now to our central question—what is the status of moral certainty, of that '*firm assent ... without any kind of hesitation or doubt of the contrary*' which we not only 'may' but 'must' give in particular cases which are not sense, mathematical, or logical cases (23)? Such 'indubitable' certainty, 'which doth not admit of any Doubt', Wilkins writes, 'may serve us as well to all intents and purposes, as that which is infallible' (23), but such a claim is ambiguous. Is 'all intents and purposes' meant to refer to the demands of conduct, religious or secular, or does the word 'all' imply speculative as well as practical purposes? The question is (*a*) whether Wilkins is qualifying the claim to certainty as one concerning assurance sufficient for acting as if *p* were true rather than as assurance sufficient for a claim that *p* is true, and (*b*) whether such assurance is thought by him to be, not merely the necessary issue of the frame of our constitution, but legitimate and rational as well.

The interchangeability of the terms 'knowledge' and 'certainty' for him suggest that whatever philosophical implications for legitimacy attach to the knowledge claim attach as well to the claim of any kind of certainty—physical, mathematical, or moral. In the absence of counter-evidence to preclude such an interpretation, there seems no reason to take it at less than its face value as a claim for a total certainty that *p* which is not unjustified.

Consider first some of the principles he puts forward concerning evidence and proof, principles which he says are 'of such perspicuity, as to need little more than the bare *Proposal* of them, and the *Explication* of their Terms, to evince the truth of them' (33). First, 'Such things as in themselves are equally true and certain, may not yet be capable of the same *kind* or *degree* of Evidence as to us' (19)[20]. Second, embodying the strong Aristotelian influence Wilkins shares with others of the period, 'Things of several kinds may admit and require several sorts of proofs, all which may be good in their kind' (20). Third, 'When a thing is capable of good proof in any kind, Men ought to rest satisfy'd in the best evidence for it, which that kind of things will bear, and beyond which better could not be expected, supposing it were true' (22). This is later rephrased as the 'duty' to 'acquiesce in such kind of Evidence as is sufficient for the Proof of it' (30). The fourth is the claim whose implications we are now considering: we 'may and must' give an assent without hesitation or doubt in cases where there is nevertheless 'a possibility, that the things may be otherwise' (23), for to do otherwise is 'irrational' (25).

One could argue that these principles need not constitute a claim for anything beyond the assurance sufficient for acting-as-if; the claim that we ought to be satisfied with such evidence as is possible in given subjects may be a simple sigh of resignation to less than total certainty that *p* is true, or to a certainty which, even if total, is unavoidable but not legitimate. In the case of some constructive sceptics—e.g. Chillingworth—the claim is simply one for an assurance sufficient for conducting our business and getting about in the daily affairs of life.[21] Is there any reason to see Wilkins, who unlike Chillingworth puts moral certainty under the rubric of knowledge, as capitulating to the sceptic's suggestion that total assurance is not justified in the absence of the in-principle highest evidence possible?

To the sceptic's requirement, Wilkins responds vehemently— 'how abhorrent such Sceptical principles must needs be to common reason, I need not say'. He explains, in a comment noted earlier:

Those who will pretend such kind of grounds for their disbelief of any thing, will never be able to persuade others, that the true Cause why they

---

[20] Italics reversed in presenting these principles.
[21] Chillingworth, *Works*, pp. 128, 140-1.

do not give their Assent, is because they have no *reason* for it, but because they have no mind to it. (22–3)

The implication here is that the absence of the highest evidence is not a reasonable ground for doubt—such evidence is therefore an unreasonable request. This is also apparent in his consideration of the principle that things which are not capable of the same kinds of evidence may nevertheless be 'equally true and certain':

That there was such a man as King Henry *the Eighth, that there are such places as* America, *or* China. I say these things may in themselves be equally true and certain with those other Matters, *That we now see and are awake, That the three Angles in a Triangle are equal to two right ones.* Though for the First of these we have only the Testimony of others, and human Tradition; whereas for the other we have sensitive proof, and Mathematical demonstration. (19)

The next sentence unequivocally points to the 'reason' for this judgement: 'And the reason is because all Truths are in themselves equal, according to that ordinary Maxim, *Veritas non recipit magis & minus*' (19-20). The conclusion, however, connects truth and rational assurance:

And therefore nothing can be more irrational than for a Man to doubt of, or deny the Truth of any thing, because it cannot be made out by such kind of Proofs of which the Nature of such a thing is not capable. (20)

The maxim which is central to his argument claims that truth is a concept whose application has a 'critical threshold', such that it is not applicable at all until it is simply and totally applicable. As a concept which is totally applicable if at all, truth has no 'degrees'—it refers to a state or condition which is not expressed gradually, and which when reached it makes no sense to talk of increasing. A proposition cannot be somewhat true—it is true, full stop, or it is not true at all. It cannot be more or less true, or more true than another which is also true.

Truth is not the only example of such a threshold concept. The legal understanding of guilt is another. One is *entirely* innocent until proven guilty. One is not partly guilty, corresponding to the degree of evidence against one—until the evidence reaches a critical threshold one is not considered by law guilty at all. There can be more evidence to support the charge after the original determination of guilt, but (though that may affect the content of the charge) that does not yield a proportionately greater degree of guilt.

What is interesting is that Wilkins seems to use the concepts of true and certain equivalently, implying that both are seen as threshold concepts. It might be thought that Wilkins is referring to objective certainty in the sense that it is equal to truth—that is, 'it is certain' equals 'it is the case' (vs. 'I am certain'). But that his claim is for the equality of *assurance* is supported by his later remarks on the second principle: 'no sober Man can deny but that several things in *Moral* and in *Natural* Philosophy are in themselves, as absolutely and as certainly true, *and firmly believ'd by us,* as any *Mathematical* Principle or Conclusion can be' (21, ital. mine from 'and . . . us'). He infers directly from this 'That it is not, ought not to be, any prejudice to the Truth or Certainty of any thing, that it is not made out by such a kind of Proofs, of which the nature of that thing is not capable' (21-2). Both remarks thus give us his claim that we can rightly be as assured in (particular) non-mathematical cases as in mathematical ones. And such seems to be his claim in the illustration of the first principle as well.

The equation of true and certain (assurance) is reinforced by his claim that 'all Truths are in themselves equal . . . And *therefore* nothing can be more irrational than for a Man to doubt of, or deny the Truth of any thing, because it cannot be made out by such kind of Proofs of which the Nature of such a thing is not capable' (19-20). He sees certainty or the irrationality of a doubt based solely on the generic nature of the evidence involved as related to the threshold nature of the concept of truth. He implies that because all truths are equal, the highest assurance one can have in any given case is equal to the highest assurance one can have in another kind of case. And such a connection would be plausible if one were arguing by it that where the evidence suffices to warrant a claim that something is true, one is unreasonable to demean it by saying that there could have been more evidence, or a different kind of evidence—e.g., that if there had been demonstration the claim to truth would have been more warranted.

We have a duty, he writes, to 'acquiesce in such kind of Evidence as is sufficient for the Proof' of something (30). The critical threshold is that point at which the evidence is 'sufficient'. Where there is more evidence, that could be considered surplus, extra—the extra is not the standard with respect to which other cases are judged to 'lack' something they should and could have. That is, at the crucial threshold the achievements are equal. He could thus be arguing not only for the sufficiency for practical purposes of the assurance attainable in cases of moral certainty, but also for the equivalence of such assurance in particular cases with the assurance attainable in (particular) cases of sense perception and mathematics or logic. That is, if certainty is a threshold concept—one which had no degrees, but was present only when a critical threshold of evidence was reached, and being at the pitch which constitutes it, did not increase with the addition of more evidence—the highest assurance we can have in any given kind of case is equal to the highest assurance we can have in another kind of case. If certainty is viewed as a threshold concept, moral certainty would not be a lower 'degree' of certainty than conditionally infallible certainty— it would be instead what he introduces it as: namely, another 'kind' of certainty (4), equal but from a different source. That difference in source would not then militate against equality in assurance or equality in legitimacy. Admittedly, Wilkins does not explicitly put forward such a proposal, nor does he provide any positive sugges- tion as to how to understand that equality of assurance (such as will be offered by later anti-sceptical thinkers), but a reading of his view of moral certainty as a threshold concept makes most sense of his claim that it is a 'kind' of certainty, equivalent to knowledge, and equal in terms of assurance to physical and mathematical cer- tainty or knowledge, as well as of his strong negative insistence that different kinds (sources) of evidence are not as such prejudicial to the truth or firmness of adherence to conclusions. And this implicit argument for a threshold notion of certainty becomes cen- tral, I shall argue, to later thinkers in their anti-sceptical appeals to 'unreasonable' doubt and the constitution of our nature.[22]

Before turning to another element of Wilkins's response to scep- ticism (the appeal to 'first principles'), it is appropriate to consider

[22] The notion of a 'threshold' concept is at least implicit in two places in Tillot- son's sermon 'Of the Faith and Persuasion of a Divine Revelation' (*Works*, 4th edn., Vol. III). He writes, for example, about 'impossibility' in such a way: 'there can be no degree of Infallibility. Infallibility is an impossibility of being deceived; but there are no degrees of Impossibility, one thing is not more impossible than another; but all things that are impossible, are equally so' (p. 430). He continues: 'I cannot possibly understand why every Man should not be contented with suffi- cient Assurance, or for what reason a Man should desire more than enough' (p. 431, ital. mine).

an objection which will be relevant to all anti-sceptical responses which depend on a threshold notion of certainty. One might argue, for example, that although truths in the abstract are all equal, we can be more or less assured of such truths, and should be more or less assured depending on the amount of evidence we possess. That is, we can and should be more or less subjectively certain (assured) of what is objectively certain (the case, the truth) in proportion to our evidence. In this vein, it has been suggested that Wilkins's claim for equal assurance is incompatible with, or renders vacuous, his requirement that we proportion assent to evidence:

> Wilkins proposes that there is an objective relation between the situation and the evidence, and that one's degree of certainty is to be proportioned to the evidence. This should mean that one is more certain of a mathematical demonstration than of what is substantiated by testimony alone. However, this is not always the case for he claims that one is as certain of the conclusions of science and history as of a conclusion in mathematics, thus breaking down the objective relation supposedly existing between evidence and assent ... This being so, the distinction between the several degrees of certainty becomes less pronounced and the proportioning of assent to evidence becomes less significant.[23]

The logical outcome of such a move, it is concluded, was 'to divorce certainty from evidence altogether, as Hume did'.

A view of certainty, and conversely, of unreasonable doubt, as threshold concepts precludes the possibility of directly proportioning certainty to evidence in a one-to-one manner, by degrees, because it precludes the notion of 'degrees' of certainty. I would argue, however, that it need not thereby open the thin edge of the wedge toward the divorce of certainty from evidence: it need not counter the thrust of a proportionality requirement. Such a requirement is intended to guarantee a non-arbitrary correlation between evidence and assurance. It is meant to preclude the divorce of evidence and assurance. It could still retain a point—even its main point—in the face of a threshold concept of certainty or unreasonable doubt as long as one requires proportion up to the critical threshold. In such a way, the requirement of proportioning assent to evidence would still rule out certainty when the evidence did not reach the critical threshold.

Wilkins speaks of a 'duty' to 'acquiesce in such kind of Evidence as is sufficient for the Proof' of a conclusion (30). The relationship

---

[23] Van Leeuwen, p. 70.

between duty and necessity is at issue again, for he had written earlier:

I appeal to the common judgment of Mankind, whether the Human Nature be not so framed, as to acquiesce in such a *Moral certainty*, as the Nature of Things is capable of. (25)

That acquiescence extends, moreover, to 'first principles', and in particular to those which are 'morally' certain. He introduces the category of 'first principles' in Chapter I, and then elaborates that understanding in Chapter IV in terms of universal consensus and 'common', 'general', or 'natural notions'.

After describing the three 'kinds' of certainty or knowledge possible, he notes that 'under each of these Heads there are several Propositions which may be styled *Self-evident* and *first Principles*' (7). His characterization of such principles makes several telling contributions to his anti-sceptical proposal. First, the term 'self-evident' means that 'they are of themselves so plain, as not to be capable of proof from any Thing that is clearer or more known' (7). Such a claim does not in itself exclude the possibility of all derivation, only derivation from premises which are clearer or more certain, and it has had forceful restatement in the twentieth century.[24] Using a sense of the term 'a priori' quite different from the modern, Wilkins goes on to say that they are '*First principles*, because they cannot be proved *a priori*; That which is first can have nothing before it' (7). It is not clear whether this second remark is intended to register a different point from that of self-evidence— either having 'nothing before it' means having nothing 'clearer or more known' before it, and so repeats the first point, or it makes the stronger claim that there can be nothing *at all* before it.

The next point he makes is that though proof is impossible, there are ways in which self-evident and first principles can be recommended. They may, he suggests

receive some kind of *Illustration* by *Instances*, and *Circumstances*, and by such universal *Effects* as do proceed from them; and from the monstrous *Absurdities* that will follow upon the denial of them. (7)

His final point in this section is that 'Such *Deductions* as do necessarily flow from these Principles, have the same kind of Certainty,

---

[24] For example, in Ludwig Wittgenstein's *On Certainty*, eds. G. E. M. Anscombe and G. H. von Wright (New York, 1969).

whether *Physical*, *Mathematical*, or *Moral*, with the Principles themselves from which they are deduced' (7). All these points will figure importantly in the claims made by later anti-sceptics concerning first principles.

Though he gives no examples at this point, it seems safe to assume that he would see his examples of mathematical and logical certainty as first principles rather than conclusions from demonstrative reasoning, and that his illustrations of moral certainty 'from the Nature of the Things themselves' (e.g. 'That *there are such Things as Virtue and Vice*. That *Mankind is naturally designed for a sociable life*—8) refer to morally certain first principles rather than morally certain conclusions from reasoning.[25]

Turning to the 'chief [i.e. religious] design' of the book in Chapter IV, Wilkins engages in two sorts of discussions which either clarify or are related to the early definition of self-evident and first principles: namely, the relevance of an argument from the 'universal consent and agreement of mankind', and the character of 'common', 'general', or 'natural notions'. Though his main concern is the religious one of showing the principles of such religion as is attainable without special revelation, and his main example is belief in the existence of God, his views on these topics are of wider application.

His proposal that 'the Universal Consent of Nations in all Places and Times, ... must needs render any thing highly credible to all such as will but allow the Humane Nature to be rational, and to be naturally endowed with a Capacity of distinguishing betwixt Truth and Falshood' (36) appeals again to Aristotle (as had his principle of suiting proof to subject-matter). 'It is laid down by the *Philosopher*', he writes, with a reference to Aristotle in the margin,

as the proper way of Reasoning from *Authority*, That what seems true to *some* wise Men, may upon that account be esteem'd *somewhat* probable; what is believed by *most* wise Men, hath a *further* degree of probability; what *most men*, both wise and unwise, do assent unto, is yet *more* probable: But what *all men* have generally consented to, hath for it the highest degree of Evidence of this kind, that any thing is capable of: And it must be monstrous arrogance and folly for any single Persons to prefer their own Judgments before the general Suffrage of Mankind. (36)

[25] Such examples may be specially relevant to the claim made by J. H. Bernard that Wilkins was an important influence on Butler ('The Predecessors of Bishop Butler', *Hermathena* IX (1894–6), pp. 75–84).

This 'highest degree of evidence of this kind' is qualified by the admission that 'ungrounded Persuasions' are ultimately distinguished from 'Dictates and Sentiments of Nature' by the test of time (39). Such a test, though retrospective, implies at the very least that the authority of universal agreement is prima-facie—that is, that there can be universally accepted 'ungrounded persuasions'; but it provides no guidance when it is most needed.

There are, however, some considerations which have more immediate bearing on an evaluation of generally held beliefs. Some are negative. For example, exceptions do not tell against the legitimacy of a conviction—consent need not be literally universal, for 'Prodigies' do not prove 'that there is no Regularity in the Laws of Nature' (40). It does not, after all, follow 'that Honey is not naturally sweet to our taste, because a sick Palate doth not judge it to be so' (41); moreover, 'Some Men are born Blind, or have lost their Sight, will it hence follow, that there is no such thing in nature as Light or Colour? Others are Lunatick or Ideots, should any Man from hence infer, that there is no such thing as Reason?' (41)

A second negative criterion appears to be the impossibility (and not the mere failure) of maintaining the belief constantly. Though his example (belief in the existence of God) may be a questionable one, his point is one that will be repeated in later general anti-sceptical arguments. Quoting Seneca, he writes that 'though they may profess this somewhat confidently in the Day-time, when they are in Company, yet in the Night and alone they have doubtful Thoughts about it'; their protestations to the contrary, it is not their 'Opinion' (43). Later uses of this point will, ironically, be inversions.

Thus construed, 'constancy and universality' is a positive mark because it reveals a number of important characteristics. First, it shows that the belief cannot be the result of a 'particular *Infirmity*, or *occasional Prejudice* in the judgment' (46)—the emphasis here is obviously on 'particular' and 'occasional'. It is significant that he tries in this context to undermine the plausibility of the suggestion that his example—belief in God—is a prejudice (though generally accepted) by undermining the plausibility of its putative *causes*. 'There is not', he claims, 'the least probability for those things which are assigned as the grounds of this Prejudice, namely, *Fear, Policy, Stipulation*' (46). Whatever one thinks of his arguments (e.g. that it is implausible that fear could lead to positing an infinitely good and merciful God—45), two things emerge as a result of his effort. First, '*stipulation* or mutual agreement' cannot be the cause for him of such beliefs as are held not only by the learned, but also by 'barbarous and savage People' who have no contact with the learned because they are (as he colourfully puts it) 'widely separated from one another, by Seas, and Mountains, and Desarts' (47). Whatever universal agreement or consensus means for him, it cannot mean what is effected by institutional policy or such mutual consensus (though he later says, not 'merely' the effect of institutions or instruction—51). Secondly, his attempt to rebut the putative causes indirectly reveals his view that without a plausible cause to account for divergence from the truth, it is not reasonable to refuse to take the prima-facie authority of universal agreement as a mark of truth. Conversely, he seeks to explain causes of contrary opinions (e.g. guilt—48).

Such 'constancy and universality' also distinguishes beliefs which are 'immediate' from those which 'require some deeper Consideration, and some skill in the Rules of reasoning' (44). Such notions as are '*general* to Mankind, and not confined to any particular Sect or Nation, or Time, are usually styled ... Common Notions ... Seminal Principles ... and innate Law ... the *Law written in our hearts*' (49).[26] These 'Apprehensions wherein all Men do agree' or '*natural Notions*' are 'generally owned and acknowledged for true, by all such as apply their Thoughts to the consideration of them' (50-1). Wilkins here uses the term 'apprehension' technically—in order to show the status of such notions he parallels them with the simple apprehensions of the external senses, which are prior to both judgements and ratiocination.[27] He implies that differences about such notions, which are 'of themselves above all other Matters most plain and perspicuous' (49), are only differences about their origin, comparable to different judgements about mutually admitted apprehensions.

Natural notions are 'innate' in the sense that they are prior to judgement or reasoning, but they require the prompting of 'Ex-

[26] Glanvill refers to 'first principles' which are 'universal and believ'd by all Mankind' as 'the Seed of Reason'; 'we cannot but assent to [them]; and we find nothing to give us occasion to doubt of the truth of them' ('Of Scepticism and Certainty', *Essays*, p. 50).

[27] Differences between Wilkins and later thinkers are indicated in Chap. 4, n. 32, below.

perience and the Instruction of others; Because Mankind is naturally designed for a Sociable Life, and to be helpful to one another
by Mutual Conversation' (52). The force (and limit) of his point is
made by asking us to imagine the predicament of 'a Person bred
up in some deep Cavern of the Earth, without any instruction from
others' (52). The naturalness of such notions is not prejudiced
simply because a condition of their being 'owned and acknowledged to be true' is explicit consideration of them, and because the
further conditions of that are 'mature Age' (i.e. the use of reason),
'the ordinary use of their Faculties', and 'the common help of
mutual Society' (53). It is quite probable that Wilkins's emphasis
on such notions being 'acknowledged to be true' is the result of the
need for the notion with which he is most concerned (namely, God)
to be consciously and explicitly acknowledged in order for natural
religion to function in the way that he, a Bishop, would find indispensable.

Willkins's view of 'first principles' will have, we shall see, interesting echoes in the thinkers to be considered in later chapters; for
the moment, however, it suffices to have noted the salient ingredients in it. Together with his account of 'moral certainty' it provides the background against which we can reconsider Locke's
position.

B. LOCKE'S RELATION TO 'CONSTRUCTIVE SCEPTICISM'

As we have seen, Hume challenged Locke's dichotomy between
'demonstration' and 'probability'. 'Mr. Locke', he writes, 'divides
all arguments into demonstrative and probable. In this view, we
must say, that it is only probable that all men must die, or that the
sun will rise tomorrow.'[28] On the contrary, he continues, 'to conform our language more to common use, we ought to divide arguments into *demonstrations, proofs,* and *probabilities.* By proofs
meaning such arguments from experience as leave no room for
doubt or opposition.' Whatever the character and status of 'proof'
in Hume's account—this will be the topic of Chapter 3—he saw
himself as introducing a necessary corrective to the view epitomized
in Locke's inadequate dichotomy. As suggested earlier, however,

---

[28] *Enquiries Concerning the Human Understanding and Concerning the Principles of Morals,* ed. L. A. Selby-Bigge, p. 56 n.

such a reading of Locke as failing to do justice to a category of arguments in which there was no room for doubt is rendered problematic in the light of claims by Van Leeuwen and others that Locke is the 'culmination' of the tradition of 'moral certainty' and 'unreasonable doubt' considered in the preceding section. It is important, then, to reconsider Locke's account, and his relation to the earlier tradition, in light of such claims.

Van Leeuwen argues that Locke's doctrine is in 'fundamental features identical with that of his predecessors' although Locke does not use the term 'moral certainty' and restricts the term 'certainty' so that it is extensionally equivalent to the term 'knowledge' (and the latter is limited to demonstrative, intuitive, and sensitive evidence). By far, the strongest warrant for putting Locke in a direct line with the earlier constructive scepticism is found in his repeated emphasis on the *practical* sufficiency of our intellectual attainments—he clearly sees practice as the key to his antisceptical response.[29] Moreover, Locke recognizes the limits of a syllogistic paradigm of reasoning.[30] Both recognitions characterized the earlier tradition. And although Locke makes knowledge and certainty co-extensive (unlike Chillingworth and Tillotson), in so doing he is doing no more than Wilkins did. So the question is whether Locke's dichotomy between knowledge and probability is meant to emphasize a distinction not present in, or compatible with, the earlier view, or whether, on the other hand, the dichotomy is mediated (rendered a continuum) through an equivalent of the moral certainty of the earlier tradition. For unless Locke's account proposes a substantive continuum, and has a category equivalent to moral certainty in its implications, it can hardly be said to be 'identical' in its 'fundamental features'. Locke's affirmation of the practical sufficiency of our intellectual achievements is sometimes taken as the overriding consideration in evaluating whether Locke continues the preceding tradition. But that affirmation, however strong, must not be allowed to obscure the possibility that Locke nevertheless had radically different assumptions which give that affirmation a different significance. In what follows, then, I will assume Locke's affirmation of the practical sufficiency of our intellectual attain-

---

[29] Woolhouse, *Locke*, pp. 10, 146-8; Locke's own view is found in his *Essay Concerning Human Understanding*, ed. Peter Nidditch (Oxford, 1975), pp. 91, 542, 564, 634, 646.
[30] *Essay* IV, xvii.

ments, and suggest further warrant for Locke's similarity with the constructive scepticism of the earlier tradition, but I will then present considerations which undermine or qualify that warrant.

I

The obvious candidate for a substantive equivalent of the earlier tradition's category of moral certainty is Locke's three highest degrees of probability. (One cannot consider Locke's category of sensitive knowledge as equivalent, because its extension is clearly not the extension of cases put by the earlier tradition under the rubric of moral certainty; the cases which moral certainty covered for them may sometimes include those covered by Locke's category of sensitive knowledge, but moral certainty also covers cases which Locke restricts to the category of probability.) Locke's admission that where any of the three highest degrees of probability obtains it is impossible not to assent, appears to show that he does not make an absolute division between knowledge and probability.[31] The three highest degrees of probability are like knowledge in that one crucial respect in which they are radically unlike the lower levels of probability. Presumably, then, they can serve as a bridge category which dissolves the apparently qualitative distinction between knowledge and probability into a quantitative one, and thus support the claim that Locke appeals, like the earlier tradition, to 'the certainty of ordinary life'. Compelling assent as they do, the highest levels of probability would, despite Locke's refusal to term them 'certainty', seem to be equal in epistemological status and force to the category of 'certainty'.

A converse way of making the same point is in terms of the relation of the highest degrees of probability to doubt. Locke and the earlier tradition agree that not all doubt that is possible is thereby reasonable. In the case of intuition, Locke writes, there is 'no room for Hesitation, Doubt, or Examination', 'no room for any the least mistake or doubt'.[32] In Demonstration the evidence is '*not* altogether *so clear* and bright, nor the assent so ready' for

---

[31] Ibid., p. 663; note that Van Leeuwen (p. 135) sees Locke's recognition of this as stronger than the preceding tradition's view which saw assent in such cases as voluntary, but Wilkins writes that one 'may *and must*' assent in such cases (p. 23, ital. mine).

[32] *Essay*, pp. 531, 684.

there is a 'great abatement of that evident lustre and full assurance' which accompany Intuition;[33] thus, mistake is possible.[34] But we are nevertheless in such a case 'put past doubting' because even in the case of sensitive knowledge, which he admits is 'not altogether so certain' as demonstration, we are put past doubting.[35] One could argue, then, that if the evidence of sense puts us 'past doubting', and according to Locke, such sense evidence not only 'passes under' but also '*deserves the name of Knowledge*',[36] then the highest degree of probability, in which we are also put 'past doubt',[37] should also deserve the name knowledge or certainty. Moreover, even in the least of the three highest degrees of probability, the evidence 'naturally determines the Judgment, and leaves us as little liberty to believe, or disbelieve, as a Demonstration does'.[38] These considerations suggest that because the highest degrees of probability are similar to knowledge or certainty with respect to indubitability, they should be considered substantively equal to knowledge or certainty.

Still another possible ground for seeing Locke as a direct culmination of the preceding tradition lies in the use of the Aristotelian principle of suiting proof to subject-matter. Recall the familiar passage in the *Nichomachean Ethics*:

Our discussion will be adequate if it has as much clearness as the subject-matter admits of ... for it is the mark of an educated man to look for precision in each class of things just so far as the nature of the subject admits; it is evidently equally foolish to accept probable reasoning from a mathematician and to demand from a rhetorician scientific proofs.[39]

Van Leeuwen suggests that Chillingworth, Tillotson, Wilkins, and Glanvill appeal to this principle as a theoretical justification for accepting moral certainty as an adequate response to scepticism.[40] Chillingworth refers to it obliquely, quoting from Grotius's use of Aristotle, with the implication that it is unreasonable to demand for one discipline proofs suited to another.[41] Tillotson writes:

[33] *Essay*, pp. 532-3.
[34] Ibid., p. 684.
[35] Ibid., p. 537.
[36] Ibid., pp. 537, 631.
[37] Ibid., p. 662.
[38] Ibid., p. 663.
[39] Book 1, Chap. 3, trans. Sir David Ross (London, 1954).
[40] Van Leeuwen, pp. 67, 69.   [41] Ibid., p. 21.

Aristotle hath long since well observed, how unreasonable it is to expect the same kind of proof and evidence for every thing, which we have for some things.[42]

He says more forcefully:

Doth not *Aristotle* say, that Things of a moral and civil Nature, and Matters of Fact done long ago, are incapable of Demonstration; and that it is madness to expect it for Things of this Nature?[43]

Contrasted with this 'madness' is the unexciting but sensible conclusion that

It is sufficient that the Evidence be such as the Nature of the thing to be proved will admit of, and such as prudent Men make no scruple to admit for sufficient Evidence for things of the like Nature, and such as, supposing the thing to be, we cannot ordinarily expect better, or greater Evidence for it.[44]

Wilkins, as noted earlier, also refers explicitly to Aristotle when he argues that '[N]othing can be more irrational than for a Man to doubt of, or deny the Truth of any thing, because it cannot be made out by such kind of Proofs of which the Nature of such a thing is not capable'.[45] His explanation:

The Philosopher hath long ago told us, that according to the divers Nature of things, so much the Evidence for them be ... He that is rational and judicious will expect no other kind of Arguments in any case than the subject-matter will bear. How incongruous would it be for a Mathematician to persuade with Eloquence ... It would be altogether as vain and improper in matters belonging to an Orator to pretend to strict Demonstration. All things are not capable of the same kind of Evidence.[46]

Van Leeuwen sees Wilkins's appeal as supporting the claim that even where different kinds of evidence are appropriate one can gain sufficient assurance for the purposes of religion and science. But Wilkins, I argued earlier, goes beyond the claim of the sufficiency of the assurance attainable, to the claim of the *equivalence* of the assurance attainable. Using the maxim *Veritas non recipit magis et minus* in conjunction with the Aristotelian principle, he suggests

---

[42] *Works*, 9th ed., 'On the Wisdom of Being Religious', p. 16.
[43] Ibid., *Rule of Faith*, p. 558.
[44] *Works*, 4th ed., Vol. III, p. 110.
[45] Wilkins, p. 20.
[46] Ibid., pp. 20–1; cf. Van Leeuwen's qualification, p. 67 n. 57.

that certainty, like truth, is a threshold concept which has no degrees. One result is that, strictly speaking, although he describes other kinds of certainty, moral certainty is not a lower level or degree of certainty—and this accounts for the claim that moral certainty is equal to the certainty of demonstration.[47]

Locke too refers to what sounds like the same Aristotelian principle when he writes:

[H]ow foolish and vain a thing it is, for a Man of narrow Knowledge ... *to expect Demonstration* and Certainty *in things not capable of it*; and refuse Assent to very rational Propositions, and act contrary to very plain and clear Truths, because they cannot be made out so evident, as to surmount every the least (I will not say Reason, but) pretence of doubting.[48]

Sharing that appreciation with Wilkins, one might expect Locke to share as well the view concerning the equivalence of the highest degree of assurance possible in each case, a view in which being put past doubt would be a threshold, all-or-nothing, category. This would render the highest degrees of probability—covering beliefs that there was such a city as Rome, and that there lived 1,700 years ago a man named Julius Caesar—as certain as knowledge. And that would adequately account for Locke's admissions that in cases of the highest probability not only do we act, but 'we reason ... with as little doubt, as if it were perfect demonstration';[49] they 'govern [not only our actions, but] our Thoughts as absolutely ... as the most evident demonstration'.[50]

2

In spite of the elements noted above, however, which can be used to support the claim that Locke was in direct line with the earlier tradition of constructive scepticism, including Wilkins, Locke was interpreted by some coming after him as failing to do justice to

---

[47] Van Leeuwen notes the use of the maxim that all truths are on a par (pp. 67, 104), but neither remarks on the implication that certainty too is seen as a threshold concept, nor sees the relevance of this for his charge that their proposed equivalence of certainty undermines the objective relation between assent and evidence and thus conflicts with their proportionality requirement.

[48] *Essay*, p. 636.

[49] Ibid., p. 661.

[50] Ibid., p. 662.

a category outside demonstration or knowledge in which there was 'no room for doubt'. He was charged as well with failing to be consistent in his conclusion that probabilities can govern our thoughts as absolutely as can demonstration, with failing to be able to justify that (correct) conclusion on the basis of his premisses.[51] These interpretations may simply have been the result of bias or misunderstanding of Locke's views. I suggest, however, that in addition to (and perhaps in tension with) those elements noted above, there are in Locke other elements which account for, or at least plausibly occasion, such interpretations, and it will be instructive to explore them.

First, despite Locke's recognition of the unavoidableness of assent in cases of the highest probability, there is reason to see in his thought the proposal of an absolute dichotomy between knowledge and probability which signals a departure from the tradition preceding him. I suggest that it is not merely the *fact* of the unavoidableness of assent which is relevant, for Locke reveals a potentially important difference in the reasons for or sources of the unavoidableness in cases of certainty and in cases of even the three highest degrees of probability. He writes:

And herein lies the *difference between Probability* and *Certainty, Faith* and *Knowledge*, that in all the parts of Knowledge, there is intuition; each immediate *Idea*, each step has its visible and certain connexion; in belief not so. That which makes me believe, is something extraneous to the thing I believe; something not evidently joined on both sides to, and so not manifestly shewing the Agreement or Disagreement of those *Ideas*, that are under consideration.[52]

I take this to introduce or emphasize a *qualitative* distinction between the two—such as precludes the notion of a continuum.[53] Even in the highest degrees of probability what makes me believe is 'something extraneous to the thing I believe'. This echoes some-

---

[51] For example, as we shall see in later chapters, this charge was made by both Thomas Reid and John Henry Newman.

[52] *Essay*, p. 655. Though the concept of sensitive knowledge is not directly or explicitly dealt with here, it is not incompatible with his characterization of knowledge.

[53] I thus take issue with claims like the following made by Shapiro: 'For Locke, knowledge ... was distinguished, *albeit not sharply*, from probability' (ital. mine) and 'Probability thus effectively became knowledge' (*Probability and Certainty in Seventeenth-Century England*, pp. 37, 42).

thing of the absoluteness of the great medieval divide between *scientia* and *opinio*, something quite foreign to the continuum proposed by Wilkins, for example. And it is, I suggest, the qualitativeness of the distinction which best accounts for the vehemence of Locke's repeated cautions. Something crucial is lacking to those cases where what makes me believe is something 'extraneous to the thing I believe'; therefore, 'the highest Probability, amounts not to Certainty; without which, there can be no true Knowledge'.[54] Even in cases where Assent 'necessarily' follows, 'it never amounts to Knowledge, no not to that which is the lowest degree of it'.[55] Moreover, even though Locke recognizes the difference between doubt that is merely possible and doubt that is reasonable, he clearly affirms that even when the probability 'puts me past doubt', I am not thereby given certainty:

[T]hough it be highly probable, that Millions of Men do now exist, yet ... I have not that Certainty of it, which we strictly call Knowledge; though the great likelihood of it puts me past doubt, and it be reasonable for me to do several things upon the confidence, that there are Men ... now in the world: But this is but probability, not Knowledge.[56]

I am suggesting that Locke's refusal to bestow the title 'certainty' on the highest levels of proability, even though assent is unavoidable there, is not simply a terminological difference between Locke and Wilkins (and perhaps the entire earlier tradition). Rather it indicates Locke's strong sense of and commitment to an unmitigated break, based on the qualitative distinction between certainty and probability.[57] It is that commitment on Locke's part which, I suggest, is incompatible with the commitment to the continuum which

[54] *Essay*, p. 546.
[55] Ibid., p. 685.
[56] Ibid., pp. 635-6.
[57] Locke's refusal to allow probable reasoning to lead in any cases to certainty sits uncomfortably, I suggest, with one of the two ways in which he speaks of 'degrees of reason'. François Duchesneau's interesting discussion of 'Locke et le savoir de probabilité' notes that one distinction between degrees of reason contrasts the higher degree which picks out necessary connections with the lower which picks out probable connections (*Essay* IV, xvii, 2), while the second distinction refers to the different 'moments ['aspects'] de l'activité rationelle' (*Essay* IV, xvii, 3); the latter highlights Locke's positive evaluation of 'sagacity' (*Dialogue* XI (1972), p. 195). On the latter view, Duchesneau concludes, 'la saisie des rapports analogiques, qui permettent de faire des raisonnements probables, accède à une perfection telle qu'elle tend à supplanter celle que l'on trouve dans la démonstration des vérités établies. L'évaluation portant sur les pouvoirs inventifs de la raison, confirme pleinement les droits du savoir de probabilité' (p. 196).

is a crucial ingredient in Wilkins's account, for such a qualitative break would be quite foreign to Wilkins. Departing from that feature is departing from *the* tradition in a significant way, however much Locke emphasizes with the rest of that tradition the practical sufficiency of our intellectual attainments.

My claim that Locke's dichotomy 'echoes' something of the earlier medieval one needs to be qualified. The medieval tradition saw the divide as the result of their claim that there were different objects for knowledge and opinion. Objects of knowledge could only be known—they were necessary conclusions of demonstration or self-evident truths. For Locke, however, it is clear that the same truths can be the subject of either knowledge or belief. For example, he contrasts two different ways of accepting the same proposition:

In the demonstration of it, a Man perceives the certain immutable connexion there is of Equality, between the three Angles of a *Triangle*, and those intermediate ones, which are made use of to shew their Equality to two right ones: ... And thus he has certain Knowledge that it is so. But another Man who never took the pains to observe the Demonstration, hearing a Mathematician, a Man of credit, affirm the three Angles of a Triangle, to be equal to two right ones, *assents* to it; i.e. receives it for true. In which case the foundation of his Assent is the Probability of the thing.[58]

No truths, then, are in themselves truths that can only be believed or only known (except intuitive truths). The same proposition can be demonstrated, hence known, or accepted on testimony or evidence less than demonstrable, and hence believed, because only probable. There is a continuum in the sense that epistemological status depends on the kind of evidence, rather than the kind of object. But Locke seems determined to distinguish kinds of evidence from degrees of evidence in a way that Wilkins, for example, does not. Probable evidence for Locke is not simply evidence that is 'less plain and clear', but rather evidence which is qualitatively distinguished from the evidence leading to knowledge. So although he challenges the medieval dichotomy, he does so, not as did his earlier predecessors, by proposing a continuum where certainty spans both the categories of knowledge and probability, or where unreasonable doubt equals certainty, but rather by proposing an

[58] *Essay*, p. 654; cf. also his example in section 5, p. 656.

equally stark dichotomy which nevertheless does not require that knowledge have its own exclusive objects.

Locke's failure to make being put past doubt an all-or-nothing phenomenon fits perfectly with his insistence on a qualitative distinction between knowledge and probability, for something is lacking to cases where what makes me believe is 'something extraneous to the thing I believe'. Moreover, even within the category of knowledge, being put past doubt is not a threshold concept for Locke. Nor are these claims by Locke inconsistent with his acceptance of the Aristotelian principle, for of itself it supports no claim to the attainment of certainty in all cases or the equivalence of all cases of highest assurance.

Finally, Locke's admission that probabilities can govern even our thoughts as fully as demonstration is not necessarily inconsistent with the qualitative distinction either. For it is not necessarily a concession on Locke's part that relates to theory, but may be going no further than to claim the legitimacy of 'thinking-as-if', or the unavoidability of particular acts of believing.

In sum, aspects of Locke's thought on probability substantively reinforce his reservations concerning the application of the word 'certainty', and thus make it plausible to interpret him as ignoring the category of 'proof', and more generally, as departing in a significant way from an account generally considered to be representative of the preceding tradition of constructive scepticism.

In the following chapter I will consider Hume's response to Locke, suggesting that the character and relevance of Hume's appeal to human nature is made clearer if one locates him in this historical perspective. In particular, (1) his response to Locke is more understandable if Locke is seen as departing from the tradition preceding him in the way I have argued, and (2) the potential implications of his 'naturalist' reply to extreme scepticism can be more adequately appreciated if approached with the particular questions in mind raised by the analysis of the preceding accounts.

3

Hume's Naturalism: Proof and Practice

HUME'S 'naturalist' response to Pyrrhonist scepticism has been interpreted by some as merely an extended *pragmatic* mitigation: whereas the Pyrrhonist concedes that we have to act on particular beliefs although they are not rationally justifiable, Hume extends the necessity to cover acts of believing in particular ways although they are not rationally justifiable. On this view Hume offers to the sceptic only a counter-description of the unavoidability of particular beliefs, a counter-description which uncritically accepts the sceptic's charge concerning philosophical legitimacy. In light of the preceding analysis of a tradition in which the notion of unreasonable doubt played an important anti-sceptical role, I want to challenge this reading of Hume by reconsidering his category of 'proof', arguing that it can shed useful light on how his 'naturalist' response to scepticism might consistently show more than simply the unavoidability or irresistibility of particular beliefs.

I will begin by considering anew Hume's description of 'proof' in terms of its achievements and implications concerning doubt and certainty. In the *Treatise* he suggests that the philosophical division of all reasoning into 'knowledge' and 'probability' leaves out the category of 'proof'. Since, he says, 'in common discourse we readily affirm, that many arguments from causation exceed probability, and may be receiv'd as a superior kind of evidence', in order to 'mark the several degrees of evidence', we ought to 'distinguish human reason into three kinds, viz. *that from knowledge, from proofs, and from probabilities*'.[1] He elaborates on the distinction between 'proofs' and 'probabilities' as follows: proofs are 'those arguments, which are derived from the relation of cause and effect, and which are entirely free from doubt and uncertainty'; probabilities are 'that evidence, which is still attended with uncertainty'.

---

[1] *A Treatise of Human Nature*, p. 124.

Moreover, although the 'gradation ... from probabilities to proofs' is in many cases 'insensible', they are separate categories; 'proof' is distinguished by 'full assurance', attaining a 'pitch of perfection' and until that point is reached it is 'only to be esteem'd a presumption or probability'.[2]

In the first *Enquiry*, Hume's recapitulation of this distinction specifically challenges Locke's division of all arguments into demonstrative and probable. On Locke's view we would have to say that 'it is only probable all men must die, or that the sun will rise to-morrow'. On the contrary, Hume continues, 'to conform our language more to common use, we ought to divide arguments into *demonstrations*, *proofs* and *probabilities*. By proofs meaning such arguments from experience as leave no room for doubt or opposition.'[3] Explaining the character of the 'experience' needed, he writes that 'where the past has been entirely regular and uniform, we expect the event with the greatest assurance, and leave no room for any contrary supposition'.[4] In line with common usage, in Section IX he calls such an inference 'certain and conclusive';[5] in Section X he reintroduces the distinction between 'proof' and 'probability', applying it to cases of 'evidence, derived from witnesses and human testimony', and concludes that where the conjunction has been constant, the proof is 'full' or 'entire', generating 'the highest certainty',[6] The question is then—what is the status of 'proof' on Hume's view; in particular, what is the status of the 'certainty' achieved by 'proof'?

Richard Popkin has shown that the distinction Hume uses had been explicitly made by several earlier writers, including the Scottish disciple of Fenelon and one-time Pyrrhonist, Chevalier Andrew Michael Ramsay, whom Hume met in France when writing his *Treatise*. Ramsay's distinction was as follows:

The source of Pyrrhonism comes from failing to distinguish between a demonstration, a proof and a probability. A demonstration supposes that the contradictory belief is impossible; a proof of fact is where all the reasons lead to belief, without there being any pretext for doubt; a prob-

---

[2] *A Treatise of Human Nature*, pp. 130–1.

[3] *Enquiries Concerning the Human Understanding and Concerning the Principles of Morals*, p. 56 n.

[4] Ibid., p. 58.

[5] Ibid., p. 104.

[6] Ibid., pp. 112, 114, 115, 110; cf. p. 44 n. (experience yields 'certainty').

ability is where all the reasons for belief are stronger than those for doubting.[7]

According to Popkin, Hume's response to Pyrrhonism, although it uses a distinction and arguments intended by others as anti-sceptical, only strengthens the philosophical thesis of Pyrrhonism. That is, Hume recognized that 'Nature does not logically refute Pyrrhonism; it only makes it unbelievable. The philosophical force of the arguments remains intact, but their psychological force is nil.'[8] The implication is that the only proper reading of the distinction between 'proof' and 'probability', for Hume, is in terms of the unavoidability or irresistibility of the conclusions of proofs. Moreover, Hume's acceptance of the 'philosophical force' of the sceptic's argument is guaranteed, for Popkin, by Hume's admission that matters of fact cannot be demonstrated. Referring to 'the sceptical view that facts cannot be demonstrated', Popkin suggests that Hume made it clear that 'if the rationalists once admit that they cannot give demonstrations for their views, then they admit these views are without foundation, and hence Pyrrhonism triumphs'.[9] Hume's consistent Pyrrhonism, then, is the uncritical acceptance of the sceptic's philosophical thesis, mitigated by the counter-description of the unavoidability of the beliefs in question.

A similar conclusion is advanced in D.C. Stove's study of Hume's view of inductive inference; the distinction between 'proof' and 'probability' cannot have any 'logical' import, although it does make the accurate psychological point that the 'degree of conclusiveness which men naturally ascribe to the predictive-inductive inference is not introspectively discriminable from that which they naturally ascribe to Barbara or *modus ponens*'.[10] Stove's argument for denying Hume's category of proof 'logical' import is that Hume is committed to inductive fallibilism.[11] This fallibilism holds that predictive-inductive inferences (including those based on constant

---

[7] *Voyages de Cyrus*, pp. 229 n.–30 n.; cited in Richard Popkin, 'David Hume and the Pyrrhonian Controversy', reprinted in *The High Road to Pyrrhonism* (San Diego, 1980), p. 136. On p. 141 Popkin even cites Hume's reference in a footnote, but only the *Treatise* version.

[8] 'David Hume and the Pyrrhonian Controversy', p. 145; cf. also his 'David Hume: His Pyrrhonism and his Critique of Pyrrhonism', reprinted in *Hume*, ed. V.C. Chapell (Notre Dame, 1968), p. 88.

[9] David Hume and the Pyrrhonian Controversy', pp. 136, 144.

[10] *Probability and Hume's Inductive Scepticism* (Oxford, 1973), p. 97.

[11] Ibid., pp. 93–7.

conjunction, as in proofs) are 'invalid [i.e., 'it is possible for them to have true premises and false conclusions'[12]] and consequently, not of the highest possible degree of conclusiveness'.[13] Stove seems then to be claiming that because proofs are not demonstrations, the 'highest certainty' Hume ascribes to them may be introspectively indiscriminable from, but cannot be, warranted certainty.

David Fate Norton's more recent study of Hume makes a more general point, but with apparently the same implication.[14] Norton dissociates Hume's admissions of the irresistibility of particular beliefs (because of the unavoidability of trust in our natural faculties) from any claims (implicit or explicit) concerning either truth or the reliability of those faculties. He contrasts Hume and his Scottish Common Sense critics, suggesting that the latter conflated psychological certainty with objective certainty or knowledge by insisting 'that what we cannot avoid *believing* must be reliable or true', and that Hume did not agree with them that unavoidable beliefs were certain.[15] Reid thought that our natural faculties were 'not fallacious' and could be 'relied on with security', and Norton takes this to be antithetical to Hume's position.[16] To admit that a particular belief in X is unavoidable, Norton writes, is quite a different thing from 'suppos[ing] that X is true or objectively certain'; Hume 'does not suppose that reality must be of a certain form because a belief that it is so cannot be shaken off'.[17] In contrast to Descartes, 'for Hume, to have no doubts is (in any circumstances), simply to have no doubts'.[18] The point then seems to be, like Popkin's and Stove's, that for Hume unavoidability is only unavoidability, to have no doubts is simply to have no doubts. Hume's mitigation of scepticism is therefore only *practical*—in the sense that it uncritically accepts the philosophical thesis of the

[12] *Probability and Hume's Inductive Scepticism*, p. 48.

[13] Ibid., p. 97. However, one could argue that Stove's own criticism of the arguments for the deductivist thesis can be applicable to the equation of non-entailment with the impossibility of the highest degree of conclusiveness (pp. 79–83); his concession that debate for and against deductivism can only 'be decided by arguments, the premises of which cannot be discovered to be true without reliance sooner or later on *intuitive* assessments of the conclusiveness of inferences' (pp. 84, 88) can also support the rejection of an analytic paradigm of certainty.

[14] *David Hume: Common Sense Moralist and Sceptical Metaphysician* (Princeton, 1982).

[15] Ibid., p. 201.

[16] Ibid., pp. 172, 172, n. 36.

[17] Ibid., pp. 290, 201 n. 18.

[18] Ibid., pp. 254–5.

sceptic, leaves the sceptic's philosophical point untouched because unaddressed.

In what follows I shall argue that a reconsideration of Hume's thought on 'proof' and 'certainty' warrants a re-evaluation of that kind of conclusion. But first I want to suggest that such an interpretation of Hume's appeal to the unavoidability of instinctive beliefs trades on an important vagueness in the phrase 'acceptance of the sceptic's philosophical thesis'. On the view of Popkin and Stove noted above, the sceptical thesis Hume is said to accept is the thesis that matters of fact cannot be demonstrated. Now Hume not only accepts that thesis, he goes beyond it by arguing that there is, in addition, no non-circular argument for matter of fact conclusions either.[19] If the sceptic's thesis is that there is no *argument* justifying those beliefs, then Hume surely accepts that thesis. But such a thesis is not necessarily a sceptical one. What is sceptical about the sceptic's challenge is the claim that *because* there is no argument, something essential is lacking—something which should be there, isn't there. So it is not at all clear, without begging the question, that Hume's acceptance of the view that there is and can be no *argument* justifying those beliefs is an acceptance of the sceptic's 'philosophical' thesis, since that view leaves open the question whether the lack of such argument is to be lamented in any way. As I noted in Chapter 1, I am not referring here simply to the fact that there are many varieties of scepticism, some more restricted than others. Rather I am pointing out that a crucial element in any definition of the sceptic's challenge is omitted if one simply stops with the claim that we do not have a particular kind of backing for a particular kind of claim, since in itself this may indicate only a sensitivity to differences in subject-matter, with no sceptical intention or implication. To refuse to see the 'lack' of argument as a lack is to fail to accept what is distinctively sceptical about the sceptic's thesis. Thus Hume's acceptance of the thesis that no 'argument' justifies those beliefs does not necessarily preclude him from offering a response to the sceptic in which 'proof' carries with it implications which critically comment on, and thereby mitigate, the sceptic's philosophical thesis.

To return then to Hume's characterization of 'proof'. As noted above, Hume characterizes 'proof' in the *Treatise* as an argument

<hr />

[19] *Enquiries*, p. 37.

which, while not demonstrative, is nevertheless 'entirely free from doubt and uncertainty'. In itself this need only be a claim about the *absence* of doubt in particular cases—we simply do not have doubt about some things. A stronger claim would be that we are *unable* to doubt in particular cases—some beliefs are irresistible. But even this, as it stands, need not constitute more than a merely descriptive claim about psychological capacities and abilities. If this is all Hume meant, Popkin, Stove, and Norton would be correct in assessing Hume's category of proof as one with only psychological import, making no critical comment on or mitigation of the Pyrrhonist thesis at a philosophical level. It would describe a psychological condition which of itself says nothing about whether we ought to try to undermine the psychological resistance we feel, or try to counteract our inability to doubt. Obviously there might be causes (drugs, electrical stimulation, etc) which can make it impossible for someone as a matter of fact to doubt a given proposition, at the same time as there are in fact good reasons for doubting it. So in itself being unable to doubt *p* says nothing about whether there are or could be *good reasons* for doubting *p*. I want to suggest, however, that there are elements in Hume which support more than either the mere absence of, or psychological inability to, doubt. And a first indication of this may be found in Hume's *later* characterization of proof.

In the *Enquiry* Hume's description of proof is slightly different from that in the *Treatise*, and it is a difference that may be instructive. Instead of saying, as he did earlier, that proofs are 'free from doubt', he says now that 'they leave no room for doubt or opposition'.[20] A page later he reiterates: such proofs 'leave no room for any contrary supposition'. To say that an argument is free from doubt is ambiguous; it might mean simply that no doubt is attached to it by the person accepting it, although doubt should be attached. To say that one is unable to doubt is likewise ambiguous; it may mean merely that a person is psychologically unable to doubt although the proposition deserves to be doubted. To say that there is 'no room for doubt', however, may be a much stronger claim; to have 'no room for doubt' may mean that there is 'no room' for anything which could significantly *count as a reason* for doubting. In a case where nothing would count in that way, persons would

---

[20] Note that Locke's use of the phrase 'no room for doubt' is limited to cases of 'Intuition'—*An Essay Concerning Human Understanding*, IV, ii, 1.

find themselves actually unable to doubt. Inability to doubt might in some cases, therefore, be importantly related to having no reasonable ground for doubting, and having 'no room for doubt' might in some cases constitute (part of) a direct philosophical reply to the sceptic.

Hume's phrase 'no room for doubt' might then be significant, signalling the possibility that Hume connected the category of proof with the idea of a lack of *reasonable* grounds for doubting (as opposed to a simple lack of doubt or psychological inability to doubt), and thus intended a response to the sceptic which, while depending on psychological description, goes beyond mere unavoidability. This would, in effect disambiguate and strengthen his earlier claim that proof is 'free from doubt'.

In what follows I want to consider two kinds of warrant for such a reading of Hume's category of proof as claiming that 'certainty' is constituted by the absence of 'reasonable' doubt—that is, not only do we experience in particular cases of matters of fact an assurance equal to that generated by demonstrations, but we are not unreasonable to do so, and, moreover, would be unreasonable not to allow ourselves to experience it. On such a reading, Hume would not be accepting an 'argument'-based paradigm of either certainty or truth.

It is clear that Hume saw his category of proof as a corrective to the view attributed to Locke that all reasoning is subject to the exhaustive dichotomy of knowledge/demonstration vs. probability. His suggestion was that Locke failed to recognize that category and consequently posited a dichotomy which led to conclusions which are, at the very least, at variance with ordinary usage (a usage, moreover, to which Hume himself adheres). Whether or not Hume was correct in attributing this failure to Locke,[21] it is important that Hume saw his reading of Locke as unproblematical, one for which he need not argue, because it means that, whatever its character and implications on his account, he sees proof as a necessary corrective and not simply a repetition or reinforcement of a category commonly assumed in philosophical circles. (That in itself seems reason enough to re-evaluate his notion of proof.)

We saw in Chapter 2 that Locke starkly and qualitatively distin-

---

[21] Cf. Henry Van Leeuwen, *The Problem of Certainty in English Thought, 1630–1690*, where Locke is said to be a culmination of the tradition in which certainty is constituted by the absence of 'reasonable' doubt, p. 123.

guishes knowledge or demonstration from probability, and that, although he concedes that in cases of the three highest kinds of probability we are put 'past doubting', he nevertheless denies that in such cases we have 'certainty'. Now either Hume was ignorant of or misunderstood Locke's view of the highest kinds of probability, or he saw his own category of 'proof' as implying more than the descriptive compulsion Locke admitted in cases of the highest probability. Moreover, Hume's own contrasts were between '*Relations of Ideas*' and '*Matters of Fact*', and between 'demonstrative reasoning' and 'moral reasoning'.[22] Hume did not, as did Locke, make the categories of knowledge and certainty coextensive by definition. There is, then, the possibility for Hume that in particular cases of matters of fact, such as were located by Locke in the category of the highest degrees of probability (and hence were not 'certain'), total certainty can be no less warranted than in cases of demonstration.

What would lend support to such a reading? Consider first Hume's view of 'reasonable' and 'unreasonable' doubt? Integral to his discussion 'Of Liberty and Necessity' in the first *Enquiry* is a detailed consideration of 'inferences ... attended with more or less degrees of certainty proportioned to our experience of the usual conduct of mankind'.[23] Hume is arguing that 'moral evidence' (here he means evidence concerning the conduct of human agents) is really on a continuum with the kind of evidence we have in cases of '*physical* necessity', and that in some instances of both kinds of evidence we can feel equally and totally assured. Thus, he says, I 'no more suspect' that some moral connections of cause and effect will not hold than I question the hitherto unvarying outcome of some physical relations. There are cases in which moral evidence is such that we can say that we 'know with certainty' that an agent will act in a particular way—e.g., will not keep his hand in a fire until it is consumed—because 'no suspicion of an unknown frenzy [on his part] can give the least possibility' to an event contrary to observed constant conjunction.[24]

The discussion is significant because it illustrates the kind of certainty Hume thinks one can obtain in a proof. His example is

---

[22] *Enquiries*, pp. 25, 35.

[23] Ibid., p. 91.

[24] Ibid. Note the conflict with Hume's claim that what is conceivable is possible (*Enquiries*, p. 26, *Treatise*, p. 89); cf. Chap. 6 below for further analysis.

obviously non-demonstrative, and his conclusion is that we are entitled to say that we 'know with certainty'. The important thing to note is that he is making a distinction here between kinds of *possibility* of error. The example clearly allows the logical possibility of error, for there is no logical contradiction in the conclusion that an agent would hold his hand in a fire until it was consumed. Yet Hume insists that nothing could give the 'least possibility' to the hypothesis of such an event. The logical possibility of error, therefore, does not constitute or give room for the supposition of the 'least possibility' of error. More important, since something more substantive could be offered in support of the possible falsehood of the conclusion than merely that its denial is not a logical contradiction, his example allows even more than the logical possibility of error. So his discussion assumes that not all cases of more-than-logical possibility of error are cases in which it is reasonable to doubt. Hume could not be intending, therefore, to correlate 'unreasonable' doubt with doubt based on the mere logical possibility of error, on the one hand, and 'reasonable' doubt with doubt based on the more-than-logical possibility of error, on the other. The crucial distinction lies *within* the category of more-than-logical possibility of error.[25]

In this discussion, then, Hume is illustrating his view that not all doubt that is possible (even more-than-logically possible) is reasonable, and that unreasonable doubt is not to be equated with doubt that is logically impossible, or merely logically possible. If this is true of conclusions about moral agency, and Hume feels the need to make the case that we can be no less certain in moral than in physical cases, then the claim that in particular cases of non-demonstrative evidence doubt is unreasonable is even more applicable to the cases of physical necessity cited as 'proofs'.

The unreasonableness of doubt in particular cases where doubt is none the less more than logically possible is reiterated in Hume's suggestion that 'none but a fool or madman will ever pretend to dispute the authority of experience'.[26] But what precisely is the 'authority' of experience? Is it merely irresistibility? If the appeal to a distinction between 'reasonable' and 'unreasonable' doubt rests, at bottom, on ungrounded instinctive responses, is it possible

[25] This is effectively a preliminary way of challenging an analytic/synthetic distinction.

[26] *Enquiries*, p. 36.

to read it as providing more than an uncritical counter-description to the sceptic? I suggest that it might provide more if implicit in the appeal to psychological/socio-linguistic fact is a particular kind of *theoretical* assessment. One element in such an assessment would be the affirmation of a connection between the impossibility of giving reasons for and against, and the illegitimacy of the request for justifying reasons in such a case. A second, reinforcing, element would be the recognition that not all possible doubt is 'reasonable' doubt. A third reinforcing element would be the affirmation of the reasonableness of continuing to believe those things (*a*) which we find ourselves unable to doubt, *and* (*b*) to which the only possible challenges are themselves no more certain than the claims they challenge. Given this threefold theoretical assessment, the entire programme could be seen as offering a response to the sceptic at a level which at least exceeds that of uncritical counter-description of the unavoidability of beliefs. Thus, without constituting an attempt to provide justification of the sort the sceptic requests,[27] Hume's discussion of proof could be read (at the very least) as introducing a category embodying an appeal to a doctrine of reasonable/unreasonable doubt which directly confronts the philosophical level of the sceptic's thesis. This would offer a way of enriching a 'naturalist' interpretation of Hume, so that Hume's programme could be seen as more than 'a project in descriptive psychology'[28] which uncritically accepts the sceptic's thesis.

Furthermore, the character of the 'authority' of experience which it is unreasonable to reject must be interpreted in light of Hume's claim two pages earlier that inductive conclusions 'may justly be inferred'[29]—i.e., they are not merely unavoidably inferred—and his claim that they can attain the 'highest certainty'.[30] And the status of both these claims can, I suggest, be illuminated by reference to Hume's understanding of certainty, as expressed outside the *Trea-*

[27] Cf. Peter Jones, 'Strains in Hume and Wittgenstein', in *Hume: A Re-Evaluation*, eds. D. W. Livingston and J. T. King (New York, 1976), p. 193; Oswald Hanfling, 'Hume and Wittgenstein', in *Impressions of Empiricism*, ed. Godfrey Vesey (New York, 1976), p. 52.

[28] This claim is made by R. W. Connon in 'The Naturalism of Hume Revisited', in *McGill Hume Studies*, eds. D. F. Norton *et al.* (San Diego, 1979), p. 121. Cf. J. Passmore's 'Hume and the Ethics of Belief', in *David Hume: Bicentenary Papers*, ed. G. P. Morice (Edinburgh, 1977), pp. 77-92, for support for a prescriptive reading of Hume.

[29] *Enquiries*, p. 34.

[30] Ibid., p. 110.

tise and first *Enquiry*. He explicitly considers, for example, such matter of fact conclusions as 'Caesar existed' and 'There is such an Island as Sicily'. Admitting that there is neither intuitive nor demonstrative evidence for these kinds of propositions, he yet asks:

> Would you infer that I deny their Truth, or even their Certainty? There are many different kinds of Certainty; and some of them as satisfactory to the Mind, tho' perhaps not so regular, as the demonstrative kind.[31]

The entailment relation is neat and formally analysable—i.e. 'regular'. But non-demonstrative reasoning, Hume here crucially concedes, can be as satisfying as demonstrative reasoning. The 'perfection' of assurance which he says is attainable through proof need not then be any less perfect than that attainable through demonstration. Is Hume here merely describing an assurance in non-demonstrative cases that is psychologically equal to that in demonstration although not as legitimate? It would seem that whatever the import of Hume's claim concerning the certainty arising in demonstrative cases, the same import attaches to the claim concerning certainty in non-demonstrative cases. *Both* must be 'satisfactory to Mind'—it is *we* who find the entailment relation assuring; the relation between premisses and conclusion must always be appropriated by a mind. Hume is therefore not downgrading the certainty available in proofs because he is not accepting an 'argument'-based paradigm of certainty or truth.

The argument that the acceptance of the sceptic's thesis (namely, that because there are no intuitive or argumentative grounds, there are no 'rational' grounds for causal beliefs) limits Hume's mitigation of scepticism to the counter-assertion of unavoidability (which has no philosophical implications concerning legitimacy) assumes that Hume canonized an intuitive or argument-based paradigm of certainty. However, Hume's explicit suggestion that there can be different evidential sources of equally satisfying certainty is one element in a rejection of such a restrictive paradigm of certainty. And his recognition that not all possible doubt is thereby reasonable doubt is a complementary and reinforcing element in such a rejection. Given such a rejection it becomes unnecessary to restrict Hume's response to the sceptic to the mere counter-assertion of unavoidability. Hand in hand with Hume's understanding of the

[31] Letter to John Stewart (Feb., 1754), *Letters of David Hume*, Vol. I, ed. J. Y. T. Greig (Oxford, 1932), p. 187.

unreasonability of doubt in particular cases where doubt is none
the less even more than logically possible, his claims about proof
can convey a philosophically critical message.

In sum, although there is neither intuition, demonstration, nor
non-circular argument for them, the conclusions of proofs are of
the 'highest certainty' and 'justly inferred', and these are attribu-
tions of more than unavoidability. So if the sceptic's thesis is that
matters of fact cannot be 'justly' inferred or certain, Hume does
not mitigate the sceptic's thesis—he rejects it. If the sceptic's thesis
is that matters of fact cannot be 'argumentatively' inferred, Hume
can be said to mitigate that thesis in more than just a practical
way. The strictly practical mitigation would have been the response—'not by argument, therefore not just or certain or true,
because not fulfilling a legitimate requirement, but nevertheless
unavoidable'. But Hume's reply is clearly not limited in that way,
and it is important to point out how much of Hume is ignored by
facile descriptions of his response as 'practical and psychological'.

In the preceding I have been attempting to show why those who
deny the possibility of philosophical import to Hume's naturalist
response to scepticism, in particular to his category of proof,
because they see 'rational justification' and 'unavoidability' as the
only two alternatives, do a disservice to Hume. But I also want to
dissociate my thesis that Hume does directly confront the philosophical thesis of the sceptic from two other variations on the
theme.

First, it has been suggested that Hume was rejecting only a very
limited notion of rationality—namely, a demonstrative or syllogistic paradigm of rationality. For example, it is claimed that Hume's
'real target in the "induction" argument' is 'one of the dogmas of
the schools amounting to the thesis that we think (as well as con-
struct arguments) in terms of syllogisms'.[32] In a similar vein it is
suggested that Hume's target was a particular rationalist conception of reasoning, illustrated by Spinoza and Leibniz, according to
which at least some matter of fact connections are necessary and
demonstrative.[33] The implication is that when Hume attempts to
undermine the notion that we justify our factual conclusions by
'reasoning', he sees such reasoning as a particular kind of syllogistic

[32] Connon, p. 133.
[33] T. Beauchamps and T. Mappes, 'Is Hume Really a Sceptic About Induction?',
American Philosophical Quarterly 12 (1975).

or demonstrative process—to undermine that is not to undermine all 'rational' justification for causal inference. But this is to limit Hume's search for 'argument', 'chain of reasoning', and 'process of the understanding'—for Hume clearly admits that there is no other argument available which does not presuppose the inductive inference in question.[34]

Secondly, even if one grants that Hume is rejecting all 'rational' justification (where 'rational' covers both demonstrative and other mediated reasoning), one might argue that the turn away from 'reasoning' or 'reason' was nevertheless not a turn away from the claim that the beliefs in question were 'reasonable'. Pall Ardal, for example, suggests, as I do, that Hume distinguished 'psychological explanation' from 'justification' and that he does not confuse 'the necessity of a belief ... with the justification'.[35] Ardal sees this as issuing from Hume's implicit commitment to 'reasonableness' as a virtue. The acceptance of causal or experimental beliefs is reasonable, on this view, because we thus favour an attitude which conduces to 'human ends and purposes' (including the end of avoiding 'confusion').[36] Such beliefs are 'inevitable and desirable', 'necessary and useful'[37]—arising and being legitimated in the same way as the rules of justice or linguistic conventions. Reasonableness of belief is not the same as truth—correspondence is not what justifies beliefs, but rather their usefulness or desirability or indispensability.[38]

Ardal admits this is a 'pragmatic' criterion. But I would argue that it is not a criterion of 'reasonable' beliefs at all—rather the question has been shifted by Ardal not from truth to reasonableness of beliefs (as was the intention), but from rationality of beliefs to rationality of actions. What sounds like saying a belief is reasonable if it is an appropriate means to a human end is really saying that it is rational to hold a particular belief if it is an appropriate means to a human end. But that it is rational or reasonable to hold a particular belief in order to achieve a particular end does not make the belief rational or reasonable—it can, after all, in parti-

[34] *Enquiries*, p. 37. But one might cite *Treatise*, p. 97 n., as evidence of an extension by Hume of the term 'rational'; cf. also Norton, p. 97 n. 4.

[35] 'Some Implications of the Virtue of Reasonableness in Hume's *Treatise*', in *Hume: A Re-evaluation*, pp. 103, 104.

[36] Ibid., p. 105.

[37] Ibid., pp. 104, 103.

[38] Ibid., p. 104.

cular cases, be reasonable to hold an unreasonable or irrational belief.

To advance beyond the interpretation that Hume responded to the sceptic's cry of 'not rationally justified' with bowed head and a counter-cry of 'but unavoidable', one needs to show that Hume's claim that such inferences are 'justly' made means more than that they are usefully, desirably, or even indispensably made. For one could claim indispensability while uncritically accepting the sceptic's implicit charge that something is lacking which it makes sense to say should be provided—that is, one could accept with the sceptic that they 'deserved' to be doubted even though we couldn't quite achieve the feat.

On the view I have been defending, Hume does mean more by 'just' and 'certain' inferences than indispensable or unavoidable ones. His claim has to do with the unreasonableness of doubting the inference. Indispensability plays a part—as a minimal condition—but it is not an adequate support for a philosophically relevant reply to the sceptic. The reply that inheres in the distinction between 'reasonable' and 'unreasonable' doubt is one that couples irresistibility of beliefs with the additional philosophically critical comments (noted earlier) that not all possible doubt is reasonable, and that the only possible challenges are themselves no more certain than the claims they challenge. Having no room for doubt means that there is no possibility of anything which could, by being more certain than the claim it attempts to jeopardize, provide a reasonable ground for doubting it. It is this kind of philosophically relevant consideration which could advance the claim beyond that of the mere unavoidability of beliefs.

Ironically, this consideration can be found in an argument which Hume offers as highlighting precisely the legitimate strength of the sceptic. The latter, he says, 'will always triumph' when he points up the following problem with any opinion which we hold based on sense evidence. Such an opinion

if rested on natural instinct, is contrary to reason, and if referred to reason, is contrary to natural instinct, and at the same time carries no rational evidence with it, to convince an impartial enquirer.[39]

Such is the 'force of the Pyrrhonian doubt' from which nothing can free us but 'the strong power of natural instinct'.[40] But what

---

[39] *Enquiries*, p. 155.   [40] Ibid., p. 162.

precisely does Hume think this impasse allows the Pyrrhonian rightly to conclude? What is the extent of the sceptic's 'triumph', the extent of the 'force of the Pyrrhonian doubt'?

On the one hand, Hume writes that the dilemma revealed by the sceptic is a topic

in which the profounder and more philosophical sceptics will always triumph, when they endeavour to introduce an universal doubt into all subjects of human knowledge and enquiry.[41]

This suggests that such doubt is reasonable, hence both belief-options are unreasonable. Moreover, the sceptic's objection concerning primary and secondary qualities, a 'sceptical topic of a like nature', 'goes farther, and represents this opinion [of external existence] as contrary to reason'.[42] These objections, he concludes, show 'the whimsical condition of mankind, who must act and reason and believe', though we cannot 'remove the objections, which may be raised against' our beliefs.[43] Though he seems to make light of this concession, by characterizing such objections as 'mere amusements' which 'can have no other tendency than to show' this whimsical condition, it seems, nevertheless, to be an admission in keeping with the former that our common sense beliefs are contrary to reason (irrational), rather than merely without foundation in reason (arational). (This concurs with the claim in the *Treatise*: 'If I must be a fool, as all those who reason or believe anything *certainly* are, my follies shall at least be natural and agreeable' (270).)

On the other hand, Hume just as explicitly limits the arena of the sceptic's triumph to showing the arationality of these beliefs, allowing the possibility that they are truth-claims which are not illegitimate. He strictly warns the sceptic to 'keep within his proper sphere'; he has 'ample matter for triumph' when he 'justly insists' that

we have no argument to convince us, that objects, which have, in our experience, been frequently conjoined, will likewise, in other instances, be conjoined in the same manner; and that nothing leads us to this inference but custom or a certain instinct of our nature; which it is indeed difficult to resist, but which, like other instincts, may be fallacious and deceitful.[44]

---

[41] *Enquiries*, p. 153.   [42] Ibid., pp. 154, 155.
[43] Ibid., p. 160.   [44] Ibid., p. 159.

It is noteworthy that in this passage Hume does not concede more than the arationality of common sense beliefs. The proper sphere, then, of the sceptic is limited to the denial of 'rational' justification and the challenge to the reliability of instinct. The latter need be taken only as a warning about our fallibility, though oddly enough Hume had earlier claimed that, on the contrary, the inductive instinct was 'infallible'.[45] The impasse in which the sceptic shows us we find ourselves does not lead Hume to say that the sceptic 'justly insists' that our matter of fact reasonings are illegitimate (though unavoidable). One explanation of why Hume does not advance the stronger view of the 'force of the Pyrrhonian doubt' is given if we see the impasse pointed to by the sceptic as turned on its head in such a way as to argue the 'unreasonableness' of the sceptic's challenge.

The sceptic's triumph as Hume portrayed it was showing, by a reasoned consideration, that our original natural belief was contrary to reason, but that the conclusion of that same reasoned consideration could not be supported by 'rational evidence ... to convince an impartial enquirer'. This, however, could be read as a description of a situation in which an original claim is advanced by a natural instinct, and a second claim, which challenges the first, is no more certain than the original claim (since it has no 'rational evidence' with which to defend itself) and so is recognized as failing to be a 'reasonable' ground for doubting the first.[46] In this case, the power of that natural instinct which mitigates the force of Pyrrhonism might be the natural inclination human agents have to take particular naturally irresistible beliefs as certain when the claims which attempt to put them in jeopardy are shown to be no more certain than the original beliefs—that is, when reference to reason does not provide 'reasonable' grounds for doubting. Thus, one could argue that the natural instinct which alone can free us from the force of Pyrrhonism is not just the psychological fact of our believing in spite of the rational objections to doing so, but rather the natural inclination to see nature and reason in such a

---

[45] *Enquiries*, p. 55.

[46] This fits well with his claims concerning scepticism with respect to abstract reasoning: 'reason must remain restless, and unquiet, even with regard to that scepticism, to which she is driven' *Enquiries*, p. 157), and 'nothing can be more sceptical, or more full of doubt and hesitation, than this scepticism itself' (158); sceptical arguments 'produce no conviction' (155).

relationship that, when there are no reasonable grounds for doubting our original instinctive beliefs, we are reasonable in continuing to believe rather than in suspending judgement.

It cannot be denied that Hume's position contains elements in tension. The vacillation in the *Enquiry* has a parallel in the *Treatise*—for he denies that he holds that 'all is uncertain, and that our judgment is not in *any* thing possest of *any* measures of truth or falshood'; he provides a rationale why sceptical reasoning cannot be sustained, yet concludes that 'all those who reason or believe any thing *certainly*' are fools, so 'In all the incidents of life we ought still to preserve our scepticism'.[47] But on his own term's the 'mitigated' scepticism he commends is a Pyrrhonism corrected not only by 'common sense' but also by 'reflection'.[48] One could argue that only such a reading as the above mitigates the sceptical thesis with 'reflection', and not merely with pragmatic needs. Moreover, such a reading seems much more in keeping with the unusually modest descriptions found in the final section of the *Enquiry* of the 'mitigated' scepticism he commends. This interpretation of the mitigation of scepticism allows the maximal philosophical mitigation, while remaining within the confines of the two species of mitigated scepticism described.[49] Moreover, the view that only practical needs mitigate the Pyrrhonist thesis seems excessively minimalistic given Hume's clearly stated concern with 'accurate and just reasoning' and the cultivation of a 'true metaphysics'.[50]

This latter concern of Hume's is hardly done justice to by those, like Ardal and Norton, who entirely separate off the realm of 'truth' from Hume's considerations. Norton's discarding of considerations of 'truth' is, I suggest, the result of, and revealed in, his implicit equation of belief or supposition that X is true with (*a*) incorrigibility, (*b*) infallibility, and (*c*) knowledge.[51] Hume clearly denied that we could 'know' X to be true, and that we could 'rationally' justify our belief that X was true—but at the same time he seems to be committed, in his notion of 'proof', to admitting that we can be 'certain' that X is true. Hume understood the difference between descriptive accounts of the anatomy of belief and

---

[47] *Treatise*, pp. 183, 184-6, 270.
[48] Ibid., p. 161.
[49] Ibid., pp. 161-2.
[50] Ibid., pp. 10, 12.
[51] Norton, pp. 278, 279, 307, 172 n. 36, 201.

infallible guarantees of truth. But it is not clear that the only legitinate alternative to such descriptive explanation is an infallible guarantee. The lack of clarity in Norton's contrasts is evident in the following comment:

> Our passions and sentiments may generally determine what we believe. But they do not, on Hume's theory, determine what we call true or false, nor are they beyond all hope of alteration or improvement.[52]

But to 'determine what we believe' just *is* to 'determine what we call true or false'. To believe *p* is to believe that *p* is true. But that does not mean that what we call true or false is necessarily thought to be 'beyond all hope of alteration or improvement'. Indeed, a compulsion to believe something to be true tells one nothing 'definitive' about the truth of the thing, if by 'definitive' we mean incorrigible or infallible. But that seems to depend on a false dichotomy, a much too limited set of options.

Hume did not say that what we believe *must* be true in the sense that it *must* be infallibly or incorrigibly true. But he did think that what we believe we believe to be true. And somehow for him there is a connection between the denial of the opinion that 'all is uncertain, and that our judgment is not in *any* thing possest of *any* measures of truth and falsehood' and the claim that Nature has determined us to judge as well as to breathe.[53] The conclusion that there are not at least implicit claims to truth and the reliability of our natural faculties in Hume needs to be supported by something other than the suggestion that the only alternative is a defence of infallible or incorrigible beliefs that something is true.

A second argument against the philosophical relevance of Hume's distinction between proof and probability is based on Hume's discussion in the *Treatise*, 'Of Scepticism with Regard to Reason'. In this section Hume first presents an argument designed to show that not only does knowledge degenerate into probabilities, but all probabilities themselves diminish to zero. The sceptic's reasoning is as follows: every judgement of probability is 'liable to a new correction by a reflex act of the mind, wherein the nature of our understanding, and our reasoning from the first probability become our objects'.[54] He continues: the 'uncertainty inherent in the subject' is compounded by the 'new uncertainty deriv'd from

---

[52] Norton, p. 307.
[53] *Treatise*, p. 183.
[54] Ibid., p. 182.

the weakness of the faculty, which judges'; this leads to a 'new doubt deriv'd from the possibility of error in the estimation we make of the truth and fidelity of our faculties'. Thus begins the fateful diminution process, because even if the last judgement is 'favourable to our preceeding judgment, being founded only on probability [it] must weaken still further our first evidence, and must itself be weaken'd by a fourth doubt of the same kind, and so on *in infinitum*; till at last there remain nothing of the original probability'.[55]

Hume's point in presenting the argument is that, since it is a correct account of how probable judgements would affect each other if they were cogitative acts, they cannot be cogitative acts. Realizing, however, that even if beliefs are seen as acts of our sensitive nature there remains a problem to be explained, he proceeds to argue that in fact each succeeding judgement becomes less effective because less vivacious (the action of the mind becomes 'unnatural' and the ideas become 'faint and obscure'). As a result, the process of diminution is slowed down and stalled entirely. Rather than cancelling themselves out, the probabilities allow belief '*sufficient for our purpose, either in philosophy or common life*'.[56]

The sceptical argument that probabilities diminish to zero has been taken to be inconsistent with Hume's distinction between proof and probabilities, and thus to indicate that because of a confusion in levels of probability he failed to follow through on a potentially fruitful distinction.[57] This particular sceptical argument, however, is considered by Hume, even in the *Treatise*, to be irrelevant; since he thinks beliefs are not cogitative acts, it is beside the point. Moreover, he abandons it, with good reason,[58] when writing the *Enquiry*. It is difficult to agree, therefore, that Hume's reference to this argument shows his failure to maintain a significant distinction between proof and probability. It must be admitted, however, that the second part of Hume's discussion still raises

[55] *Treatise*, p. 182.

[56] Ibid., p. 185.

[57] Ian Hacking, 'Hume's Species of Probability', *Philosophical Studies* 33 (1978), appears to take this argument to prove that Hume failed to follow through on the distinction between species of probability.

[58] Cf. Hacking, p. 30; Stove, p. 132; Robert Imlay, 'Hume's *Of Scepticism with Regard to Reason*: A Study in Contrasting Themes', *Hume Studies* 7 (Nov., 1981), pp. 125-6. See also Owen Raynor's 'Hume's Scepticism Regarding "Probable Reasoning" in the *Treatise*', *Southern Journal of Philosophy* (Fall, 1964), for a criticism of such attacks on Hume's argument.

questions. Even if one grants Hume that beliefs are acts of our sensitive nature, his explanation of why probabilities do not diminish to zero does not positively account for the reinforcing character of probabilities, which seems to be a necessary element in the distinction between proof and probability. What Hume does is to show why the process of extinction is slowed down and stalled; what he needs, however, to provide positive support for his category of proof is not only the claim that probabilities do not diminish to zero, but the stronger claim that they can actually be reinforcing.

Hume's account of belief in this section, therefore, is not sufficient, even at a descriptive level, to explain how the 'highest certainty' of a 'proof' could be generated by probabilities. Elsewhere, as we have seen, he suggests that probabilities accumulate so as to result in 'full' or 'entire' assurance; the addition of probabilities can yield 'perfection' of confidence. In the absence of any account of how probabilities could legitimately reinforce each other (such as that offered by Richard Price in criticism of Hume[59]), such conclusions about the force of accumulating probabilities can be read as psychological description of the accumulating force of ideas through the continued mechanism of association.[60] On the other hand, Hume's conclusion that probabilities can result in belief sufficient for our purpose even in 'philosophy' might imply that the reinforcement of probabilities is considered by him to be legitimate, and so support more than a descriptive reading of the certainty of proof.

In sum, I have examined elements in Hume's thought which can plausibly be read as supporting an epistemologically significant category of 'proof'—in particular elements providing warrant for a reassessment of Hume's category of 'proof ' in terms of a doctrine of 'reasonable' and 'unreasonable' doubt, as well as elements which support a claim that Hume rejected an argument-based paradigm of certainty. In the process, the locus of elements which would conflict with, or undermine, an epistemologically significant category of 'proof' has been made clearer. For example, his failure to provide any account of how probabilities could be *legitimately*

[59] David Raynor, 'Hume's Mistake—Another Guess', *Hume Studies* 7 (Nov., 1981), pp. 164-6. Cf. Chap. 4, n. 28, below.

[60] Cf. Thomas Jessop, 'Hume: Philosopher or Psychologist? A Problem of Exegesis', *Rivista Critica di Storia Della Filosofia* (Oct.-Dec. 1967), pp. 424-6.

reinforcing needs to be remedied in any account which seeks to maintain a consistent epistemological distinction between proof and probability (and I will be showing later that Reid and Newman attempt to do so).

By focusing attention on those aspects of Hume's thought which support an epistemologically significant distinction between proof and probability one points to 'naturalist' elements which locate Hume in a continuing British tradition of response to scepticism emphasizing appeals to human nature and the unreasonableness of doubt in cases where doubt is none the less even more-than-logically possible.[61] Whether or not one concludes that these aspects are decisive in a unified interpretation of Hume, or that they point to irreconcilable strains in his thought, it is at least clear that such aspects need to be duly appreciated; they illustrate the potential in his thought, capable of being reconstructed and developed as an anti-sceptical response.

We have seen even in this chapter, however, that these aspects which offer more than unavoidability in response to the sceptic are in tension with other elements in Hume's thought. This tension was perceived by later anti-sceptical thinkers like Thomas Reid and makes plausible his attack on Hume in spite of the naturalist elements they share. Chapter 6 will indirectly continue the exploration of Hume's mitigated scepticism by considering Reid's explicit suggestion that Hume was inconsistent in several respects—for example, with regard to (1) the ability to maintain a theoretical commitment to scepticism, and (2) the relation between conceivability and possibility.

---

[61] Hacking claims that Hume was 'the first and apparently the last to make' the distinction between two species of probability (p. 32). I argue in the preceding and following chapters that it was made by various seventeenth-century figures, and continued by T. Reid and J.H. Newman.

4

Reid: 'Proof' and 'Probable' Reasoning

THE Scottish Presbyterian minister Thomas Reid (1710–96) is best known as the founder of a school of 'Common Sense' philosophy which was expressly directed to a refutation of Hume's scepticism. Combining the positions of parish minister and professor of philosophy at King's College, Aberdeen, Reid gave evidence in his early 'Philosophical Orations' (1753–62) of some central themes of his later writing. His first major work, *An Inquiry Into the Human Mind*, published in 1764, was the most illustrious outgrowth of the weekly discussions (most often on Hume's philosophy) of the 'Wise Club', a philosophical society he helped found at Aberdeen. His student and biographer Dugald Stewart writes that Reid thought his talents best employed 'in combating the schemes of those who aimed at the complete subversion of religion, both natural and revealed'; in the philosophical context of the time, Hume's scepticism was the obvious target.[1] Its immediate effect, though not extensive, was significant enough to establish his reputation as a philosopher and to warrant an invitation from Glasgow to take up the chair of moral philosophy vacated by Adam Smith at Glasgow. He retired from his teaching duties in 1780 and began to prepare his lectures for publication, resulting in the *Essays on the Intellectual Powers* (1785) and the *Essays on the Active Powers* (1788), works which Stewart characterizes as revealing intellectual habits which 'rank among the rarest gifts of the mind', in union with 'the curiosity of a naturalist, and the eye of an observer'.[2] Though Hume was the initial stimulus for his writings, they constitute a more thoroughgoing and comprehensive response to scepticism, addressed to the fundamental assumptions of a tradition pre-

---

[1] 'Account of the Life and Writings of Thomas Reid, D.D.', at the beginning of the *Works of Thomas Reid, D.D.* (3rd edn.), ed. William Hamilton (Edinburgh, 1852), pp. 32, 7; see also the *Dictionary of National Biography* XVI, pp. 879–82.
[2] *Works*, p. 32.

ceding Hume—a response whose influence has continued to the present.[3]

Attention to Reid's response to scepticism has deservedly been renewed in this century, but it is usually seen only in terms of (1) his account of 'first principles' and the intuitive faculty of 'common sense' which picks them out and (2) his alternative to perceptual representationalism. Little attention is given to his account of reasoning, presumably because Reid himself spent proportionately less time and energy enunciating an understanding of reasoning which could have relevance for, and a role in, a reply to scepticism. Now that we have seen the tradition preceding him, however, in which the response to scepticism emphasized a category of 'moral certainty' and 'proof' and hence focused on reasoning as well as on immediate beliefs, it seems appropriate to approach Reid from this new perspective, to reconsider his understanding of reasoning for its potential contribution to his naturalist response to scepticism. I suggest that although Reid did not explicitly adopt the terminological distinction between demonstration, proof, and probability which characterized earlier accounts, he did effectively use a category equivalent to proof in his discussion of non-demonstrative reasoning—and that category illustrates the rationale behind his entire response to scepticism. By examining how his account of proof relates to the preceding tradition, as well as to his view of non-inferential 'first principles', we shall achieve an enhanced understanding of his position as a whole.

The heart of Reid's proposal concerning the certainty possible in cases of reasoning is laid out in his chapters 'Of Probable Reasoning' (3) and 'Of Mr. Hume's Scepticism With Regard to Reason' (4) in the seventh essay, 'Of Reasoning', of the *Essays on the Intellectual Powers*. (We will see that both chapters were among those annotated by Newman.) Reid's major claim is that in cases where conclusions are reasoned to, there are *two* separate sources of certainty: 'probable' evidence can yield certainty no less than can 'demonstrative' evidence. That claim to equality, I shall argue in this chapter, covers both assurance and legitimacy, and is

---

[3] C. S. Peirce's 'Critical Common-Sensism' and G. E. Moore's thought are obvious examples. Cf. Ronald E. Beanblossom's 'Introduction' to *Thomas Reid's Inquiry and Essays* for a discussion of Reid's influence (eds. Keith Lehrer and Ronald E. Beanblossom (Indianapolis, 1975), pp. xxxix–li), as well as his article 'Russell's Indebtedness to Reid', in *The Monist* 61 (1978).

supported by critical comment on the sceptic's challenge at the same philosophical level at which the challenge is formulated. That is, Reid's defence of non-demonstrative certainty does not argue merely for equal assurance in demonstrative and non-demonstrative cases, while accepting the sceptic's charge of the unjustifiability of certainty in the latter. In the following chapter I will consider the relation of this understanding of non-demonstrative certainty to the other elements of his 'naturalist' account.

A. 'PROBABLE' REASONING AND CERTAINTY

Reid departs in the chapter 'Of Probable Reasoning' from his proclaimed deference to ordinary language and adopts instead an admittedly peculiarly philosophical sense of the term. He writes:

> In common language, probable evidence is considered as an inferior degree of evidence, and is opposed to certainty: so that what is certain is more than probable, and what is only probable is not certain. *Philosophers consider probable evidence*, not as a degree, but as a species of evidence which is *opposed, not to certainty, but to another species of evidence called demonstration.*[4]

He repeats the contrast in the following chapter as well: 'Philosophers understand probability as opposed to demonstration; the vulgar as opposed to certainty' (485: VII,4). That his point was to some extent prescriptive is shown by comparison with his friend Lord Kames's restriction of certainty in reasoning to demonstration in his apparently philosophical discussion of knowledge, opinion, and belief in his *Sketches of the History of Man*. Kames wrote: 'Reasoning that produces certainty is termed *demonstration*; and is termed *probable*, when it only produces probability.'[5]

Reid illustrates his point as follows:

> That there is such a city as Rome, I am as certain as of any proposition in Euclid; but the evidence is not demonstrative, but of that kind which

---

[4] *Works*, 482: VII,3 (ital. mine). References to Reid will be to the one-volume *Works of Thomas Reid, D.D.* (3rd edn.), ed. William Hamilton (Edinburgh, 1852); for easier reader reference I will follow the page number by Essay and Chapter (in the case of the *Essays on the Intellectual Powers*) or Chapter and Section (in the case of the *Inquiry*).

[5] Dublin, 1775, Vol. III, Book III, Sketch I, 'Principles and Progress of Reason', p. 107.

philosophers call probable. Yet, in common language, it would sound oddly to say, it is probable there is such a city as Rome; because it would imply some degree of doubt or uncertainty. (482: VII,3)

His explanation of the capacity of probable reasoning to generate certainty is that the process is a cumulative one:

The strength of probable reasoning, for the most part, depends not upon any one argument, but upon many, which unite their force, and lead to the same conclusion. Any one of them by itself would be insufficient to convince; but the whole taken together may have a force that is irresistible, so that to desire more evidence would be absurd. (482)

The force such arguments have, however, is not merely cumulative—that is, it is not merely linear and additive. He makes the point graphically:

Such evidence may be compared to a rope made up of many slender filaments twisted together. The rope has strength more than sufficient to bear the stress laid upon it, though no one of the filaments of which it is composed would be sufficient for that purpose. (482)

Such reasoning is understood, therefore, as *convergent* and *reinforcing* reasoning—it is configurational rather than linear and additive—and such an understanding is a significant development on Reid's part.

Models of cumulative reasoning are not uncommon—in fact any suggestion that the testimony of two is worth more than the testimony of one is a claim about the power of cumulative reasoning. Robert Boyle (1627–91), for example, illustrated a cumulative model when he wrote that in English courts of law:

a second testimony added to the first, though of itself never a whit more credible than the former, shall ordinarily suffice to prove a man guilty; because it is thought reasonable to suppose, that though each testimony single be but probable, yet a *concurrence of such probabilities* ... may well amount to a moral certainty, i.e., such a certainty, as may warrant the judge to proceed to the sentence of death against the indicted party.[6]

The character of such accumulation or 'concurrence', however, can be understood either according to an additive or a convergent model.

A detailed analysis of the 'concurrence' was offered by Bishop

---

[6] *Works*, Vol. IV, p. 182, ital. mine (cited in Van Leeuwen, *The Problem of Certainty in English Thought*, p. 102 n.).

Joseph Butler (1692-1752) in his *Analogy of Religion* (1736).[7] The 'Introduction' opens with a decisive statement of the distinction between 'demonstrative' and 'probable' evidence, positing 'moral certainty' as the highest degree of probability and culminating in the now familiar dictum that 'probability is the very guide of life'. Chapter VII of Part II, addressed to 'The Particular Evidence for Christianity', contains Butler's clearest statements of the force of probable reasoning, beginning with a very general sketch of the character of a cumulative case:

Thus the evidence of Christianity will be a long series of things, reaching, as it seems, from the beginning of the world to the present time, of great variety and compass, taking in both the direct and also the collateral, proofs, and making up, all of them together, one argument. (275)

The potential shift from a cumulative model highlighting the number and variety of elements to a convergent, reinforcing model is revealed in the conclusion that 'the conviction arising from which kind of proof may be compared to what they call *the effect* in architecture or other works of art; a result from a great number of things so and so disposed, and taken into one view'.

The shift from cumulative to convergent models centres on the notion of *seeing relations* between items *within 'one view'*. 'Nor need any one of the things mentioned ... be considered as a proof by itself', he continues, 'yet all of them together may be one of the strongest' (281), because

the proper force of the evidence consists in the result of those several things, considered in their respects to each other, and united in one view. (293)

He sums up with his most explicit statement of a position in which there is more than a mere accumulation of pieces of evidence:

judging by the natural rules, by which we judge of probable evidence in common matters, they amount to a much higher proof, upon such a joint review, than could be supposed upon considering them separately, at different times ... For probable proofs, by being added, not only increase the evidence, *but multiply it.* (306, ital. mine)

The emphasis on 'joint review' and the marked contrast between 'increase' and 'multiply' highlight the potential reinforcing and con-

---

[7] *Analogy of Religion, Natural and Revealed, to the Constitution and Course of Nature* (London, 1889). Further references to Butler will be to this work.

vergent character of the proof, as opposed to the simple additive power.

Butler is pointing to a phenomenon similar to that argued for by Reid, but only with Reid do we get the use of the image of the rope and the elements of which it is made. It is an image which is striking, as we shall see, both because it is repeated later by other thinkers[8] and because it has important implications for the question of the legitimacy of non-demonstrative certainty.

It is significant that in November 1738 Reid made a lengthy 'abstract' of the *Analogy*,[9] and although his reference to Chapter VII consists only in jotting down the title (a practice followed only in three of the fifteen chapters, the other twelve receiving careful notes), he has a detailed account of the 'Introduction'. In addition to the references to probability and moral certainty, it includes two other themes which will be seen as central to Reid's view: (1) the 'first principles of our nature' through which 'we unavoidably judge or determine' various things,[10] and (2) the rejection of abstract speculation. The latter methodological theme is expressed, for example, in Butler's claim that we should

instead of that idle and not very innocent employment of forming imaginary models of a world, and schemes of governing it, turn our thoughts to what we experience to be the conduct of Nature with respect to intelligent creatures; which may be resolved into general laws or rules of administration, in the same way as many of the laws of Nature respecting inanimate matter may be collected from experiments. (7)

[8] It is interesting to note that C. S. Peirce, familiar with Reid's works, adopts this kind of example too. He writes: 'Philosophy ought to imitate the successful sciences in its methods, so far as ... to trust rather to the multitude and variety of its arguments than to the conclusiveness of any one. Its reasoning should not form a chain which is no stronger than its weakest link, but a cable whose fibers may be ever so slender, provided they are sufficiently numerous and intimately connected.' ('Some Consequences of Four Incapacities', in *Journal of Speculative Philosophy* 2 (1868), reprinted in *Charles S. Peirce: Selected Writings*, ed. Philip P. Wiener (New York, 1958), pp. 40-1.)

[9] No. 3061, 10 of the Birkwood Collection of Reid manuscripts, King's College Library, Aberdeen; (hereafter cited as Birkwood).

[10] J. H. Bernard has suggested that Wilkins's *Of the Principles and Duties of Natural Religion* has 'more resemblance both in thought and phraseology with the *Sermons* and the *Analogy* than can be reasonably ascribed to chance' ('The Predecessors of Bishop Butler', *Hermathena* IX (1894-6), p. 76). Book I, Chap. III, of Wilkin's work, he argues, yields the principle of Butler's 'Introduction' to the *Analogy*, and Wilkins's psychological doctrine (78) and use of Grotius (77), are found in Butler's works, indicating a debt to Wilkins not generally recognized. A general recognition of the similarities is noted in the life of Wilkins (*Dictionary of National Biography* XXI, p. 267).

It is Butler's methodology which Hume admires in the Introduction to his *Treatise*, including him among 'some late philosophers in England who have begun to put the science of man on a new footing',[11] and which Reid notes in one of his approving references to Butler, citing his negative use of analogy.[12]

Butler's point about the force of probable reasoning is a twofold one. First, precisely because of the complexity of the convergent, reinforcing case the advantage lies on the side of those seeking to undermine such proof:

for it is easy to show, in a short and lively manner, that such and such things are liable to objection, that this and another thing is of little weight in itself; but impossible to show, in like manner, *the united force of the whole argument in one view.* (308, ital. mine)

That is, a convincing or adequate *analysis* of the force of the case is difficult, if not impossible. Secondly, although he calls the 'moral certainty' achievable in such proofs 'full assurance' and 'full conviction' (72) and 'ground for an expectation without any doubt of it' (73), his emphasis is on the sufficiency of the proof for purposes of behaviour, or to 'influence the actions of men who act upon thought or reflection' (174; see also 223, 256, 258, 264-5, 274, 275, 312, 315, 326).

Reid does not directly address the question whether convergent, reinforcing, probable reasoning is unanalysable and implicit. But in other contexts he makes two claims which seem to imply the illegitimacy of requiring an *analysis* of such reasoning in order to justify it. First, he distinguishes between the tasks of the philosopher and non-philosopher. Secondly, he insists repeatedly on an anti-élitist approach.

Contrasting the philosophical and non-philosophical tasks, he writes of the operations of abstracting and generalizing, suggesting that

The practice of them is, and must be, familiar to every man that uses language; but it is one thing to practise them, and another to explain how they are performed; as it is one thing to see, another to explain how we

---

[11] *A Treatise of Human Nature*, p. xvii.
[12] *Works*, 237: I, 4. The other very approving reference shows Reid's dependence on Butler's argument against Locke's position on identity, p. 350: III, 6.

see. The first is the province of all men, and is the natural and easy operation of the faculties which God has given us. The second is the province of philosophers. (396: V,3)

We all have 'the power of making accurate distinctions, and of forming general conceptions', and in the same way as 'Nature has given eyes to all men, and they can make good use of them; but the structure of the eye, and the theory of vision, is the business of philosophers', so 'Nature has given those powers to all men ... but they leave it to the philosophers to give names to them, and to descant upon their nature' (441: VI,4). Just as seeing properly cannot depend on properly analysing our seeing, so we can reason well without being able to analyse our complex convergent and reinforcing process of reasoning. Reid emphasizes the uncommonness of such analysis ('not one in ten thousand can give a reason for it' (458: VI, 6)). It is not clear whether he would make the stronger claim that our reasoning is radically implicit—that is, that it is impossible for anyone, even the reflective philosopher, ever to make such a convergent case totally or sufficiently explicit—but he does on occasion suggest it, as when he writes that 'To think that a thing cannot be because we do not comprehend the manner how it may be, is a way of thinking very unbecoming a Philosopher.'[13] And this would fit well with his anti-élitist claim that 'the knowledge that is necessary to all, must be attainable by all' (481: VII,2).

His anti-élitist argument is intended to deny that the judgements or beliefs we need for common survival depend on reasoning or education (416: VI,1; 449: VI,5; 451: VI,5). What puts all on a level is a use of reason which is not discursive (456: VI,6)—in that realm 'every man is a competent judge' (438: VI,4; 422: VI,2). Since 'the greatest part of men hardly ever learn to reason; and in infancy and childhood no man can reason' (260: II,5), Reid turns away from reasoning to a non-discursive legitimation of indispensable beliefs. But such an anti-élitist argument could also support the claim that where reasoning does take place, analysis cannot be required for its justification.

Reid's position on the second aspect of Butler's point—the status of the certainty achieved—is the subject of the remainder of this chapter. The first step in the determination of that point is to set forth in Reid's own words the most relevant characteristics of such

---

[13] Birkwood, 2131, 2/III/2.

certainty. His view of the force of probable reasoning is couched in terms that seem to connect psychological and epistemological considerations: it can have a 'force that is irresistible, so that to desire more evidence would be absurd' (482: VII,3). Even in non-demonstrative cases we can come to

the highest degree of evidence, when all doubt vanishes, and the belief is firm and immoveable. This degree of evidence, the highest the human faculties can attain, we call certainty. (482)

Thus even in cases short of demonstration 'the evidence *may be equal to that of demonstration*' (483, ital. mine).

Already it can be seen that whatever the status of the certainty possible to probable reasoning on Reid's view, he witnesses to his place in an established tradition of responses to scepticism. Though he does not use the term 'proof' or 'moral certainty' he effectively distinguishes an intermediate category between demonstration and probability, for the claim that probable reasoning generates a certainty *equal* to that of demonstration is a claim that it is no longer merely probability—it deserves to be, and is being, qualitatively distinguished from reasoning which yields conclusions of a particular degree of probability and so remain uncertain. He is thus in a direct line with those who believed, like Wilkins, that 'That kind of *Assent* which ... doth not admit of any reasonable Cause of doubting, is called *Knowledge* or *Certainty*.'[14] More specifically, his claim that the evidence can be 'irresistible', so that it would be 'absurd' to require more, echoes Wilkins's claim that the mere possibility of doubt generated by the lack of demonstrative entailment does not constitute reasonable ground for doubt—we cannot doubt just because the 'contrary is not impossible, and so does not imply any Contradiction'.[15] His admitted admiration of Tillotson would clearly extend as well to the latter's explicit claim that the 'bare Possibility that A Thing may be, or not be, is no just Cause of doubting whether a Thing be or not'.[16]

Reid not only shares their rationale, he continues a tradition of the examples or illustrations used. As examples of conclusions which may be so reliably attested to 'that a man must be a fantastical incredulous fool to make any doubt of them' Wilkins cites

[14] *Of the Principles and Duties of Natural Religion*, 7th edn. (London, 1715), p. 4.
[15] Ibid., p. 24; cf. pp. 22–5.
[16] *Works*, 9th edn., p. 559.

the beliefs 'That there was such a Person as Queen *Elizabeth*; That there is such a Place as *Spain*.'[17] Moreover, 'equally true and certain' with the conclusion 'That the three Angles in a Triangle are equal to two right ones' is the conclusion 'that there are such places as *America*, or *China*'.[18] Tillotson's examples are that the sun will rise and that there are such places as America and Spain.[19]

Reid's continuation of that tradition in important respects is clear. The seventeenth-century notion of moral certainty, being beyond reasonable doubt, like the category of 'proof' introduced by Hume intermediate between demonstration and probability, parallels Reid's own effective distinction between the three categories. Moreover, with Wilkins, Reid would agree that one need only 'appeal to the common judgment of Mankind, whether the Human Nature be not so framed, as to acquiesce in such a *Moral certainty*, as the Nature of Things is capable of'.[20] That appeal to the frame or constitution of human nature is central to the seventeenth-century tradition and to Reid. The status of that moral certainty, however, for the seventeenth-century figures is not clear. Sometimes it is argued merely that it provides sufficient assurance for religious needs or practical affairs of life; at other times, as with Wilkins, it is equated with knowledge. Reid's position on this question remains to be determined, and that provides the next topic for consideration.

B. 'PRACTICAL' CERTAINTY

Certainty, for Reid, is the highest degree of evidence 'human faculties can attain': it is the 'highest degree of evidence, when all doubt vanishes, and the belief is firm and immovable' (482: VII,3). We need to confront him with the question of the status of that certainty, for such a characterization is ambiguous with respect to the extent of the achievement being claimed. The question of the status of the certainty for which Reid is arguing actually resolves itself into two separate questions, each of which reveals a different sense in which 'practical' certainty can be understood.

[17] *Natural Religion*, p. 9.
[18] Ibid., p. 19, reversed italics.
[19] *Works*, 9th edn., p. 559; 4th edn., Vol. III, p. 431.
[20] *Natural Religion*, p. 25.

We need first to determine whether on Reid's view this 'degree of evidence, the highest the human faculties can attain' is (total) certainty that p (is true), or instead is only sufficient (though not entire) conviction to warrant required *actions*. The latter is what I mean by 'practical' in the first sense—i.e. merely behavioural, acting-as-if, without actually being certain that p. 'Practical' certainty in this first sense is contrasted with 'speculative', 'theoretical', or (total) certainty that p (is true).

But even if one argues for more than that kind of practical certainty, it is possible for such certainty to be considered 'practical' in a second sense because even a claim to total certainty that p can be supported by the 'practical' warrant of needs or unavoidability (rather than theoretical evidence or argument). 'Practical' in this second sense is contrasted, not with theoretical certainty that p, but with justified or legitimate certainty that p. There can be at least two kinds of practical warrant for a certainty that p: (1) hypothetical or conditional needs for related action (e.g. moral or religious) or (2) categorical or unconditional need (e.g. irresistibility or unavoidability). The determination of 'practical' in this sense is a second and very different question because one could hold with certainty that p (rather than merely act-as-if p were true) on the basis of either of these kinds of 'practical' warrant (rather than theoretical evidential warrant). That is, one can hold with certainty that p (rather than merely act-as-if p without certainty that p), yet hold that such assurance is unjustified or illegitimate because it has only 'practical' warrant.

Certainty that p is of course closely bound up with practice—as will be made clearer later—but I would argue that it need not therefore be 'practical' in either of the two senses introduced above, and that for Reid it is not restricted to the 'practical' in either of those two senses. In what follows I will consider the evidence both for Reid's intentions in this matter, and for his achievement. The determination of his intention is asymmetrically related to the determination of the extent of his achievement—that is, his achievement does not necessarily reveal the character of his intention, for he may simply have failed to achieve his aim, but in so far as he offers what can be plausibly read as support for a more ambitious intention, one can use that as evidence for such an intention.

1. Practical vs. Theoretical

The irresistible force that probable evidence has for Reid might be understood in principle in a variety of ways. It might mean that in the face of appropriate evidence one is *forced to*, cannot help but

(1) act as if *p* is true
(2) be certain that it is safe to act as if *p* is true
(3) be certain that it is necessary to act as if *p* is true
(4) be certain that it is safe to believe that *p* is true
(5) be certain that it is necessary to believe that *p* is true
(6) be certain that *p* is true.

To which of these does Reid see the force of probable reasoning to correspond most closely? He is himself responsible for the ambiguity concerning his position since often his discussion sounds very Lockean in terms of the pragmatic limit on the achievement. For example, he writes that

the man who makes the best use he can of the faculties which God has given him, without thinking them more perfect than they really are, may have all the belief necessary in the conduct of life, and all that is necessary to the acceptance with his Maker. (485: VII,4)

The claim is that all we need is certainty sufficient to warrant the action necessary in human affairs ('in the conduct of life'), a claim repeated often by Reid.[21] What is not clear is whether the implication is that such certainty is *all* we can attain. The certainty possible to probable reasoning is at least practical in this sense—it at least covers (1) through (3). The question is whether it is more, whether it is a certainty that *p* is true.

Since Reid does not explicitly consider the distinction between practical and more-than-practical certainty (as Newman will later do), we can expect little in the way of a direct and explicit answer to the question as it is posed. But he does claim that induction can in principle generate 'as full conviction as demonstration itself' (481: VII,3)—a claim also made in his 'Brief Account of Aristotle's Logic'.[22] And as noted earlier, he claims that the certainty possible to probable reasoning can be '*equal* to that of demonstration'—an illustration of the 'irresistible' strength of a particular kind of convergent, reinforcing case is that of testimony:

[21] *Works*, 259, 260: II,5; 326: II,20; 398: V,4.
[22] *Works*, p. 712.

When there is an agreement of many witnesses in a great variety of circumstances, without the possibility of a previous concert, the evidence may be equal to that of demonstration. (483)

This is a straightforward claim for total theoretical assurance—certainty that p is true—since that is what is claimed for demonstration. And there is no reason not to take this at face-value. A second and very different question from that of the practical vs. theoretical achievement is that of the status of the claimed certainty that p is true, for the equality being claimed could be seen either in terms of assurance or in terms of legitimacy as well.

To understand Reid we now need to address the question of the second sense of practical. He is clearly concerned with the practical warrant of the unavoidability of 'the constitution of our nature'. Here the contrast is between 'practical' certainty—understood as 'necessary' but illegitimate—and legitimate certainty. The question is whether his claim for certainty expresses only a description of unavoidable assurance, while accepting the sceptic's charge that such assurance lacks justification. To say that in probable reasoning we reach a point at which 'all doubt vanishes' is not necessarily more than to claim that we reach a point at which there is a total absence of doubt, or a point at which we are unable to doubt. But, as we saw earlier, the absence of doubt and the inability to doubt say nothing, according to the sceptic, about whether the doubt should vanish, whether there might nevertheless be good reasons for doubting, or whether we ought to try to revive some of the vanishing doubt. If the irresistibility of the belief is only the force of unavoidability, with no challenge to the sceptic's request for justification, Reid's understanding of the achievements possible to probable reasoning has no relevance for a reply to the sceptical challenge at the level at which the challenge is formulated. If, on the other hand, it directly challenges the sceptic's request for justification it can constitute an important part of an anti-sceptical response. We turn then to the question of the philosophical status of the total assurance—that is, the level of Reid's reply to the sceptic.

2. *Irresistible Assurance* vs *Legitimate Assurance*

Reid remarks over and over again that even sceptics believe what non-sceptics believe—they not only act the same way, they believe the same things. This is sometimes seen as evidence of confusion on Reid's part, as if he saw such an observation as an argument against the sceptic. One could, however, start from the other direction, and assume that since Reid recognized that, he also recognized that his own response had to intend and argue for more than the mere irresistibility of assurance if it was to differ significantly from the sceptic's. I suggest that the claim for equality, in addition to being a straightforward claim for total theoretical certainty that *p* is true (rather than merely practical), is also a prima-facie straightforward claim for equal legitimacy. That is, it is a claim that there is no way in which they are not equal, except in terms of the obvious difference in their sources, and Reid's explicit claim that probable evidence is opposed not to certainty but to demonstrative evidence implies that the difference in sources is not prejudicial to the certainty achievable. The claim to equality should therefore not be reduced to a claim for only one dimension of equality (i.e. assurance) unless it has to be. The unreduced claim should be taken as accurately reflecting Reid's intention as long as further analysis of his position does not preclude him from arguing for more than the irresistibility of assurance, with no claim for equal legitimacy. (Obviously the case is better made if there are in addition positive suggestions which point to and plausibly support the stronger claim.) Such an analysis follows, centring on a reading of convergent probable reasoning as a 'threshold' category and its relation to 'unreasonable' doubt.

C. CONVERGENT REASONING — A 'THRESHOLD' CATEGORY

The core of Reid's argument is the notion of convergent, reinforcing reasoning, and I suggest that the image of a rope and filaments is used precisely to illustrate not only the reinforcing character of probable reasoning but its 'threshold' character as well. A threshold concept, as noted earlier, is one whose application has a 'critical threshold', such that it is not applicable at all until that threshold is reached, and when reached it is simply and totally applicable. It is thus a concept which is applicable totally if at all. It has no 'degrees'—it refers to a state or condition which is not expressed gradually (by degrees), and which when reached it makes no sense to talk of increasing. We saw in Chapter 2 that some of the seventeenth-century figures treated the concept of 'truth' as a threshold concept, without degrees. A proposition was not judged true at all until it was able to be judged true, full stop. It was not rather true, hardly true, or somewhat true—part of it might be true, but it was not partially true. It was true or it was not. Such a notion of truth was explicitly linked, by Wilkins, for example, to a notion of certainty, rendering the latter a threshold concept as well. And by extension, the notion of 'being beyond reasonable doubt' can be considered a threshold concept.

For Reid the rope and filaments image is especially suited to show not only that (1) though none of the filaments individually could bear the requisite weight, together they can, but also that (2) even though an iron bar could also lift the weight, the rope can be 'sufficient'. And where a rope can do the job, it should not be faulted for not being an iron bar. Though there could be more evidence, one can nevertheless have sufficient strength for a proof without it. Though Newman, as we shall see, was much more explicit about certainty as a threshold category, Reid's point is clear: once the weight to be carried is determined, the important question is whether there is sufficient evidence to bear that weight—*not* whether there could have been more. The claim that it is 'absurd' to doubt is a claim that where there is more evidence, it is surplus—the *extra* cannot be the standard with respect to which other cases are judged to *lack* something they should have.

Moreover, if certainty is seen as a threshold concept, Reid's requirement of a proportionality between evidence and belief is not incompatible with a claim for equal certainty (both in terms of legitimacy and assurance) in both demonstrative and non-demonstrative cases. We saw earlier the suggestion that the seventeenth-century figures' attempt to claim equal certainty in both cases conflicted with their emphasis on a proportionality requirement. To repeat, Van Leeuwen writes:

Wilkins proposes that there is an objective relation between the situation and the evidence, and that one's degree of certainty is to be proportioned to the evidence. This should mean that one is more certain of a mathematical demonstration than of what is substantiated by testimony alone. However, this is not always the case for he claims that one is as certain of the conclusion in science and history as of a conclusion in mathematics, thus breaking down the objective relation supposedly existing between evidence and assent . . . This being so, the distinction between the several degrees of certainty becomes less pronounced and the proportioning of assent to evidence becomes less significant.[23]

The logical outcome of such a move, he continues, was 'to divorce certainty from evidence altogether, as Hume did'.

Now if this was a real problem for people like Wilkins, it would be a problem for Reid as well, for Reid wants to acknowledge both the importance of a proportion between evidence and assent and the equality of certainty in demonstrative and non-demonstrative cases. While demonstrative evidence has no degrees, probable evidence does—'from the very least, to the greatest, which we call certainty' (482: VII,3). Moreover, assuming a sound and unprejudiced understanding, '[e]very degree of evidence perceived by the mind, produces a proportioned degree of assent or belief' until we reach the point where 'all doubt vanishes, and the belief is firm and immoveable'. This, the highest degree of evidence 'human faculties can attain, we call certainty' (482). He insists that belief should be proportioned to evidence.[24] How, then, can that be reconciled with a claim for equal certainty in both demonstrative and non-demonstrative cases?

The two claims can be reconciled if one sees the point at which 'all doubt vanishes' as a critical threshold. When it is reached, certainty exists—there are no degrees of certainty before that, or after. When the critical threshold is reached all the achievements are equal in the sense that doubt vanishes. Belief has degrees, confidence grows—the explosive material gets hotter and the rope gets stronger. But at the point at which 'all doubt vanishes' the assurance can be equal, and, to repeat, the claim that it is 'absurd' to doubt is a claim that the evidence of demonstration is surplus and cannot be the standard with respect to which other cases are judged to 'lack' something they should have. It is a claim, therefore, that the legitimacy of that assurance can be equal. An understanding of certainty as a threshold concept precludes the possibility of directly proportioning certainty to evidence in a one-to-one manner by degrees, precisely because it precludes the notion of degrees of certainty altogether. But as noted in Chapter 2 in the examination of Wilkins, this need not counter the intention of a proportionality requirement—which is to guarantee a non-arbitrary correlation

[23] *The Problem of Certainty in English Thought*, p. 70.
[24] *Works*, 234: I,3; but cf. 238: I,5; 434: VI,4; 447–8: VI,5.

between evidence and assurance. A proportionality requirement can retain its main point as long as one requires proportionality up to the critical threshold; the proportionality requirement can still rule out certainty when the evidence does not reach the critical threshold. Thus an understanding of certainty as a threshold concept allows Reid both to require proportionality of assent in a non-vacuous way, and yet to claim that non-demonstrative certainty is equal to and equally legitimate with demonstrative certainty.

D. OBJECTIONS TO CONVERGENCE?

Reid's understanding of the converging, reinforcing character and force of probable reasoning, which is central to his claim that the certainty of probable reasoning can be legitimately equal to that of demonstration, seems, however, to be at odds with, or challenged by, an admission he makes two chapters earlier. At the beginning of the essay 'Of Reasoning', in the chapter 'Of Reasoning in General, and of Demonstration' he writes:

> In every chain of reasoning, the evidence of the last conclusion can be no greater than that of the weakest link of the chain, whatever may be the strength of the rest. (476: VII,1)

That very admission, however, has been used as an argument against a view (identical to Reid's in the relevant respects) of converging, reinforcing probable reasoning issuing in certainty. John Hick, for example, argues:

> The steps of an argument are not like the steps of a ladder; they are more akin to the links of a chain from which something is suspended. And a chain of reasoning can be no stronger than its weakest link; probable arguments never suffice to establish a certain conclusion.[25]

How then does Reid's admission relate to his later claim that probable reasoning can issue in certainty equal to that of demonstration?

There are three options. First, the admission might simply be in contradiction with the later claim. Second, the admission might force us to interpret the later claim as intended by Reid to refer to a different level—that is, whereas the admission is a philosophically considered opinion, the later claim is a claim about psychological

[25] *Faith and Knowledge* (Ithaca, 1957), p. xv.

assurance with no implications about legitimacy. Third, the admission and the later claim might be reconciled as consistent claims on the same philosophically relevant level. Obviously the first option should be seen as a last resort. The second option should be avoided if possible since it relegates Reid's point to one with no real power against the sceptic. So some reconciliation should at least be attempted.

A first attempt at reconciling the two discussions could be made by suggesting that Reid intended the admission to apply only to linear or deductive reasoning—that is, we might restrict the admission to 'chains' of reasoning and deny that probable reasoning consisted for Reid in a chain. But before determining the plausibility of this reconciling strategy in this case, I want to suggest that the strategy may be relevant to another admission similar to the one above which likewise needs to be reconciled with the claim that probable reasoning can issue in certainty equal to that of demonstration. That admission is found in a discussion 'Of First Principles in General' which, though it does not directly address reasoning, bears in a similar manner on the question of the certainty possible to probable reasoning.

In his attempt to show that *all* reasoning depends on 'first principles', Reid writes that 'some first principles yield conclusions that are certain, others such as are probable, from the highest probability to the lowest' (435: VI,4). His explanation is apparently unproblematic: 'In just reasoning, the strength or weakness of the conclusion will always correspond to that of the principles on which it is grounded.' This correspondence, however, is understood by Reid quite literally in a univocal fashion:

As water, by its gravity, can rise no higher in its course than the fountain, however artfully it be conducted; so no conclusion of reasoning can have a greater degree of evidence than the first principles from which it is drawn. (436: VI,4)

The result is that only reasoning based on 'necessary truth whose contrary is impossible' (436) can yield 'certain' conclusions; reasoning based on non-necessary principles can, in contrast, yield only 'probable' conclusions. Even the most 'accurate and profound reasoning can never yield a certain conclusion' from first principles which are not necessary truths (436).

This admission, like the one noted above about links in a chain, seems to contradict (or reduce to mere psychological description) the claim that probable reasoning can issue in certainty equal to that of demonstration. But it can be clarified somewhat by looking more closely at one of Reid's examples:

> In games of chance, it is a first principle, that every side of a die has an equal chance to be turned up; and that in a lottery every ticket has an equal chance of being drawn out. From such first principles as these ... we may deduce, by demonstrative reasoning, the precise degree of probability of every event in such games. (436)

The noteworthy words are 'we may deduce, by demonstrative reasoning'. Reid is here claiming correctly that in a deductive or linear process of reasoning the premisses can transfer only their own degree of probability to the conclusion drawn from them. He is highlighting the limits of demonstration, its purely formal nature, and the problem of the status of the premisses even in cases of demonstration. One could then argue that there is no contradiction between Reid's claim about the certainty possible to probable reasoning and the admission that even the most 'accurate and profound reasoning can never yield a certain conclusion' from nonnecessary premisses because the latter admission refers only to the limits of *deductive* reasoning. This seems likely given his claim that 'The conclusions *deduced* by reasoning from first principles, will commonly be necessary or contingent, according as the first principles are from which they are drawn' (442: VI,5, ital. mine).

Moreover, even if Reid's summarizing remark—'as there are some first principles that yield conclusions of absolute certainty; so there are others that can only yield probable conclusions' (436: VI, 4)—covers both demonstrative and probable reasoning, it leaves open the possibility that probable reasoning can issue in certainty equal to that of demonstration as long as the word 'probable' is taken in the strictly philosophical sense he later emphasizes and so is not contrasted with certainty as such but only with the certainty of-a-particular-source. This is more plausible given the fact that the claim on page 482—'there are first principles of necessary truths, and first principles of contingent truths. Demonstrative reasoning is grounded upon the former, and probable reasoning upon the latter'—is immediately followed by emphasis on the philosophical use of the term 'probable' which he is adopting.

This reconciling strategy of suggesting that Reid refers only to deductive reasoning may be plausible, then, in relation to this discussion of first principles, but Reid seems to have excluded that possibility in the case of the claim that the evidence of the conclusion can be no greater than that of the weakest link in the chain. That is, the suggestion that we need not consider probable reasoning to be a 'chain' seems ruled out because immediately following the admission about the chain Reid proceeds to divide up all reasoning into demonstrative and probable—implying that until that point he had been discussing reasoning in general. This seems to commit him to seeing all reasoning as consisting in a 'chain' of some length. And this is borne out by an earlier reference to 'the power of reasoning, that is of drawing a conclusion from a chain of premises' (434: VI,4).

Another, and more suggestive, strategy for reconciliation would be to argue that Reid was making two points which were consistent (whether or not he was fully aware of their relation is not clear) in the following way. The admission that the weakest link in the chain limits or dictates the strength of the conclusion could be understood as an admission on Reid's part of what was correct in the sceptic's charge—namely, that probable reasoning has no entailment relation and can never overcome what he had earlier referred to as the 'defect' of the logical dubitability of some first principles (436). That defect, he had argued—namely, that the contrary is not a logical contradiction—cannot be eliminated by demonstrative reasoning. Here he could be taking that admission further by admitting that it cannot be eliminated by *any* kind of reasoning. But the claim in the later chapter on probable reasoning could be seen as a recognition that the so-called 'defect' is not a defect prejudicial to certainty. The undeniable *absence* of entailment is not a relevant *lack*. The ineluctable weak link in reasoning (whether demonstrative or probable) from non-necessary premises which limits the strength of the conclusion is that the contradictory of the conclusion remains logically possible. This is supported indirectly by Reid's reference to the hypothetical objection in a legal proceeding that 'It has never been proved that the most distinct memory may not be fallacious ... yet this is one link in the chain of proof against the prisoner; and if it have no strength, the whole proof falls to the ground' (444: VI,5), for his point is the absurdity of allowing such a 'weak link' to preclude certainty. That weak link must be faced for what it is. But what it is is not incompatible with certainty because certainty requires only that the evidential 'fila-ments' converge sufficiently to 'bear the stress laid upon it'—not that there could be no greater strength. The two discussions then together could (rather than contradicting each other or making claims at a different level) be making the claim that probable reasoning can issue in certainty equal to that of demonstration despite its logical dubitability. In what follows further warrant for such a construal will be examined.

E. CERTAINTY AND 'UNREASONABLE' DOUBT

I suggested above that Reid's image implies that where a rope can do a job it should not be faulted for not being an iron bar, and that this supports the view that he sees the certainty possible to 'probable' reasoning as providing more than mere counter-descrip-tion of assurance equal to that of demonstration. A number of other elements in his thought support it as well—namely, those elements which suggest that neither the logical dutitability of a conclusion, nor all cases of the more-than-logical dubitablity of a conclusion, necessarily preclude certainty. But before addressing that, it is important to consider a preliminary, but nevertheless fundamentally important, point for Reid, concerning the possibility of certainty in probable reasoning—namely, that certainty does not require infallibility.

Reid's initial response to Hume's scepticism concerning reason is to make very clear concessions concerning our fallibility:

That man, and probably every created being, is fallible; and that a fallible being cannot have that perfect comprehension and assurance of truth which an infallible being has, I think ought to be granted. It becomes a fallible being to be modest, open to new light, and sensible, that by some false bias, or by rash judging, he may be misled. (485: VII,4)

His emphasis on our fallibility is remarkable throughout his writ-ings, and is not sufficiently appreciated by some commentators.[26] In fact, Reid faults Hume for 'not being sceptical enough' when Hume allows that 'the rules of demonstrative sciences' are 'infalli-

---

[26] For example, C. S. Peirce, 'Issues of Pragmatism', in *The Monist* (1905), re-printed in *Philosophical Writings of Peirce*, ed. Justus Buchler (New York, 1955), pp. 290–4; also note pp. 296–9. See also David Fate Norton, *David Hume: Common Sense Moralist and Sceptical Metaphysician*, p. 172, n. 36.

ble', since they are after all 'discovered by our fallible and uncertain faculties, and have no authority but that of human judgment' (486). For Reid, then, our fallibility clearly extends to all our reasoning—both demonstrative and probable. Reid's precarious project is to do justice to our fallibility even in cases of demonstrative reasoning, while defending the possibility of total certainty even in cases of non-demonstrative reasoning. That is, Reid highlights our fallibility, and so cannot hold that demonstration is, by its nature, unassailable; but he also wants to argue that fallibility as such does not prevent us from reaching certainty in either demonstrative or non-demonstrative cases. All that can be legitimately inferred from the fact of our fallibility is that 'human judgments ought always to be formed with an humble sense of our fallibility in judging' (485).

To the sceptic who allows that demonstration can provide certainty, but that probable reasoning cannot (and such sceptics were common because a preoccupation with the pre-eminence of Aristotelian syllogism was maintained till Reid's time[27]), Reid's implicit argument is the following:

(*a*) total certainty is admitted to be possible at least in cases of demonstration;

(*b*) but infallibility is not possible in any case—demonstrative or probable;

(*c*) therefore, fallibility cannot preclude total certainty.

In other words, at least *in so far as* total certainty is admitted to be possible in cases of demonstration, it ought likewise to be admitted that our fallibility cannot legitimately be used as a reason to deny the possibility of total certainty in non-demonstrative cases.

To the more radical sceptic who suggests that fallibility precludes certainty in all cases of reasoning (the kind of sceptic Reid understands Hume to be), Reid counters that the equation of certainty with infallibility is totally idiosyncratic; whereas 'philosophers understand probability as opposed to demonstration' and 'the vulgar as opposed to certainty', Hume (like Descartes) understands it 'as opposed to infallibility, which no man claims' (485). Hume's conflation of two very different concepts is the result, according to Reid, of two misunderstandings of the legitimate import of our fallibility.

The first misunderstanding concerns demonstrative certainty.

---

[27] See Wilbur Samuel Howell, *Eighteenth-Century British Logic and Rhetoric* (Princeton, 1971), esp. Chap. II and pp. 262–3, 379–95.

Reid's quibble that the imperfection of our faculties could not turn a demonstration into a probable argument—'What is really demonstration, will still be so, whatever judgment we form concerning it' (485)—is a reversion on his part to consideration of demonstration in the abstract and idealized. His conclusion that a mistake in demonstrative reasoning destroys the demonstration rather than turns it into another kind of argument (e.g. probable) fails to address Hume's anxiety with precisely that possibility of mistake. Against Hume's real concern, then, Reid's real answer is that demonstrative certainty must be possible because presumably not even Hume could deny that 'One who believes himself to be fallible, may still hold it to be certain that two and two make four', for instance (485). Our fallibility, therefore, can only exact from us the admission that we ought always to be cautious in our examination and corroboration of reasoning processes.

Hume's second misunderstanding consists in 'subjecting every judgment to an infinite number of successive probable estimations' (486) and attempting to use a single source of uncertainty as if it were a new one again and again (487). Once we have considered 'our liableness to err in our first judgment' of something, and have accordingly very cautiously examined and corroborated it, we 'have allowed to it all the effect that reason and the rules of logic permit' (487). It is not legitimate to suggest that the recognition that our judgement that *p* is a fallible judgement further infirms our initial judgement that *p* because, Reid suggests, 'to take credit twice in an account for the same article is not agreeable to the rules of logic' (487). Whereas Hume sees each succeeding judgement as compounding the uncertainty so that the conviction of the initial judgement is, in principle, totally obliterated, Reid suggests that the succeeding judgements can go either way. They can, depending on the circumstances, either strengthen or decrease the initial probability. In defence of the former possibility Reid argues:

The first judgment may be compared to the testimony of a credible witness; the second, after a scrutiny into the character of the witness, wipes off every objection that can be made to it, and therefore surely must confirm and not weaken his testimony. (487)

On the other hand, my second judgement might reveal things which make me less confident in my initial judgement. But even when the succeeding judgements are unfavourable to the initial judgement,

Reid says, their effect is not to annihilate utterly the initial judgement; rather they have less and less impact on it. The unfavourable judgement is 'a presumption against the first judgment', the second 'will be only the presumption of a presumption; and the third, the presumption that there is a presumption of a presumption' (488). Thus such presumptions undermine, rather than reinforce, themselves. (This latter suggestion resembles Richard Price's criticism of the same point in Hume.[28]) Hume too admits that the total extinction possible in principle is stalled in fact, but whereas Reid sees this as the result of a philosophically relevant consideration, Hume seems to see it as the result simply of a diminution of psychological strength.

Reid has one other kind of argument, presented earlier in the book, which is relevant here as well. Reid argues that our faculties, like our senses, can be 'imperfect' and 'fallible' without being 'fallacious' in their nature[29]—that is, they are not necessarily distortive. Certainty, he claims, cannot be precluded by the fallibility of the senses because the possibility of anything that would count as a recognition that we were once wrong depends on acknowledging the certainty of at least some of our judgements; it is, after all, only by the information of the senses that errors in our judgements can be discovered (335: II,22). For parallel reasons, the fallibility of our faculties could not preclude the certainty of at least some of our judgements (at the very least, the certainty of the judgement that we have been wrong; at best, the certainty of the judgement that we were wrong to believe a particular proposition).

Reid's sensitivity to our fallibility in cases of demonstration is maintained along with the claim that fallibility *as such*, while providing the possibility of a ground for doubt, does not provide an actual ground for doubt in *any* case. It is also maintained along with the claim that the logical dubitability which attaches to non-demonstrative reasoning does not imply that doubt of the conclusion is therefore reasonable.

---

[28] Price, *A Review of the Principal Questions in Morals*, ed. D. D. Raphael (Oxford, 1974). Price writes concerning Hume's argument for the continual diminution of evidential force: 'As much of this strange reasoning as is not above my comprehension, proves just the reverse of what was intended by it.... [T]he subsequent reflection on the uncertainty attending this judgment which we make of our faculties, diminishes not, but contributes to restore to its first strength, our original assurance; because the more precarious a judgment or probability unfavourable to another appear, the less must be its effect in weakening it' (p. 96 n.).

[29] *Works*, 447: VI,5; 335, 338: II,22.

Reid does not deny a difference between demonstrative and non-demonstrative reasoning *in the abstract*. He admits that in demonstration 'the inference is necessary, and we perceive it to be impossible that the conclusion should not follow from the premises', whereas in probable reasoning 'the connection between the premises and the conclusion is not necessary, nor do we perceive it to be impossible that the first should be true while the last is false' (476: VII,1).[30] The point is that if *ex hypothesi* the premises of demonstrative and non-demonstrative arguments are both correct, and we make no mistake in our reasoning process, the conclusion in a demonstration is guaranteed in a way that is not possible in probable arguments. Even if it is possible trivially to turn any argument into a demonstration, by adding a premiss to the effect that the initial premises imply the conclusion, the reasons for which we can be wrong in probable reasoning are not simply the reasons for which we can be wrong in demonstrative cases.

That difference *in itself*, however, says nothing about the reasonableness or unreasonableness of doubting the conclusion *in a particular case*. For example, 'a long train of demonstrative reasoning' can issue in conclusions which are 'very remote and unexpected' (417: VII,1). This highlights the possibility of going wrong, and is illustrated by reference to the procedure even a mathematician would adopt to corroborate his conclusions (440: VI,4). His point is that however perfect the entailment relation *in the abstract*, the necessity of personal (hence fallible) appropriation of any and every argument means that one can have good reasons to doubt what might as a matter of fact be necessarily true (and conversely, one could have good reasons to believe what might in fact be neces-

---

[30] Reid is ambivalent about the character of premises in demonstrations. He notes that 'demonstrative reasoning can be applied only to truths that are necessary, and not to those that are contingent' (*Works*, 477: VII,1). This seems to be a claim that the premises of demonstration must be necessary ones, but this conflicts with his admission noted earlier that we can 'deduce, by demonstrative reasoning' from non-necessary premises (436: VI,4). His article, 'A Brief Account of Aristotle's Logic', divides Aristotelian syllogism according to the status of the premises as follows: those whose premises are 'certain' are called 'apodictical' syllogisms or 'demonstrations', while those with 'probable' premises are called 'dialectical' syllogisms (*Works*, 705). Hamilton comments critically that premises of demonstration 'must not only be *true* and *certain*, but *necessarily* so', ignoring Reid's further comment that 'In all demonstration, the first principles, the conclusion, and all the intermediate propositions, must be necessary, general, and eternal truths' (ibid.).

sarily false).[31] Moreover, the subject's moral and intellectual states are related in an important way for Reid, as shown by his approving quotation of Berkeley's 'just' observation 'That though a demonstration be never so well grounded, and fairly proposed, yet, if there is, withal, a strain of prejudice, or a wrong bias on the understanding, can it be expected to perceive clearly, and adhere firmly to the truth?' (283: II,10). He summarizes both points as follows:

When a demonstration is short and plain; when the point to be proved does not touch our interest or our passions; when the faculty of judging in such cases, has acquired strength by much exercise, there is less danger of erring; when the contrary circumstances take place, there is more. (487: VII,4)

There is, as he sees it, less danger or more—never none.

In so far as demonstration can achieve total certainty, therefore, it cannot be because of the nature of demonstrative entailment in the abstract, but rather because in a given case we have no reason to doubt the correctness of the premises or the process of reasoning. The recognition by an individual of his or her poor track record in a given intellectual arena (or the likelihood of relevant biases) may well provide an actual ground for doubt in a given case, even a case of demonstration. Thus, contextualization (or the necessity of personal appropriation of arguments) is epistemologically, and not merely psychologically, significant. By thus making the reasonableness of doubt of a conclusion a function of contextual appropriation he puts all arguments on a continuum and precludes the a priori confinement of reasonable doubt to non-demonstrative cases. For this reason, demonstration is not a guarantee that doubt of the conclusion cannot be reasonable. But the sceptical implication of this move is avoided because by taking the emphasis away from the abstract form of the argument and attaching it to context, he guarantees that the fact that an argument is not demonstrative is not in itself an actual ground for doubt. For Reid, then, the critical line between 'reasonable' and 'unreasonable' doubt of a conclusion depends on actual rather than possible

---

[31] This shows that Reid did not make the mistake, which has been attributed to many anti-sceptics, of believing that 'the logical impossibility of error in beliefs concerning the impossible and the necessary' was a 'bulwark against scepticism' (Keith Lehrer, 'Why Not Scepticism?' in *Essays on Knowledge and Justification*, p. 351 (reprinted from *The Philosophical Forum* 2.3 (1971), pp. 283-98)).

grounds for doubt. This allows that conclusions of both demonstration and probable reasoning can be subject to either determination. In particular it allows the possibility that the logical dubitability of a conclusion (that its denial is not logically contradictory) does not in itself introduce reasonable ground for doubt into any cases of reasoning. His view of the relation between 'conceivability' and 'possibility' shows that he thinks this is actually the case.

In his chapter on 'Mistakes Concerning Conception' (IV,3), Reid concentrates at length on one of the mistakes he cites—namely, the view

that our conceptions of things is a test of their possibility, so that, what we can distinctly conceive, we may conclude to be possible; and of what is impossible, we can have no conception. (376)[32]

His target is the 'short road to the determination of every question about the possibility or impossibility of things' which consists in the test: 'If we can conceive the thing, it is possible: if not, it is impossible' (377). His aim is to show that conceivability is not the test of possibility, and he does this in two different ways. First, he argues that conceivability is not the test of possibility because we can conceive what is necessarily false or logically impossible. He supports that claim with a variety of examples, referring to the conception of explicitly contradictory propositions in geometry (378), and to the implicit conception of contradictory propositions (when one conceives a necessarily true proposition, one conceives at the same time its contradictory—a logically impossible, necessarily false proposition (378)). The latter admission, he notes, is made even by Hume, who thereby 'contradicts' his explicit reliance on the maxim 'that whatever we conceive is possible'. Finally, the most graphic evidence against that maxim with respect to logical possibility is illustrated in demonstrations *ad absurdum*:

[32] Another mistake he cites is the belief that conception is the first act of the intellect, rather than analysis of a complex whole (106–7: II,§4; 376: IV,3; 418: VI,1; see also his Orations III and IV (*The Philosophical Orations of Thomas Reid* (1753–62), ed. D. D. Todd, trans. Shirley M. Darcus (1977) from the Latin translation by W. R. Humphries (Aberdeen University Press, 1937)). In this respect his position differs from Hume's atomism and agrees with Newman's approach in which analysis follows a wholistic perception or judgement; Newman explicitly says 'Certain philosophers say that the first element ⟨act⟩ of thought is not a simple apprehension, but a judgment. What I have here said agrees with this idea' (*Philosophical Notebook* II (Louvain, 1970), p. 71, also pp. 8, 73. Angle brackets in this and subsequent quotations indicate Newman's interlinear additions.

Mathematicians often require us to conceive things that are impossible, in order to prove them to be so ... Conceive, says Euclid, a right line drawn from one point of the circumference of a circle to another, to fall without the circle; I conceive this, I reason from it, until I come to a consequence that is manifestly absurd; and from thence conclude, that the thing which I conceived is impossible. (379)

Thus, we can conceive what is necessarily false in the process of showing it to be necessarily false. In sum, we can conceive what is logically impossible, what is merely logically possible, and what is more than logically possible. Conception cannot discriminate between logical possibility and logical impossibility.

But Reid's point, reiterated in the charge that one's 'being able to conceive a thing is no proof that it is possible' (379), is also made in a second way—namely, in terms of a distinction between what is conceivable and a stronger sense of possibility. He argues that conceivability is not the test of possibility because we can conceive things which, though logically possible, may be impossible in other ways. That is, the test of positive conceivability not only fails to rule out the logically impossible—it fails to rule in all kinds of possibility. Reid makes the contrast in the following example:

It is possible, you say, that God might have made an universe of sensible and rational creatures, into which neither natural nor moral evil should ever enter. It may be so, for what I know: but how do you know that it is possible? (379)

The contrast is between what *may be possible* and what *is possible*. Reid's claim that 'were we ever so certain that a thing may be, this is no good reason for believing that it really is'[33] certainly means that possibility is not a ground for believing a thing to be actual, but it may also mean that the determination of what *may* be possible is not the same as the determination of what *is* possible. Such a universe without moral or natural evil is conceivable; it may even be logically possible since it implies no logical contradiction. But, Reid asks, is it possible in any stronger sense? Neither conception nor logical possibility tells us anything about 'real' possibility, possibility in the world as we know it. What *may* be possible tells us nothing about what *is* possible in this stronger sense. That this is Reid's intention is clear from his concluding statement:

[33] *Works*, 397: V,3.

I cannot admit, as an argument, or even as a pressing difficulty, what is grounded on the supposition that such a thing is possible, when there is no good evidence that it is possible, and, for any thing we know, it may in the nature of things be impossible. (379)

Note the crucial contrast between 'the supposition that such a thing is possible' and 'good evidence that it is possible'.[34]

Reid's repetitiveness on the issue is striking and clearly highlights the difference between conceivability and a stronger sense of possibility. The 'short road' fails to do justice to a determination which is necessarily more difficult than simple reference to distinct understanding or logical consistency. To distinguish in this way between conceivability and possibility (whether or not Reid was misreading the intention of those he criticizes in this respect[35]) is to argue that logical possibility as such tells one nothing about what constitutes 'real' possibility. This, moreover, seems to be a first step toward the recognition that the determination that something is more-than-logically possible as such tells one nothing about whether it is reasonable or unreasonable to assume as a basis for doubt—the recognition, that is, that not all more-than-logically possible grounds for doubt are reasonable in every case. And this far more important recognition is suggested by Reid's use of a 'tribunal' or jurisprudential model of reasoning to illuminate his view of certainty.

Reid's use of jurisprudential illustrations implies that he sees certainty as compatible with the admission that it is more than logically possible that the proposition in question is false, since in legal cases there is more than just the logical possibility of reasons for and against the defendant's innocence (413: VI,1).[36] The motif

---

[34] In his chapter on 'Possibility', Alan R. White makes a distinction between 'existential' possibility and 'problematic' possibility which I think is useful in explaining Reid's point; he concludes: 'A root cause of scepticism is the failure to see that although problematic possibility implies existential possibility, the converse does not hold. Sceptical arguments based on the premise that it is possible for something to be otherwise than it appears to be provide no reason for the conclusion that it is possible that something is otherwise than it appears to be, much less for the conclusion that something actually is other than it appears to be.' (*Modal Thinking* (Oxford, 1975), p. 15.)

[35] Cf. Hamilton's footnote, *Works*, 377: IV,3.

[36] An excellent discussion of the relation between models of evaluation of evidence and developments of legal thought in the seventeenth century is found in Barbara J. Shapiro's *Probability and Certainty in Seventeenth-Century England*. Chap. V. Louise Marcil-Lacoste also discusses the jurisprudential model in Reid,

that runs throughout his references to the mind as a tribunal is that a witness's testimony is to be given the benefit of the doubt— innocent until proven (entirely) guilty. A judge would find it 'absurd' to admit as worthy of being taken into account the challenge that, for instance, memory has *not* been proven *not* fallacious— and, he concludes starkly, 'what is absurd at the bar, is so in the philosopher's chair' (444: VI,5). In particular, the judge gives the benefit of the doubt to a witness until it can be shown that the witness's testimony *in this case* is subject to particular objections; that is, this particular instance of the witness's testimony must be impugned if it is to incline the judge to discount it (234: I,2). Sceptical pleas *in general*, as opposed to those with particular warrant, are not relevant (259: II,5). The doubt that is reasonable is the doubt that applies to the particular case at hand—what has been called 'case-specific' as opposed to 'generic' doubt.[37].

Thus in a court of law and in philosophy, Reid concludes, the possibility of reasons against a conclusion (that is, the more-than-logical possibility that the conclusion is false) does not in itself necessarily constitute 'reasonable' grounds for doubt. The admission that contrary evidence is possible does not for Reid leave 'room for doubt' in some cases (413: VI,1). He does not align 'unreasonable' doubt with demonstration or the mere logical possibility that the conclusion is false, on the one hand, and 'reasonable' doubt with the more-than-logical possibility that the conclusion is false, on the other hand.

The preceding considerations find natural expression in Reid's claim that probable reasoning can 'have a force that is irresistible, so that to desire more evidence would be absurd' (482: VII,3), and warrant a reading of it as arguing for a non-demonstrative certainty which is legitimately equal to demonstrative certainty. The point is that to ask for more evidence, in the face of particular configurations of accumulated probabilities, is only 'reasonable' (i.e. not 'absurd') if one assumes that total legitimate certainty is only provided by demonstration. Only if one holds allegiance to a demonstrative paradigm of certainty does one need to see the absence of

---

Claude Buffier and Thomas Reid: Two Common-Sense Philosophers (Kingston, 1982), pp. 93, 134–6, 154; see pp. 137–40 for the relation of the tribunal motif to the inductive method.

[37] See Nicholas Rescher, *Scepticism*, pp. 48, 100–8.

entailment in probable reasoning as a lack which would preclude total certainty, as legitimate as that in demonstration. Reid, however, writes early on that 'Every branch of human knowledge hath its proper principles, its proper foundations and method of reasoning', illustrating his point by reference to the differences between evidential requirements of historians, antiquarians, and mathematicians (234: I,3). Moreover, he is well aware that 'It is a common observation, that it is unreasonable to require demonstration for things which do not admit of it' (482: VII,3). Clearly we are *unable* to have demonstration in cases of matters of fact, and it is unreasonable to require what is impossible. This is not a Reidian resignation to 'less than the best', however, because it is explicitly coupled with an analysis of the limits of demonstration or syllogism such as make it an 'unreasonable' standard for certainty.

In his 'Brief Account of Aristotle's Logic', Reid points to the limits of syllogism in terms of the central principle underlying syllogism—*Dictum de omni et nullo*. He writes:

The general principle in which the whole terminates, and of which every categorical syllogism is only a particular application is this, *That what is affirmed or denied of the whole genus may be affirmed or denied of every species and individual belonging to it.* This is a principle of undoubted certainty indeed, but of no great depth. Aristotle and all the Logicians assume it as an axiom, or first principle, from which the syllogistic system, as it were, takes its departure; and, after a tedious voyage, and great expense of demonstration, it lands at last in this principle, as its ultimate conclusion.[38]

The circularity of syllogism—its inability to transcend its initial premises—is the main reason why syllogism cannot be made the standard for all determinations.[39]

Moreover, and this is crucial to Reid's case, such syllogistic reasoning is not able in principle to be a standard for concrete determinations because there is a prior and more fundamental non-syllogistic use of reason without which the syllogistic enterprise cannot go on. This point is made in his account of Aristotle's logic in a variety of ways. His diatribes on the unfruitfulness of logic as

---

[38] *Works*, p. 702.

[39] In his introduction to Reid's account of Aristotle, Kames writes that Aristotle's 'artificial mode of reasoning' is 'superficial' because 'what he gives as a conclusion or consequence, is not really so; it is not *inferred* from the fundamental proposition, but is *included* in it' (*Sketches of the History of Man*, Appendix, p. 148).

compared with Baconian/Newtonian methodology make the point in a very general way.[40] From a different angle, and more specifically, he gives an example of a syllogism whose conclusiveness 'common sense pronounces, and all Logicians must allow', but which is 'somewhat unpliable to rules, and requires a little straining to make it tally with them'.[41] He then suggests that

> an attempt, by any method, to demonstrate that a syllogism is conclusive, is an impropriety somewhat like that of attempting to demonstrate an axiom. In a just syllogism, the connection between the premises and the conclusion is not only real, but immediate; so that no proposition can come between them to make their connection more apparent ... In a word, an immediate conclusion is seen in the premises by the light of common sense; and where that is wanting, no kind of reasoning will supply its place.[42]

Similarly, one must gain expertise in detecting 'sophistical' syllogisms, determining which rules are transgressed.[43]

These points were actually the same made, and made more pointedly, by Locke in Chapter XVII of Book IV of his *Essay*. Although Reid does not recognize or admit his congeniality with Locke on these points, he does give credit to Locke for the 'judicious and seasonable' counsel that 'the improvement of our reasoning power

---

[40] Reid's Philosophical Oration of 1753 contains a foreshadowing of this criticism; Todd argues that 'most of Reid's erroneous assessment of formal logic' can be excused—he was, after all in the 'good company, of Descartes, Bacon, the Port Royal logicians, and Locke (p. G-11). Nevertheless, he argues, Reid 'certainly ought to have known that the scholastic logicians did not regard the syllogistic as an instrument for making empirical discoveries ...'. In this respct it is interesting to note Jonathan Barnes's claim that the 'task of explaining [the] apparent inconsistency [between Aristotle's prescriptions concerning demonstration in the *Posterior Analytics* and the method he actually follows in his treatises] is recognized as a classical problem of Aristotelian exegesis' ('Aristotle's Theory of Demonstration', in *Articles on Aristotle: 1, Science*, eds. J. Barnes, M. Schofield, and R. Sorabji (London, 1975), p. 65). Barnes sees it necessary to argue that the non-obvious explanation of this prima-facie inconsistency is that, contrary to a common but usually unexpressed assumption, 'the theory of demonstrative science was never meant to ... describe how scientists do, or ought to, *acquire* knowledge: it offers a formal model of how teachers should *present and impart* knowledge' (p. 77). Cf. M. F. Burnyeat, 'Aristotle on Understanding Knowledge', for a 'corrective' to Barnes's thesis, based on the distinction between knowledge and understanding (*Aristotle on Science, the Posterior Analytics*, ed. Enrico Berti (Padua, 1981), pp. 115-20).

[41] *Works*, p. 609.

[42] Ibid., pp. 700-1. Cf. D. C. Stove, *Probability and Hume's Inductive Scepticism* (Oxford, 1973), pp. 84, 88 for the role of intuition in demonstration.

[43] *Works*, p. 707.

is to be expected much more from an intimate acquaintance with the authors who reason the best [e.g. Chillingworth], than from studying voluminous systems of logic'.[44] This point is of great importance to Reid, and clearly an Aristotelian one, yet he indicates no appreciation of Aristotle.[45] In general, Reid's preoccupation with the limits of syllogism seems to have obscured his appreciation of 'naturalist' elements in Aristotle's work—e.g. the 'naturalist' potential of the category of *phronesis*, a potential fully exploited later by Newman.

For Reid to say that it is 'unreasonable' to demand entailment or demonstration is also to say that it is 'unreasonable' to fault probable reasoning for its absence. In other words, only if one canonizes a demonstrative or intuitive paradigm of certainty does one have reason to claim that probable reasoning can at best issue in 'practical' or less than total legitimate certainty. Reid's recognition of the limits of syllogistic reasoning constitutes a rejection of such a paradigm of certainty. Such a rejection affirms that the line between 'reasonable' and 'unreasonable' doubt is not drawn between demonstrative and probable reasoning, but rather within each of those categories, and supports the conclusion that in particular cases of probable reasoning 'the evidence may be equal to that of demonstration' (482: VII,3)—equally total and equally legitimate certainty that *p*. It allows Reid to go beyond the 'practical' certainty which even the sceptic concedes is possible, and allows his response to the sceptic to be more than simple counter-description.

[44] *Works*, p. 709.

[45] Reid's selective appropriation of Aristotle is evident in his concentration on the objectionable elements in his theory (e.g. *Inquiry*, Chap. V, §8 and VI,§6), neglecting to note as Aristotelian those insights with which he concurs (e.g. that we should be satisfied when we have 'all the evidence that the nature of the thing admits' (132: V,§8)).

5

Reid: Proof, First Principles, and Practice

IN the preceding chapter I have been examining Reid's defence of
the certainty possible to non-demonstrative reasoning, detailing its
implicit and explicit support at length. At the very least this could
be seen as redressing a neglect of that element on the part of his
commentators. But if that element were a discrete and peripheral
one whose importance was therefore proportional to the brevity of
Reid's explicit treatment of it, the neglect would be deserved and
the foregoing examination would remain an academic exercise. In
Reid's case, however, brevity of explicit treatment of a topic should
not be allowed to obscure its possible importance—after all, his
explicit treatment of 'common sense' in the *Essays* is, if anything,
even more brief than that of 'probable reasoning'. On the contrary,
the importance of his understanding of non-demonstrative certainty lies in its intimate connection with the more conspicuous
and widely studied elements in his programme—namely, 'common
sense' and its 'first principles', and his attack on the 'theory of
ideas' (in particular, perceptual representationalism).

Some would see Reid's attack on the 'theory of ideas' as his chief
contribution to philosophy—indeed, Reid himself refers to it as the
signal 'merit of ... *my philosophy*'.[1] That attack, however, was
motivated by a more pressing and fundamental concern with the
status of the constitution of human nature, or the sanction of 'the
natural'. What is wrong with the representationalist theory of ideas,
according to Reid, is that it 'contradicts the immediate dictates of
our natural faculties, which are of higher authority than any
theory' (431: VI,3); it contradicts the natural principle of trust in
our faculties (445: VI,5). That concern likewise motivated his
attack on a demonstrative paradigm of certainty, informing his
understanding of the potential of non-demonstrative reasoning.

---

[1] Letter to Gregory, *Works*, p. 88; cf. also Stewart's citing of a letter to Gregory
(20 Aug. 1790), p. 23.

Thus, the relation of his perceptual theory to his understanding of non-demonstrative certainty is a significant though indirect one—that is, they both issue from the same fundamental motivation.

The connection of his understanding of common sense and its first principles (which is central to his response to scepticism) with his understanding of non-demonstrative certainty is, on the other hand, both direct and twofold. I shall argue first in what follows that although common sense and reasoning are two different employments of 'reason', so that common sense does not directly concern itself with reasoning processes, reasoning does play a role with respect to first principles—in terms of corrigibility, adjudication, and thus indirect justification. Secondly, and more importantly, I shall argue that Reid's equivalent of the category of 'proof' is an illustration and specification of his view of the status of 'the natural', of the constitution of human nature which underlies his understanding of first principles as such. Moreover, since he admits at the end of the chapter on probable reasoning that 'the far greatest part, and the most interesting part of our knowledge, must rest upon evidence of this kind' which philosophers call 'probable' (484: VII,3), of which 'the greatest part' is evidence from testimony (482), it is an especially important illustration.

Thus, underlying his whole anti-sceptical programme is an appeal to the sanction of 'the natural', and analysis of his category of non-demonstrative certainty uncovers that substratum. Because it is a specification of the more general discussion of common sense and first principles, and because it has been less explored than his account of perception, that category can provide a useful alternative approach for illuminating his overall position. The relation between his understanding of non-demonstrative certainty and his view of the sanction of 'the natural' is mediated by the categories of common sense and first principles, so I will consider in turn (1) the relation of reasoning to common sense in terms of his claims about their respective jurisdictions, (2) his concessions concerning the relation of reasoning to first principles, and (3) the relation of non-demonstrative certainty to the sanction of 'the natural' as that is revealed in his understanding of the first principles of common sense.

A. COMMON SENSE AND REASONING

In contrast to his treatment of the word 'probable', where he explicitly adopts a peculiarly philosophical usage, Reid rejects the philosophical understanding of the word 'sense' and adopts instead the popular usage—namely, sense as *judgement*. Theodor Haecker has suggested that the word 'sense' is one of the 'heart-words' (*Herzworte*) of the English language, comparable in function to the Greek *logos*, the French *raison*, etc.[2] Such 'heart-words' are critical elements in a particular language which reveal the 'invisible and individual spirit of a people'; they reveal 'its greatest care, grief, longing, suffering, joy, and desire' and are effectively 'untranslatable'.[3] He explains:

... one can say of the English language, that one of its heart-words is *sense—sense*, an unmistakably individual, richly organized concretion of sensuality and spirituality, of pragmatic intelligence and of the intellectual-sensuous faculty, such as has been developed in no other language.[4]

Reid's particular use of the word 'sense'[5] can thus be a significant and revealing element in his response to scepticism.

'In common language', Reid writes, 'sense always implies judgment'; 'good sense is good judgment' and 'common sense is that degree of judgment which is common to men with whom we can converse and transact business' (421: VI,2).[6] Common sense is not a 'new principle' (422), but rather something with which we are all familiar, for some degree of it 'is necessary to our being subjects of law and government, capable of managing our own affairs, and answerable for our conduct toward others' (422). Such general characterizations employ a language strikingly similar to that used

[2] Haecker, *Vergil, Vater des Abendlandes* (Leipzig, 1931), pp. 117–21.

[3] Ibid., p. 117.

[4] Ibid., p. 118. Haecker's exact formulation is as follows: '... wie man von der englischer Sprache sagen kann, daß eines ihrer Herzworte "sense" ist, sense, ein unverkennbar individuelles, reich organisiertes Konkretum von Sinnlichkeit und Spiritualität, von pragmatistischer Geistigkeit, von geistig-sinnlichem Organ, das in keiner andern Sprache gewachsen ist und darum am besten seinen Sinn in seiner eigenen Gestalt, ob im moral sense oder im common sense, ausdrücken kann....'.

[5] His use is shared by Newman, though not by Hume (cf. Hume's *Treatise*, p. 470).

[6] See Marcil-Lacoste for a useful summary of references to the variety of ways Reid uses 'common sense' (faculty, set of principles/beliefs, theory, etc.), *Claude Buffier and Thomas Reid*, pp. 74–5 nn.

by the seventeenth-century figures noted earlier, as well as to that adopted after him, to refer to the quality of common or good sense.[7]

Reid calls our attention to four specific characteristics of common sense. First, it is 'purely the gift of Heaven'—it cannot be learned or acquired by education (425, 422). Second, it is not merely a practical gift, but has a theoretical or speculative focus as well—not only does it make us 'capable of acting with common prudence in the conduct of life', it makes us 'capable of discovering what is true and what is false in matters that are self-evident' when they are 'distinctly apprehend[ed]' (422). Even Hume is twice invoked in support of the claim that common sense keeps us on the 'right path', secure from 'illusion' in *both* the theoretical and moral realms (424). Third, the possession of such common sense entitles us 'to the denomination of reasonable creatures' (425).

But by far the most important characteristic of common sense is its relation to 'reason', and here I suggest that Reid maintains what is arguably a stipulative and non-popular sense of the term 'common sense' despite his appeal to popular usage. He explains the relation between common sense and reason by allocating common sense to one of the two employments of reason:

we ascribe to reason two offices, or two degrees. The first is to judge of things self-evident; the second to draw conclusions that are not self-evident from those that are. The first of these is the province, and the sole province of common sense; and therefore it coincides with reason in its whole extent, and is only another name for one branch or one degree of reason. (425)

The claim is double-edged, for it gives common sense the entire province of judging self-evident truths, but *only* that province. Since it is because the 'sole province of common sense' is judgement of things self-evident that common sense 'coincides with reason in its whole extent', the latter phrase refers to the whole extent of common sense rather than the whole extent of reason. Although 'sense, in its most common, and therefore its most proper meaning, signifies judgment' (423), Reid goes further by restricting common sense to one kind of judgement—judgement of things self-evident. He does not see common sense as informing or guiding reasoning processes in any way—and it is arguable that such a view represents

[7] See Birkwood 2131, 4/I/2 where he explicitly contrasts the Schoolmen's view with his own.

a departure from its 'most common, and therefore its most proper meaning'.

Because common sense is an office of reason it cannot oppose reason.[8] But the relation between common sense and *reasoning* is less straightforward. Reid's characterization of them as two offices of reason with distinct objects implies 'separate but equal' employments and jurisdictions. One expects the difference in objects to rule out the possibility of conflict or support from both directions. His suggestion that a reasoned conclusion cannot 'receive any confirmation from common sense, because it is not within its jurisdiction' (425) fits that expectation, but the preceding claim that the conclusions of 'just reasoning from true principles cannot possibly contradict any decision of common sense' allows asymmetry in the relation. And he confirms the asymmetry, and rejects the model of 'separate but equal' jurisdictions, by distinguishing between the conclusion of a reasoning process and the process itself (or the grounds of the conclusion), and allowing that a reasoned conclusion can be rejected by common sense (even when we are unable to 'show the error of the reasoning' process) if the conclusion conflicts with common sense. Although strictly speaking Reid can still claim that the reasoning *process* is not within the jurisdiction of common sense, he effectively dissolves the limits of the jurisdiction of common sense by thus putting all reasoned conclusions within its domain. The priority of common sense—as the 'first born of Reason' (425)—thus refers not only to the role of self-evident principles as the foundation of all reasoning, but also to a superiority of common sense over reasoning in cases of conflict. The claim is more restricted than it might at first sight appear since Reid keeps to his stipulative definition of common sense as the judge only of self-evident truths. As his mathematical example shows, in order to be summarily rejected in the absence of reasoning to show the error involved, the conclusion of reasoning must contradict a self-evident truth—and even for Reid most truths are not self-evident. But since far more than mathematical and logical truths are considered by him to be self-evident, the intuitive judgements of common sense retain a kind of superiority.

---

[8] He does, however, in the *Inquiry*, sometimes contrast 'reason' with 'common sense'—e.g. 108: II,§5; 127: V,§7.

B. FIRST PRINCIPLES AND REASONING

Whereas the first way in which reasoning was related to common sense put the conclusions of reasoning within the jurisdiction of common sense, the second way concerns the principles of common sense themselves and gives a kind of priority to reasoning. Although reasoning does not pick out or determine first principles, it is relevant to their corrigibility, adjudication, and hence to their indirect justification.

The relation between reasoning and first principles is made most clear in the *Essays*, where for Reid the impossibility of an infinite regress guarantees that 'all knowledge got by reasoning must be built upon first principles', for

[w]hen we examine, by way of analysis, the evidence of any proposition, either we find it self-evident, or it rests upon one or more propositions that support it. The same thing may be said of the propositions that support it, and of those that support them, as far back as we can go. But we cannot go back in this track to infinity. Where then must the analysis stop? It is evident that it must stop only when we come to propositions which support all that are built upon them, but are themselves supported by none—that is, to self-evident propositions. (435: VI,4)

Sometimes he speaks of 'first' principles as simply the propositions assumed in any dialogue, agreement on which is required before people can reason together[9]—but he does not think first principles are such merely because they happen to be treated as first principles by their respective advocates. First principles are for Reid those self-evident propositions which are 'the foundation of all reasoning and of all science'—for example, that the senses and testimony are reliable guides (230: I,2). The only understanding of first principles for which the question of the relation of reasoning makes sense is that of first principles as propositions, axioms, or beliefs. But, though this is Reid's dominant view of first principles, it is not his only view; so before continuing the examination of the relation of reasoning to first principles, it is important to digress briefly to consider the vacillation in Reid's account of first principles.

1. Propensities or Propositions?

Reid articulates the concept of 'first principles' in the *Inquiry* in terms of 'principles of the human constitution' (97: I,§1). Although

[9] *Works*, 422: VI,2; 435-7: VI,4.

his initial formulation is open to a reading of first principles as axioms or propositional premises—the arts of the poet, painter, moralist, and statesman, he claims, cannot 'ever stand on a solid foundation, or rise to the dignity of a science, until they are built on the principles of the human constitution' (97)—it is immediately clear that such principles are to be seen in terms of propensities, powers, tendencies, and dispositions. He equates 'principles' with 'powers and faculties' (98), for example, and groups together in Humean fashion 'instincts, habits, associations, and other principles' (99). He urges us to 'consider the phaenomena of human thoughts, opinions, and perceptions, and endeavour to trace them to the general laws and the first principles of our constitution' (100: I,§3), which principles are 'simple and original principles' of our constitution of which the only account to be given is that they result from the 'will of our Maker' (99). (His many references to 'laws' of our constitution share in any ambiguity attached to his use of 'principle'.[10]) The view of principle as an actuating power or tendency is also expressed in his claim that sensation and memory are 'original principles of belief' while imagination is not (106: II,§3).

Such original principles of our constitution 'irresistibly govern the belief and the conduct of all mankind' (102: I,§5)—for example, the 'inductive principle' is the 'natural, original, and unaccountable propensity to believe [or the 'original principle by which we believe' (198: VI,§24)], that the connections which we have observed in time past, will continue in time to come' (113: II,§9). In the conclusion of the *Inquiry* he claims that in the course of the examination of the five senses he has 'taken notice of several original principles of belief' (209: VII). Such principles are therefore tendencies either to particular beliefs or to types of beliefs; they are original propensities rather than beliefs, axioms, or propositions which function either as initial premises in particular inquiries or as a propositional framework for reasoning in general.

Reid allows, however, an even broader notion of first principles. Such powers or propensities need not be propensities to either particular or general types of beliefs—they can be propensities to think in particular ways without having the corresponding belief. For example, in explaining how we come to discover such principles he refers to an instance of just such a tendency:

[10] Letter to James Gregory, *Works*, p. 75.

By our constitution, we have a strong propensity to trace particular facts and observations to general rules, and to apply such general rules to account for other effects, or to direct us in the production of them. (97: I, §1)

Moreover, he writes that 'every man ... is determined, by the constitution of his nature, to give implicit belief' to consciousness, to 'trust' that consciousness does not deceive him (100: I,§3). Such an 'implicit belief' is a tendency to treat consciousness as reliable— it is not a consciously held belief. This view of first principles is exemplified in his discussion of the two 'principles' of 'veracity' and 'credulity', the first a 'propensity to speak truth' and the second a 'disposition to confide in the veracity of others' (196: VI,§24). In neither case does the original principle necessarily involve a belief.[11]

According to the *Inquiry*, then, first principles can be understood as non-propositional in three ways: (*a*) tendencies to particular beliefs or judgements, (*b*) tendencies to general types of beliefs or judgements, and (*c*) tendencies to think or treat things in various ways without a corresponding belief. Whether or not Reid recognized these as different possibilities, it is clear that he did not distinguish them in his discussion.

The non-propositional view of first principles finds support in the *Essays* as well as in the *Inquiry*; for example, he writes:

We are so made that, when two things are found to be conjoined in certain circumstances, we are prone to believe that they are connected by nature, and will always be found together in like circumstances. (332: II,21)

To the question 'How then is our belief to be regulated before we have reason to regulate it?' he replies:

It is regulated by certain principles, which are parts of our constitution. Whether they ought to be called animal principles, or instinctive principles, or what name we give to them, is of small moment; but they are certainly different from the faculty of reason. (333)

The echo of Hume here is remarkable.

Even within the *Inquiry*, however, there emerges another view of

---

[11] Cf. Nicholas Wolterstorff, 'Can Belief in God Be Rational If It Has No Foundations', in *Faith and Rationality: Reason and Belief in God*, eds. A. Plantinga and N. Wolterstorff (Notre Dame, 1983), pp. 149–51. Wolterstorff here, and in an unpublished manuscript entitled 'Thomas Reid on Rationality', has interesting discussions of Reid on this point.

first principles, with which the preceding view alternates—namely, a view of first principles as themselves beliefs or propositions. He refers early on to

certain principles ... which the constitution of our nature leads us to believe, and which we are under a necessity to take for granted in the common concerns of life, without being able to give a reason for them— these are what we call the principles of common sense. (108: II,§6)

Thus, according to the *Inquiry*, the original or first principles of our constitution, our constitutive propensities, lead us to believe the first (propositional) principles of common sense. It is to the latter 'first principles' that we are led by the impossibility of an infinite regress—there is a necessity of 'assenting to them' if we are ever to prove anything (130: V,§7).[12]

The shift back and forth between the views of first principles as tendencies of our constitution and as propositional statements or beliefs is apparent also in his listing of first principles in the Essay VI, Chapter 5. First proposing a propositional first principle, he writes: 'Another first principle appears to me to be—*That there is a certain regard due to human testimony*' (450). But he adds that the 'wise Author of nature hath planted in the human mind a propensity to rely upon this evidence before we can give a reason for doing so', elaborating:

The natural principles, by which our judgments and opinions are regulated before we come to the use of reason, seem to be no less necessary to such a being as man, than those natural instincts which the Author of nature hath given to regulate our actions during that period. (451)

The parallelism suggesting that we have natural or instinctive principles which govern our beliefs in the way that instincts govern our actions before we can reason implies that the principle in question is not the proposition that testimony is generally reliable, but rather the propensity to take it as generally reliable; that is, the propensity to rely on it. Because the two—propensity and belief—are connected, Reid slides back and forth between the view of first principle as constitutive propensity and the view of first principle as that to which we are pushed by the need to avoid an infinite regress.

---

[12] Cf. *Works*, 185: VI,§20. One of Reid's earliest printed references to first principles is found in his Philosophical Oration II (1756): they are there equated with 'common notions' and compared with mathematical axioms—that is, they are explicitly propositional, p. C-6.

A Humean view of actuating first principles of our nature, dominant in the *Inquiry*, is thus embedded in a residual way in what is in the *Essays* explicitly a discussion of first principles as self-evident propositions. That explicit or focal discussion remains Reid's leading one in the *Essays*, however, and in that context the question of the relevance of reasoning becomes a pressing one.

2. Self-Evidence and Corrigibility

We are forced back, according to Reid, to self-evident first principles since we cannot trace back supporting propositions 'to infinity'; we 'must stop only when we come to propositions, which support all that are built upon them, but are themselves supported by none, that is, to self-evident propositions' (435: VI,4). The self-evidence of first principles is the result of lack of support from other propositions: 'the judgment follows the apprehension of them necessarily' because 'the proposition is not deduced or inferred from another; it has the light of truth in itself, and has no occasion to borrow it from another' (434).

The determination of self-evident propositions, as noted earlier, is the prerogative of the employment of common sense or intuitive judgement. Because 'there is no searching for evidence; no weighing of arguments' (434), philosophers and lay people are on a par. The power of reasoning 'resembles the power of walking, which is acquired by use and exercise', whereas

the power of judging in self-evident propositions, which are clearly understood, may be compared to the power of swallowing our food. It is purely natural, and therefore common to the learned and the unlearned; to the trained and the untrained. It requires ripeness of understanding, and freedom from prejudice, but nothing else. (434)

Mistakes, however, are possible, and from both directions—we can accept as first principles those which are not, and not accept those which are. Because 'vulgar prejudice' can pass for a first principle, while a genuine first principle may 'by the enchantment of words, have such a mist thrown about it, as to hide its evidence, and to make a man of candour doubt of it' (231: I,2), he is insistent that they be examined and sifted (231; 234). He is clearly not allowing as first principles any and all principles which happen to be treated as first or taken up without support—he is after 'what is really a first principle' (231).

Because (in addition to willful prejudice) mistakes are possible, differences of opinion about first principles are possible—and since the differences concern first principles themselves 'reasoning seems to be at an end' (422: VI,2). Reid's use of the word 'seems' here is quite deliberate, for it adumbrates a point made more clearly in a later section; repeating the identical phrase (437: VI,4) he retains the word 'seems' both times, for it is the burden of that later section (437-41) to show that reasoning is not actually at an end. It is applicable in particular ways. As preface to a consideration of those ways I will examine first how Reid thinks reasoning is not applicable.

What is decidedly not applicable is 'proof'. His repetition of the point that first principles neither admit of nor need proof is made increasingly specific—what is ruled out is 'direct' or 'apodictical' proof.[13] Elsewhere apodictical is equated with 'demonstrative'.[14] In itself this is clearly not the same as excluding the relevance of *all* reasoning. Reid does not, however, merely want to exclude deductive or demonstrative reasoning—as noted earlier, he wants to exclude more, for first principles are 'supported by none' (435: VI,4). Moreover, in so far as he distinguishes between deduction and inference in the claim that first principles are 'not deduced or inferred' from others (434), he is claiming that they are not derived in any way, even non-deductively, from other propositions.

A brief digression on Reid's response to the Aristotelian notion of first principles may be useful at this point. In spite of his modest descriptive title it appears as if Reid set out to provide a critical appraisal, rather than merely a 'Brief Account of Aristotle's Logic'.[15] In that account, his discussion of Aristotelian syllogism is an uncompromising one—he never gives the impression of holding back criticism in order simply to describe the Aristotelian position. He presents Aristotle's view of first principles, however, without any critical comment whatsoever. Since that presentation contains language, at least, which seems at odds with Reid's own account of first principles, it is worth considering it further.

---

[13] *Works*, 230-1: I,2; 422: VI,2; 439, 441: VI,4; but cf. 230: I,2 where he says 'seldom'.
[14] 'Brief Account of Aristotle's Logic', in *Works*, p. 705.
[15] This was first published in 1774 in Kames's *Sketches of the History of Man*, then included in the *Works*.

The Aristotelian position on first principles as laid out by Reid is as follows:

All demonstration must be built upon principles already known, and these upon others of the same kind; until we come at last to first principles, which neither can be demonstrated, nor need to be, being evident of themselves.... These are not innate, because we may be, for a great part of life, ignorant of them: nor can they be deduced demonstratively from any antecedent knowledge, otherwise they will not be first principles.[16]

Aristotle, he continues,

concludes, that first principles are got by induction, from the informations of sense. The senses gives us informations of individual things, and from these by induction we draw general conclusions.

That 'first principles are got by induction' might seem at odds with Reid's claim that first principles are not 'deduced or inferred' or 'supported' by other propositions. How can such self-evidence be compatible with being arrived at 'by induction' from particular sense informations?

Perhaps the simplest explanation for the lack of any criticism by Reid of Aristotle's position is that he recognized that Aristotelian induction was not enumerative (or otherwise probabilistic) induction, but rather was 'intuitive induction'. In the latter the perception of individual particulars is followed by a process of abstraction of properties and an intuitive apprehension of a conclusion about the properties and their relations. The intuitive apprehension yields a necessary universal generalization. The generalization is not 'justified' by the particulars (since reinterpretation of the particulars need not affect the conclusion), though the particulars served as the occasion for the intuition of the necessary conclusion.[17] Such intuitive induction of first principles would clearly not be at odds with Reid's view of their self-evidence, and Reid could quite straightforwardly agree with it. Reid's claims about the intuition of first principles could then as easily be couched in the Aristotelian language of induction.

The question at issue is not whether Reid correctly interpreted

---

[16] *Works*, p. 705.
[17] Cf. Aristotle's *Analytica Posteriora*, 81b, 100a (trans. G. R. G. Mure), and *Topica*, 105a: 13–19 (trans. W. A. Pickard-Cambridge), in the *Works of Aristotle*, ed. W. D. Ross (Oxford, 1928).

Aristotle, but rather whether his view was compatible with his account of Aristotle, and it should be admitted that Reid's formulation of Aristotelian induction of first principles leaves itself open to a reading of induction as resulting in generalizations which are not necessary, and which could not survive in the face of a concession that perception of the particulars was not veridical. I suggest, however, that Reid's view of self-evidence could be compatible with even that view of induction (itself weaker than Aristotle's own). What Reid sees at stake for Aristotle is the maxim 'That there is nothing in the understanding which was not before in some sense.'[18] What is at stake for Reid is that first principles are not supported by other propositions in such a way as to derive their evidential validity from them. Even non-intuitive induction of first principles is compatible with Reid's view of self-evidence if (but only if) one can consider the sense particulars (the premises) as themselves no more certain than the induced first principle (the concluding generalization)—and Reid does give some warrant for seeing that as the crucial element in self-evidence. For example, when in the *Inquiry* he charges Descartes with inconsistency in refusing to ask for proof that consciousness cannot deceive, he says of the proposition that 'thoughts cannot be without a mind or subject' that it is

liable to the same objection: not that it wants evidence, but that its evidence is no clearer, nor more immediate, than that of the proposition to be proved by it. (100: I,§3)

So Reid could allow even non-intuitive induction as long as it were admitted that the premises are no more certain than the conclusion. The generalization in such a case would have the same status as the perception of the particulars. 'Not supported' by other propositions would translate 'not supported by propositions more basic'.

Given the denial that first principles are 'supported' by or 'deduced or inferred' from other propositions (or from more basic propositions), how can 'reasoning' be relevant? In Essay I, Chapter 2, 'On Principles Taken for Granted', Reid suggests that 'illustration' is relevant and hints at 'ways by which the evidence of first principles may be made more apparent' (231). Promising to show how more fully later on, he says only that

[18] *Works*, p. 705.

they require to be handled in a way peculiar to themselves. Their evidence is not demonstrative, but intuitive. They require not proof, but to be placed in a proper point of view. (231)

On the one hand, the term 'intuitive' evidence suggests that he is here referring exclusively to common sense or non-reasoned judgement as the arbiter, but, on the other hand, the fact that the contrast is with 'demonstrative' evidence and 'proof' makes it less obvious what alternative is intended. His examples retain the open-endedness of the meaning of placement in a 'proper point of view', since later he suggests that Tillotson 'takes ... the proper method of refuting an absurdity, by exposing it in different lights, in which every man of common understanding perceives it to be ridiculous', in which method there is 'much good sense' but not 'one *medium* of proof' (459: VI,6)—but only a page earlier he had used 'reasons' interchangeably with 'any *medium* of proof' (458). It is only in the chapter 'Of First Principles in General' (VI,4) that it becomes absolutely clear that reasoning in its ordinary sense of discursive judgement is relevantly applicable to first principles.

In that chapter, in answer to the question 'Is there no mark or criterion, whereby first principles that are truly such, may be distinguished from those that assume the character without a just title?', he responds with conviction and definitiveness that

Nature hath not left us destitute of means whereby the candid and honest part of mankind may be brought to unanimity when they happen to differ about first principles. (437)

A page later he 'hopes' that there are 'rational means' available to us to 'correct' or 'confirm' our judgements in such cases; he then repeats the confident claim about the relevance of 'reasoning':

although it is contrary to the nature of first principles to admit of direct or *apodictical* proof; yet there are certain ways of reasoning even about them, by which those that are just and solid may be confirmed, and those that are false may be detected. (439)

And he concludes with another unqualified claim that 'there are ways of reasoning, with regard to first principles, by which those that are truly such may be distinguished from vulgar errors or prejudices' (441).

Reid's position is then, on the one hand, that first principles are self-evident, not admitting or needing 'proof' and not derived from or supported by other propositions, and, on the other hand, that reasoning is relevant to them in terms of confirmation and correction, allowing adjudication in cases of disagreement. How can the requirement of lack of support be reconciled with the possibility of confirmation and correction?

Confirmation constitutes a justification, but it is retrospective rather than prospective; that is, it is a justification for maintaining a belief already held, rather than a justification for adopting a belief. One might then want to see Reid's point as the exclusion of all prospective justification of first principles. But that cannot be right, because the notion of correction or corrigibility of first principles implies that he allows justification for adopting an improved or corrected (presumably the correct) alternative, and that is equal to allowing prospective justification for first principles as well. His point is better seen, I suggest, in terms of two other distinctions which cut across the prospective/retrospective divide: namely, the distinction between direct and indirect justification and the distinction between logically prior premisses and psychologically prior premisses.

Prospective justification of a conclusion can be either direct or indirect. Direct justification occurs in those cases where evidence directly supporting the conclusion (i.e. evidence for the substantive content of the proposition) is used by the agent to reach the conclusion. The conclusion in such a case is both psychologically and logically dependent on the evidential premisses. Alternatively, one might prospectively justify a conclusion by reference to reasons which do not bear directly on the substantive content of the proposition—i.e. reasons for accepting a conclusion of a particular type, or a conclusion with particular characteristics or consequences. Consider, for example, the indirect justification of a proposition because of a particular kind of desirability or necessity. This indirect justification does not imply logically prior premisses for the conclusion (though it does allow psychologically prior premisses).

The distinction between direct and indirect justification applies as well to retrospective justification. The acceptance of a conclusion which is not actually, or cannot be, reached by reasoning can nevertheless be justified (confirmed) retrospectively by an inference *directly* supporting the conclusion (counting as evidence for the substantive content of the proposition).[19] Such direct retrospective support allows that even though the conclusion is not psychologically dependent on the premises (because the agent did not use them to reach the conclusion), it is nevertheless logically dependent on or supported by them. By contrast, the acceptance of a proposition not capable of being reached by reasoning can be justified retrospectively by reference to reasons which do not bear directly on the substantive content of the proposition—e.g. retrospective indirect justification of a proposition because of a particular kind of desirability or necessity. Such indirect retrospective justification allows reasoning to be relevant to a conclusion without implying logically prior premises.

Direct prospective justification is clearly ruled out by Reid's view of self-evident as meaning not supported by other propositions. Unless his intention is simply to exclude conscious or psychological dependence on premises, direct retrospective justification would also conflict—and the claim that they are 'supported by none' implies that he wants not only lack of conscious mediation, but also lack of logically prior premises. But both indirect prospective and indirect retrospective justification are possible ways in which reasoning can be relevant to first principles, without depriving them of their status as principles which are not logically dependent on reasoning from more basic propositions.

Reid's catalogue of means of confirmation, correction, and adjudication assumes in all cases 'a sound mind free from prejudice, and a distinct conception of the question' (438: VI,4). Although he begins by reminding us that nature has furnished us with the notion of ridicule to expose 'absurdity' (in as keen a manner as 'argument' exposes 'error'—438), this appeal to non-reasoning is actually only a small part of his case. In his unpublished manuscripts he explicitly recognizes the limits of ridicule.[20] By contrast, far more space and attention are given to delineating the ways in which 'reasoning' as such is relevant—and those ways constitute indirect justification.

The first is the argument that 'a first principle which a man rejects, stands upon the same footing with others which he admits' (439). It is an attempt to show inconsistency, not between a conclusion of reasoning and a first principle, or between first principles,

---

[19] Cf. Lawrence Bonjour, 'Externalist Theories of Empirical Knowledge', in *Midwest Studies in Philosophy* V, eds. P. French *et al.* (Minneapolis, 1980), pp. 53-4.

[20] See Birkwood 2131, 4/I/8: 'Mere laughing is no Argument...'.

but the inconsistency of not accepting principles which stand on an equal footing in so far as a reason for accepting or rejecting one applies with equal force to all. The importance of such an argument to Reid is shown by its repetition in both the *Inquiry* and elsewhere in the *Essays*.[21] It is particularly interesting here because it has implications for first principles which just a bit earlier seemed to be exempted from the possibility of adjudication. That is, his discussion of resolution of disagreement considered those who believe 'that there is a real distinction between truth and error, and that the faculties which God has given us are not in their nature fallacious' (438). In other words, it seemed that the first principle concerning trust in our faculties was one about which agreement was necessary before any possibility of adjudication of conflicts could arise. But the argument that it is illegitimate to treat unequally principles on the same level is clearly meant to address the issue of disagreement about trust in faculties as well.

The second means he considers is another form of argument for consistency or coherence—namely, an argument *ad absurdum*, based on the recognition of the interconnectedness of the web of our beliefs. A proposition, especially a first principle, does not stand 'alone and unconnected':

It draws many others along with it in a chain that cannot be broken. He that takes it up must bear the burden of all its consequences. (439)

Although Reid puts this quite simply, it is probably one of the most important ways of correcting beliefs, even when the connection is understood in a linear manner as the reference to 'chain' might suggest. It is obviously even more important when the interconnectedness is understood in a horizontal and converging fashion.[22]

In addition to those two means he considers three marks of first principles which can be used in reasoning about their legitimacy. The first, paralleling one of the early 'principles taken for granted' (Essay I, Chap. 2) which will be considered in more detail later, is that

---

[21] See *Works*, 100: I,§3; 129-30: V,§7; 183: VI,§20; 447: VI,5. In Chap. 9 below, it will be shown that Newman uses a similar argument, claiming that one cannot divide the mind and its gifts.

[22] Cf. Philosophical Oration II (1756), p. C-5.

the consent of ages and nations, of the learned and unlearned, ought to have great authority with regard to first principles ... When we find a general agreement among men, in principles that concern human life, this must have great authority with every sober mind that loves truth. (439)

Several things ought to be said about this important element in his thought, which has been the subject of so much unsympathetic comment. First, though the authority of general agreement is put forth as a relevant consideration in confirming and correcting first principles, Reid is quick to admit that the authority is only prima-facie. It is a benefit of the doubt given in favour of the belief in the absence of the determination of a plausible cause for such widespread error—in cases of such general agreement, to charge a deviation from the truth 'of which no cause can be assigned, is highly unreasonable' (440). The same point was made by him earlier in Essay I, Chapter 2:

A consent of ages and nations, of the learned and vulgar, ought, at least, to have great authority, unless we can show some prejudice, as universal as that consent is, which might be the cause of it. (233; cf. 457: VI, 6)[23]

Moreover, the entire chapter 'On Prejudices, the Causes of Error' (VI, 8) makes clear the prima-facie character of the authority of general opinions.

Such unanimity as Reid refers to is a prima-facie *mark* of true first principles—it is not what constitutes their truth.[24] But it should be emphasized that it is a prima-facie mark of *truth* none the less, for Reid's concern is with the truth of those principles and not just their status as genuinely underived. Unanimity implies that such principles are not the result of reasoning, for not all men are at the age of reason and not all that are do reason—so such unanimity is the mark of an underived principle. But Reid is not satisfied with offering marks of principles which are genuinely first only in the sense of being genuinely underived or genuinely unanimous. Although his question about the judgement of first principles is initially phrased in ambiguous terms—he asks about a criterion

---

[23] See John Wilkins (see Chap. 2 above), *Of the Principles and Duties of Natural Religion*, 7th edn. (London, 1715), for a discussion of the relevance of universal consent (pp. 36, 39, 41) and an illustration of Reid's point (pp. 46–7, where he attempts to rule out putative causes of the prejudice).

[24] Paul Vernier argues persuasively for this, in 'Thomas Reid on the Foundations of Knowledge and His Answer to Skepticism', in *Critical Interpretations of Reid*, eds. Stephen Barker and Thomas Beauchamp (Philadelphia, 1976), pp. 17–18).

'whereby first principles that are truly such, may be distinguished from those that assume the character without a just title' (435: VI, 4)—the contrast is later clearly drawn between 'those that are truly such' and 'vulgar errors or prejudices' (441). He is searching not just for means of achieving 'unanimity' (437), but that 'the real lovers of truth may come to unanimity' (438). Thus, unanimity and lack of derivation are distinguished from truth.

His concern for true first principles as opposed to merely unanimous ones is supported, and can only be supported, by maintaining a realism about truth. What then can we make of his reply to the potential objection he himself raises at one point—namely, 'Is truth to be determined by most votes?' (439). He does not, after all, simply say 'no'. Instead, he points to the limits of his claim for the relevance of consensus or authority—it can be a 'useful handmaid ... This is all she is entitled to, and this is all I plead in her behalf' (440). It is as if Reid is saying that as long as it is recognized that the authority of consensus is prima-facie, the 'determination' of truth may well be a matter of 'most votes'. This is, however, compatible with the realism he espouses as long as he distinguishes between the definition of truth and the determination of truth, as long as he maintains an in-principle distinction between truth and its determination by us.

Reid's second mark of a first principle is that of being held prior to reasoning and instruction. For example,

the belief we have, that the persons about us are living and intelligent beings, is a belief for which, perhaps, we can give some reason, when we are able to reason; but we had this belief before we could reason, and before we could learn it by instruction. (441)

His point is that the belief is held prior to reasoning and instruction. It is interesting, however, that he uses this particular example since it has rather a peculiar status among his list of first principles. It is, on the one hand, a first principle for which he admits justification might be possible (448: VI, 5), and on the other hand, it is a first principle which depends on other first principles (e.g. the principle *That design, and intelligence in the cause may be inferred with certainty, from marks or signs of it in the effect*' (457: VI,6)). Reid's point about first principles in general seems to be that not only are they not psychologically dependent on previous reasoning, and not only are they not supported by other propositions, but they cannot be supported by other propositions. So the first principle about other minds is unusual, and clearly not at the same level as other first principles (cf. 346: III,4).

He claims thirdly that necessity in conduct is a separate mark. Perhaps his point is to highlight the necessity involved, since in principle it is possible for a belief not necessary to conduct to be universally held, and thus held prior to reasoning and education. But in an important sense, this third mark is coextensive with the second, and both can be seen as implied in the mark of universality.

The relevance of reasoning in these indirect ways is thus clearly admitted by Reid. He not only exemplifies the relevance in his own thought, he explicitly provides guide-lines for it. Even in the *Inquiry* where his view of reasoning in relation to common sense is sometimes more negative than in the *Essays*, he argues for the restoration of a 'cordial friendship' between the two (101: I,§4). His extreme ejaculation 'I despise philosophy, and renounce its guidance; let my soul dwell with common sense' is found in the context of a conditional—*if* philosophy 'hast not power to dispel those clouds and phantoms which [it] hast discovered or created', *then* and presumably only then should it be rejected (101: I,§3). He goes on to say that 'instead of despising the dawn of light, we ought rather to hope for its increase ...' (101: I,§4), arguing that it is not clear that philosophy ought to be condemned:

I have found her in all other matters an agreeable companion, a faithful counsellor, a friend to common sense, and to the happiness of mankind. This justly entitles her to my correspondence and confidence, til I find infallible proofs of her infidelity. (104: I,§8)

The claim that 'common sense holds nothing of philosophy, nor needs her aid' and that philosophy cannot rightly 'call to her bar the dictates of common sense' is rhetoric addressed to those philosophers who 'have waged open war with Common Sense, and hope to make a complete conquest of it' (101: I,§4). To extreme objections Reid tends to make extreme responses—but he practises in this case better than he preaches.

Moreover, the 'union and subordination' he prescribes has to be understood in ways compatible with his request for a 'cordial friendship'—for friendship is impossible in the face of a certain kind of subordination, in the absence of a certain kind of mutuality. Such mutuality is found in the circular relationship between common sense and reasoning. Common sense and its first principles are in one sense prior and fundamental to reasoning. Moreover, the role of intuitive judgements within the steps of the reasoning process implies a superiority of common sense. But if we can be mistaken about first principles and if reasoning can help us to distinguish error from truth in these cases, as Reid allows, there is an implicit fundamental reliance on the legitimacy of reasoning. Reasoning and common sense can be seen as complementary—both are legitimated by the sanction of 'the natural' and both can be seen as rules for 'taking for certain'. Reasoning is validated by common sense in so far as we have first principles about natural laws of what 'counts as certain'. But reasoning can also indirectly correct common sense's determinations. So mutual interdependence obtains.

Highlighting the ways in which Reid sees reasoning as a complement to common sense in terms of confirmation and correction of first principles clarifies his claims for their self-evidence and thus redresses unfair assessments of them.[25] His personal modesty and lack of dogmatism in presenting his own position, evidenced so often in his writing,[26] are mirrored in his view of the corrigibility of the judgements of common sense and the scope of intuition.

C. REASONING AND HUMAN AGREEMENT

A third way in which reasoning is related to common sense and its first principles is perhaps the most important for an appreciation of Reid's overall response to scepticism—namely, the relation between the certainty possible to non-demonstrative reasoning and the status of 'the natural' as it is revealed in his understanding of the first principles of common sense. I shall argue that the category of non-demonstrative certainty exemplifies for Reid a 'rule' of 'what counts for certain' in the human practice of justification, and that

[25] S. A. Grave's discussion of 'common sense' likewise suggests that Reid's position is neither uncritical nor anti-philosophical (*The Scottish Philosophy of Common Sense* (Westport, Conn., 1973; originally Oxford, 1960), Chap. II, esp. pp. 123-32. See Chap. 4, n. 26, above.

[26] He writes 'I shall humbly offer in the following propositions what appears to me to be agreeable to truth in these matters, always ready to change my opinion upon conviction' (435: VI,4). Again, 'I shall rejoice to see an enumeration more perfect in any or in all of those respects' since '[s]uch enumerations, even when made after much reflection, are seldom perfect' (441, 452: VI,5). See also Birkwood 2131, 4/I/2, 2/III/1, and his letter to Hume (18 Mar. 1763), *Works*, p. 92.

such rule-governed practice is at the heart of the notion of 'universal agreement'. The sanction of such agreement illustrates the status of the sanction of the dictates of human nature, so the sanction of non-demonstrative certainty in his account (especially the view of 'unreasonable' doubt that informs it) can illuminate his understanding of first principles, in particular the character and role of 'human (universal) agreement' in his response, at the same time as his understanding of the character and role of such agreement can clarify his view of the status of non-demonstrative certainty.

Determining the relation between Reid's view of non-demonstrative certainty and his naturalism involves pinpointing the locus and character of his appeal to the sanction of 'the natural'. I suggest that that is found in the concept of 'human agreement' which I will introduce through a brief review of the list in Essay I, Chapter 2, of 'principles taken for granted', paying special attention to the last two.

The first principle to be taken for granted is 'that I *think*, that I *remember*, that I *reason*, and, in general, that I really perform all those operations of mind of which I am conscious' (231). The second is that 'we know the past by remembrance' (231); the third, 'that, by attentive reflection, a man may have a clear and certain knowledge of the operations of his own mind' (232). These principles, it should be noted, concern only the *exercise* of the faculties or operations, not their testimony.[27] The fourth principle is 'that all the thoughts I am conscious of, or remember, are the thoughts of one and the same thinking principle, which I call *myself* or my *mind*'—the principle, that is, of 'continued existence and identity' (232). Five and six: 'that there are some things which cannot exist by themselves, but must be in something else to which they belong, as qualities, or attributes' (232); 'that in most operations of the mind, there must be an object distinct from the operation itself' (233).

An unmistakable shift comes with the final two categories of things to be 'taken for granted'. The seventh heading is the general claim that

We ought likewise to take for granted, as first principles, things wherein we find an universal agreement, among the learned and unlearned, in the different nations and ages of the world. (233)

[27] This should clarify the first principle in his second list, VII,5.

Instead of the usual straightforward statement of a first principle, Reid gives us here a statement about first principles—we should take as first principles 'things wherein we find an universal agreement'. His examples of such agreement are striking: belief in 'the existence of a material world', the belief 'that every thing that begins to exist, and every change that happens in nature, must have a cause', and 'that there is a right and wrong in human conduct'. His later discussion of first principles 'in general' (Essay IV, Chap. 4) addresses the bearing of universal agreement using the very same examples cited here, and much of the same language about their characteristics. Two points about such agreement, brought out in the preceding section's consideration (B) of that later discussion are first made in this early discussion of universal agreement—namely, that (1) the authority of such agreement is prima-facie, and (2) such agreement is a *mark* of truth, rather than what constitutes it.

Statement seven expresses the prima-facie authority of universal agreement. Reid expressed more explicitly the import of such universality in an early unpublished piece in which he wrote that 'The Universality of the first principles of Knowledge which Philosophers have either called in Question or have laboured with difficulty to prove is no small Argument of their Being Natural and Constitutional'.[28] Statement seven is a principle indicating (though not explicating) the sanction of 'the natural' at the same time as it is validated by that sanction—implicitly Reid argues that it is itself 'natural and constitutional'. I shall argue in what follows that it is a principle whose applications are first principles, and a principle which underlies and encompasses all his first principles.

Universality for Reid is both an indicator of and an 'argument' for the naturalness of such principles. But how is such universality determined and what is the authority of the natural? Universality is obviously not in principle determinable by polling people, questionnaire-fashion, for such principles as are 'universal' in the relevant sense are none the less challenged at times. Examples of universal agreement are, rather, determined by reference to two sources: some opinions are

evident, from the whole tenor of men's conduct, as far as our acquaintance reaches, and from the records of history, in all ages and nations, that are transmitted to us.

[28] Birkwood, 2131, 4/I/8 (1765?).

There are other opinions that appear to be universal, from what is common in the structure of all languages. (233; cf. 440: VI,4)

The unique character of Reid's examples of universal agreement and their 'evidence' belies his claim that he is discussing agreement in 'opinions'—it suggests rather that he is referring to agreement *in what we do*. Such universal agreement is evident from the tenor of human conduct and the structure of language, *not* from being attested to by sense, memory, or testimony. Sense and testimony are not related, for example, to the belief in a material world, that every event has a cause, or that there is a right and wrong, in the way that sense and testimony are relevant to other kinds of beliefs held by reasonable men (for example, that there is a building in front of me, that Julius Caesar existed, or that there is such a city as Rome). The 'evidence' of the former is evidence *that* such beliefs are held universally, not evidence for the content of the beliefs.

Such agreement is not the result of evidence—it is agreement in how we treat evidence. It is akin to what Wittgenstein calls agreement in 'form of life' or 'judgments' rather than 'opinions',[29] determining what is to count as evidence from sense, memory, and testimony. The universal agreement noted in the above-mentioned unpublished piece makes this even clearer, for he gives as examples 'Credulity. Induction. Memory. Consciousness. Perception'— clearly references to a form-giving level prior to that of conclusions based on evidence.

Reid's understanding of the relevance of what is common in language deserves some comment here as well, for it is complex both with respect to the authority of common language and the extent of its informativeness as regards 'the natural'. On the first point his most straightforward position is that ordinary language has the benefit of the doubt in its favour: until it is 'proved' to be wrong it 'ought to be used, and ought not to give place to a phraseology invented by philosophers' (221: I,1). More specifically, the operations of the understanding have 'corresponding' forms of speech which would not be found in language unless the operations were common to mankind (238: I,5); moreover, the 'most common' is the 'most proper meaning' (423: VI,2). On the other hand, ordinary language is inherently problematical because of its generation

---

[29] *Philosophical Investigations*, trans. G. E. M. Anscombe (New York, 1958), §§ 241–2.

and purpose. It is developed 'in the early periods of society' by 'rude and ignorant men ... to express their wants, their desires, and their transactions with one another', and 'can reach no farther than their speculations and notions' (474: VI,8).[30] Even now 'we can only expect, in the structure of languages, those distinctions which all mankind in the common business of life have occasion to make' (238: I,5). As a result 'philosophy teaches us ... to distinguish things which the vulgar confound' (336: II,22), and meanings can be 'so common and so well authorized in language' that though misleading they cannot easily be avoided (223: I,1).

The position seems to be asymmetrical, nicely summed up in the following formulation:

There may be distinctions that have a real foundation, and which may be necessary in philosophy, which are not made in common language, because not necessary in the common business of life. [He refers in the *Essays* to numerous instances.[31]] But, I believe no instance will be found of a distinction made in all languages, which has not a just foundation in nature. (224: I,1)

But the asymmetry is a factual one—in principle he allows that philosophy can challenge and rightly undermine distinctions which exist in common language as long as it proceeds in a particular fashion (224).

What we learn from ordinary language is therefore defeasible in principle, and can be misleading in fact, but it is at least more than what can be learned from syntax. Often Reid seems to restrict the 'structure' of language to things like distinctions between subject and object, noun and adjective, or elements like plurals, adverbs, prepositions, and conjunctions.[32] But that is not the limit he envisages, for he writes as well of learning about human practices—for example, making promises and contracts, offering testimony or supplication (238: I,5). He elaborates on the relevance of the constitution of language by referring to 'Words that imply a moral faculty [*sic*] that Imply Taste. That imply a Notion of Cause and Effect to be found in all languages.'[33]

---

[30] Reid refers here (474) to Wilkins's work on language (*An Essay towards a real Character and a Philosophical Language*, 1668), praising him even more on p. 403: V,4. (There is an unrelated reference to Wilkins in II,3.)

[31] See 265: II,7; 310: II,16; 336: II,22; 348: III,5; 475: VII,1; 223: I,1.

[32] Cf. 224: I,1; 233: I,2; 238–9: I,5; 440: VI,4.

[33] Birkwood, 2131, 4/I/8.

Agreement is expressed in practice and language—practice and language embody agreement. Not as if there were *first* agreement, and *then* expression in practice and language—the agreement is *evident* in the practice and language. Number seven thus underlies and encompasses the preceding six principles to be taken for granted.

Although number eight is like number seven (and unlike the first six) a general claim about things to be taken for granted, it is obviously intended to convey a different message. He writes in number eight:

> I shall also take for granted such facts as are attested to the conviction of all sober and reasonable men, either by our senses, by memory, or by human testimony. (233: I,2)

What is the difference between seven and eight? It might simply be the difference between 'universal' and 'all sober and reasonable men'. But this seems implausible both because the remainder of the contrast is not identical, and because in any case his understanding of 'universal' would always exempt the reasonable. The difference seems to lie elsewhere—namely, in the contrast between the two types of beliefs, with two types of relation to evidence. The evidence of the examples of first principles in number seven is evidence from conduct and language—evidence *that* such beliefs are held universally, not evidence for the content of the beliefs as seems to be the case in number eight. The formulation of principle eight implies that all those particular facts attested to by sense, memory, and testimony are to be taken as separate first principles. But that this cannot, without contradiction, be Reid's intention, is shown by considering the case of testimony. A plausible example of a belief accepted by reasonable men on the basis of testimony—namely, that there is such a city as Rome—is actually used by him to illustrate a conclusion of 'probable' reasoning (482: VII,3); to see such beliefs as themselves first principles conflicts with his requirement that first principles be unsupported by other propositions. Two options are possible. The first is that he is here introducing, admittedly in a misleading fashion, what he takes to be his main point—namely, that

> although some ... have disputed the authority of the senses, of memory, and of every human faculty ... [they] pay the same regard to the authority of their senses, and other faculties, as the rest of mankind. (233: I,2)

The first principles at issue in number eight would thus be the first principles of trust in our senses, memory, and testimony. As such they would parallel his later formulation of first principles in Essay VI, Chapter 5: trust in memory, trust in senses, trust in faculties in general, especially reasoning, and trust in testimony. That our senses can in general be trusted is at the same formal level as that there is an external world—not learned from experience, or from its being attested to by the senses or other faculties. Such trust is a 'practice' evident in conduct and language. The second option is that number eight simply gives particular examples of conclusions accepted on the basis of those first principles which would then be included under number seven. In either case the eighth statement, like the first six principles, finds a place under the rubric of the seventh—that is, it is subsumable under the appeal (always prima-facie) to universal agreement, or agreement in 'what we do'.

Principle seven is thus in an important sense the core of Reid's response to scepticism. The conceptual connection between universal agreement and human practices whose 'rules' can be described is what explains the connection between the category of non-demonstrative certainty and first principles—the common ground is the dependence on the sanction of 'the natural'. The category of non-demonstrative certainty embodies a 'rule' of 'taking for certain' in non-demonstrative cases. It is a particular exemplification of the trust we have in our faculties—a description of what we count as being certain in such cases, a description of a 'rule' generated by a 'practice'. Non-demonstrative certainty is thus defended by Reid in the same way as his other epistemological claims—it illustrates the heart of his response to scepticism.

But even if one grants that for Reid normativity is related to naturalness, and hence to universal agreement, there remain a number of open questions. The ultimate source of the normativity is still undetermined, as is Reid's view of the relation between 'practice' and 'necessity'.

6

Reid: The Sanction of the Natural

THE point of the preceding chapter was to suggest that Reid's notion of 'universal agreement' reveals his reliance on the embeddedness of beliefs, implicit or explicit, in socio-linguistic practice. The legitimacy of such beliefs is not for him the result of a special intuitive insight, or a special kind of 'seeing' that they are correct, as if their truth were evident in what could be seen by looking at them in isolation and inspecting their phenomenological characteristics. They are 'evident' in universal practice. Their 'evidence' is 'self-evidence' in the sense that it does not depend on other more basic propositions supporting them. Reid could then say, with Wittgenstein, that

Giving grounds, however, justifying the evidence, comes to an end;—but the end is not certain propositions striking us immediately as true, i.e. it is not a kind of *seeing* on our part; it is our *acting*, which lies at the bottom of the language-game.[1]

It might be thought, however, that my emphasis on Reid's attention to the agreement evidenced in the 'tenor of our conduct' and our language misrepresents a fundamental methodological commitment of Reid's. Before proceeding to further analysis of the role in Reid's naturalism of the notion of 'practice' in order to illuminate the authority of 'the natural', it is appropriate to consider this objection.

One form this objection might take raises the question of the relation of Reid's theological commitment to his methodological commitment. It has been suggested, for example, that a decisive difference between Reid's naturalism and Hume's centres on the question of Reid's appeal to God, the Author of our constitution: 'Hume and Reid differed in substance as well as words, for Hume rejected that supernaturally founded or motivated reliance on natural belief—that curious supernatural naturalism—which char-

---

[1] *On Certainty*, §204, see also §110.

acterizes the works of Reid.'[2] Reid's naturalism, it is true, cannot be assessed properly without taking into account the importance of his religious beliefs to his theory of human nature, but I suggest that an appreciation of his theological frame of reference must not be allowed to obscure the import of his appeal to the natural.[3] His reliance on natural belief is, I would argue, neither supernaturally founded nor supernaturally motivated, and this is best shown by examining his response to Descartes.

Reid emphatically rejects the Cartesian appeal to God to prove the veracity of our faculties, explaining that Descartes argues

that our senses are given us by God, who is no deceiver; and therefore we ought to believe their testimony. But this argument is weak; because, according to his principles, our senses testify no more but that we have certain ideas. (286: II,10)

In addition to this inadequacy he points to its vicious circularity:

It is strange that so acute a reasoner did not perceive that in this reasoning there is evidently a begging of the question.
For, if our faculties be fallacious, why may they not deceive us in this reasoning as well as in others? And, if they are not to be trusted in this instance without a voucher, why not in others?
Every kind of reasoning for the veracity of our faculties, amounts to no more than taking their own testimony for their veracity. (447: VI,5; cf. also 273: II,8)

Recognizing this circularity, the thrust of his attempt to avoid it is at heart a rejection of the possibility of proof or reasons for the veracity of the faculties. Louise Marcil-Lacoste provides a most useful discussion of this rejection in terms of both his notion of self-evidence and the inductive codification of principles.[4] Reid's position is clearest when he writes:

---

[2] David Fate Norton, *David Hume: Common Sense Moralist and Sceptical Metaphysician*, p. 208. Since his admission, p. 203 n., fails to affect his conclusion, his position is apparently that Reid differs from Descartes only in so far as Descartes sees the guarantee as a conclusion of an argument whereas Reid sees the guarantee as a first principle; I am challenging the notion that they had a similar guarantee.

[3] Daniel Schulthess, *Philosophie et sens commun chez Thomas Reid: 1710–1796* (Berne, 1983), has a sensitive account of Reid in light of his theological commitment and in relation to the theological tradition preceding him (esp. Chaps. III, VIII), but he seems at times not to appreciate differences between Reid and Descartes (pp. 349, 82–3).

[4] See 'Dieu garant de véracité ou Reid critique de Descartes' (*Dialogue* XIV, 4 (1975), pp. 584–605), as well as *Claude Buffier and Thomas Reid*, pp. 146–9.

He who is persuaded that he is the workmanship of God and that it is a part of his constitution to believe his senses, may think that a good reason to confirm his belief: but he had the belief before he could give this or any other reason for it. (329: II,20)

Belief in God cannot be a reason for trusting our faculties since we trust (and not unrightly) before we can have this reason. Here and elsewhere he implicitly distinguishes between prospective and retrospective roles for the appeal to God, allowing that though it may confirm one's trust,[5] it is not necessary either to generate or legitimate that trust. Belief in God is not of the same status as belief in the veracity of the faculties, nor is it evidentially prior—it is instead the result of reasoning from first principles. The relation of trust in our faculties to belief in God is, therefore, not one of epistemological dependence.

Ontological dependence is, therefore, implicitly distinguished from epistemological dependence. Admittedly, the divine authorship of our constitution is responsible for the functioning of our faculties—we are, for Reid, the workmanship of God—but we can come to know of that authorship only after we have trusted our faculties, so such trust cannot be epistemologically dependent on belief in God. In sum, though Reid may be guilty of other kinds of circularity, he cannot be charged with the kind of circularity for which he criticised Descartes.[6] His theological tenets do not inform his methodological commitment in that way; as Marcil-Lacoste concludes: 'inductively speaking, Reid's appeal to common sense would still be possible even without his reliance on a Deity'.[7] The discussion of Reid's view of the relation between theory and practice which follows will provide further support for such a conclusion.

An objection to my analysis of his methodological commitment can assume a more important form—one which directs itself to the question of introspection. Reid does, to be sure, claim in the *Essays* that the primary tool in generating a philosophy of mind, the 'main

---

[5] For example I take it that such retrospective use is what is referred to in the *Inquiry*, 184: VI,§20 and 198: VI,§24.

[6] See Marcil-Lacoste, 'Dieu garant de véracité ...', pp. 592–605, and *Claude Buffier and Thomas Reid*, p. 149, for a discussion of problems with Reid's attempt to use the teleological argument. Cf. Reid's *Lectures on Natural Theology* (1780), ed. Elmer Duncan (Washington, DC, 1981).

[7] Marcil-Lacoste, *Claude Buffier and Thomas Reid*, p. 146.

source' of information, is 'accurate reflection' on the mind's activities.[8] 'Subservient' to that are two other methods: attention to
the structure and status of language and attention to the actions
and opinions of men, since they 'may sometimes give light into the
frame of the human mind' (238-9: I,5). I suggest, however, that
Reid's *de facto* reliance on the latter two strategies belies his proclaimed methodological hierarchy, and I will defend that suggestion
below. However, in so far as his methodological commitment to
'accurate reflection' is expressed in terms of introspection of individual psychology, two remarks should be made at the outset.
First, it may well be part and parcel of the problem attending any
attempt at innovation from within a necessarily limiting context.[9]
For that reason his account should be read with the sympathy with
which he approached other philosophical accounts; despite defects
they were to be studied and valued, he said, because

They have made many openings that may lead to the discovery of truths
which they did not reach, or to the detection of errors in which they were
involuntarily entangled. (101: I,§4)[10]

Reid clearly proposes to do 'anatomy' (i.e. description), for 'it must
be by anatomy of the mind that we can discover its powers and
principles' (98: I,§1).[11] But what needs to be determined is what
kind of anatomy he is committed to, and whether that commitment
carries in its train (or is motivated by) a confusion between causal
explanation and justification. Anatomy as such is no response to a
sceptic; it must be part of or placed in the context of a philosophi-

---

[8] *Works*, 238: I,5.
[9] Cf. Reid's 'Introduction' to the *Inquiry* where he writes: 'The language of
philosophers, with regard to the original faculties of the mind, is so adapted to the
prevailing system, that it cannot fit any other; like a coat that fits the man for whom
it was made, and shows him to advantage, which yet will set very awkward upon
one of a different make, although perhaps as handsome and as well proportioned'
(98: I,§2). The problem is also pointed to by Richard Rorty, *Philosophy and the
Mirror of Nature* (Princeton, 1979), p. 58 n., and expressed quaintly by Wittgenstein
when he writes: 'My account will be hard to follow: because it says something new
but still has egg-shells from the old view sticking to it' (*Culture and Value*, ed. G. H.
von Wright (Oxford, 1980), p. 44e).
[10] Cf. Stewart's life of Reid, *Works*, pp. 15, 22, 23, 28, for a similar call for a
sympathetic reading.
[11] Even though he implicitly parallels anatomy of mind with that of body, his
strictures against analogies between mind and matter (*Inquiry*, Chap. VII; *Essays
on the Intellectual Powers* (hereafter *E.I.P.*), Essay I, Chap. 3) show that we cannot
determine by the use of such an analogy what he takes anatomy of mind to be.

cal theory about the status of the anatomy. I suggest that Reid has, at least implicitly, placed it in such a context, but that some effort is required to determine what, despite limitations, remains of value in his attempt to show the philosophical relevance of the appeal to the constitution of human nature.

Second, the role of introspection and the tool of 'accurate reflection' on the mind's activities are crucially qualified by him in the *Inquiry* when he writes:

if a philosopher could delineate to us, distinctly and methodically, all the operations of the thinking principle within him, which no man was ever able to do, this would be only the anatomy of one particular subject; which would be both deficient and erroneous, if applied to human nature in general. For a little reflection may satisfy us, that the difference of minds is greater than that of any other beings which we consider as of the same species. (98: I,§2)

Thus, even though he admits that the determination of 'the operations of other minds' must, being ambiguous, be interpreted by what each perceives within himself (98), such introspective perception is not sufficiently generalizable to form the basis of a philosophy of mind. It is difficult in the face of this qualification to see introspection as the surest methodology (and this is borne out, as we shall soon see, by his manner of criticizing Locke). Lest one argue that Reid shifted his position between the *Inquiry* and *Essays*, it should be noted that the unusual fact that both works were written late in life (the *Inquiry* was written when he was 54) renders less plausible the suggestion of a significant shift in evaluation of methodological commitments.

To return then to the determination of the 'anatomy' or description Reid saw necessary—his criticism of 'a priori' methodology gives some indication of his view of the formal character of such anatomical study. An early unpublished piece makes this criticism clear:

I thought it most decent and proper to write not in the Synthetical but in the Analytical Method; That is, not to lay down my conclusions first and then seek for facts to confirm them; But to take the facts in the order that the Senses present them and consider what may be inferred from them.[12]

He continues, interestingly: 'I have not indeed affected to shew my Method in the titles of the several Sections ... nor have I taken any

[12] Birkwood Collection, 2131, 2/III/1.

pains to point out my Method by tedious transitions, conceiving it Essential to a Philosophical work to have included but not essential to make ostentation of it.'

His attention to methodology is thus central to his project, and he repeatedly expresses his indebtedness to Baconian/Newtonian emphases on description vs. a priori creative hypothesizing.[13] Reid could say, as easily as Bacon did, that

we have no authority arbitrarily to prescribe laws to man's intellect, or the general nature of things. It is our office, as faithful secretaries, to receive and note down such as have been enacted by the voice of nature herself.[14]

But there are many alternatives to a priori prescription, and I suggest that the particular method of description actually relied on by Reid is not always the method called upon explicitly. For example, despite claims about the priority of introspection, he argues against Locke on the basis of *what we count as knowledge* rather than by appeal to introspective anatomical description. He writes:

Neither do I think that knowledge is confined within the narrow limits which Mr. Locke assigns to it; *because* the far greatest part of *what all men call knowledge*, is in things which neither admit of intuitive nor of demonstrative proof. (426: VI,3, ital. mine)

Locke's assignment, according to Reid, ignores the social 'facts', and this a priorism infects his entire programme with scepticism. Such a criticism is just what one would expect given Reid's explicit position on the relevance of universal agreement, and the general and continued appeal throughout both the *Inquiry* and the *Essays* to the construction of language, universal belief, and the presuppositions of action.[15] And it shows that 'accurate reflection' and

---

[13] His indebtedness to Baconian/Newtonian methodology is expressed repeatedly in his Philosophical Orations I and II (1753, 1756) as well as in the *Inquiry*: I; VI,§24 and in the *E.I.P.* (I, 2–4). Marcil-Lacoste's work is an explicit attempt to emphasize the implications of Reid's methodology, arguing that 'the majority of commentators have failed to see the importance of the link between the Reidian method and doctrine, while some have denied this link altogether' (*Claude Buffier and Thomas Reid*, p. 77; cf. also pp. 76-7 nn. 8–10, and pp. 131-45). Cf. L. L. Laudan's 'Thomas Reid and the Newtonian Turn of British Methodological Thought', in *The Methodological Heritage of Newton*, eds. Robert E. Butts and John W. Davis (Oxford, 1970).

[14] Preface to Book V, 'Anticipation of the Second Philosophy', *Works* XIV, ed. Basil Montagu (London, 1831), p. 428.

[15] See *Works*, 110: II,§7, in addition to all the references noted in Chap. 5 above.

'anatomy of the mind' can be addressed to social practice as well as to individual psychology.

Even if these qualifications concerning methodology support a reading in which the notion of 'human agreement' points to the sanction of the natural, it is still necessary to consider what is revealed by the natural and what constitutes the philosophical relevance of a natural 'practice'. I will begin by examining Reid's numerous charges of the sceptic's inconsistency—charges made in both the *Essays* and the *Inquiry*.[16] The most obvious candidate for the locus of inconsistency is the conflict between 'theory' and 'practice', and his charge has seemed to many a naïve one, missing the sceptic's real point. I want to argue in what follows that the formula 'theory vs. practice' is simplistic, masking a variety of versions of possible inconsistency which need to be distinguished. Moreover, I want to argue that Reid's work has in addition the heart of another kind of charge of inconsistency which, to retain the parallelism, one could term a conflict between 'theory and theory', or a conflict within the realm of theory. This conflict within the realm of theory illuminates the relation between theory and practice which informs Reid's discussion. Determination of the real import of his response to scepticism requires analysis of both kinds of charge of inconsistency—and hence analysis of the various ways in which the notion of 'practice' can enter into a response to scepticism. Until the relevant distinctions are made justice cannot even begin to be done to Reid's account, and the question of Reid's view of the ultimate sanction of the natural cannot be fruitfully asked or answered.

A. THEORY VS. PRACTICE

Since Reid clearly thinks that 'want of faith, as well as faith itself, is best shown by works' (489: VII,4), it is all too easy to read his charge of the sceptic's inconsistency as if he thought the only consistent sceptic was one like Pyrrho the Elean who 'if a cart ran against him, would not stir a foot to avoid the danger, giving no credit to his senses' (102: I,§5), one who, believing there is no external world, would 'run his head against a post' (234: I,2) and not 'avoid the fire' (489: VII,4). But his charge of inconsistency is

[16] *Works*, 102: I,§5; 109–10: II,§6; 121: V,§2; 127–8: V,§7; 184: VI,§20; 234: I,2; 432: VI,3; 447: VI,5; 448: VI,5; 489: VII,4.

clearly not so naïve as to be the claim that the sceptic believes *p* and acts according to not-*p* (or vice versa) where what is at issue is a first-order belief like 'there is no post in front of me' or 'there is no external world'—for he recognizes and affirms over and over again that the sceptic too finds himself 'under a necessity of believing with the vulgar' (432: VI,3). Such beliefs, he says repeatedly, are irresistible.[17] Presumably this would include 'vulgar' beliefs like the belief that the faculties are reliable. He does not deny that the sceptic too can and does concede the necessity of such beliefs. He does not therefore charge a conflict between theory and practice at that level, because at that level there is no conflict—the sceptic practises what he necessarily believes. Reid's point is therefore a different one.

A second way in which theory and practice can conflict is through an inconsistency between action and a metabelief about the justification of any beliefs in question. That is, a sceptic can hold that there is an external world, and even that his faculties are reliable, while holding the metabelief that each of those beliefs is unjustified (though unavoidable). And he can hold that metabelief while carefully stepping around the post he believes is in front of him. Reid's charge at the very least concerns the inconsistency between such metabelief and action.

Such inconsistency, however, can take two forms, and it is central to Reid's account that he charge the sceptic with the latter form. The first form is that of *contingent* action contrary to the metabelief in question; the second is that of *necessary* or *unavoidable* action contrary to the metabelief. Reid's point clearly concerns the latter; he writes that even in the case of a first-order belief which sceptics reject 'in speculation' (that is, by means of the metabelief that it is unjustified), there is a 'necessity of being governed by it in their practice' (447: VI,10). There is not only a necessity to believe certain first-order propositions, there is as well a necessity to act contrary to the sceptical metabelief about their lack of justification. Reid's charge is that the sceptic exemplifies the truth that it is not in his power *not* to act contrary to the metabelief—he necessarily acts contrary to it, and that necessity or unavoidability says something philosophically relevant about the status of the metabelief. The formal structure of his charge is that, while

[17] *Works*, 102: I,§5; 110: II,§7; 121: V,§2; 126: V,§7; 132: V,§8; 184: VI,§20; 234: I,2; 416: VI,1; 447: VI,5; 454: VI,6; 455: VI,6; 458: VI,6; 485: VII,4.

action-contrary-to-a-metabelief *simpliciter* says nothing about the status of the metabelief, the necessity of such action has implications contrary to the sceptic's claim that our necessary beliefs are none the less unjustified. What might those implications be?

Reid is facing the objection that even if the sceptic is forced to act in all things like the non-sceptic, and, consequently, to have those beliefs which are necessary to such action and to act against his sceptical metabelief, he might nevertheless maintain a sceptical metabelief. That is, it seems possible that a sceptic can act contrary to the metabelief that his first-order beliefs are unjustified, while continuing to believe that it is unjustified to hold those first-order beliefs. But in Reid's account there is the outline of a further argument against the sceptic, developing the implications of the previous argument. That is, his claim that it is descriptively impossible to act in line with the metabelief suggests another consideration which transforms the charge from one of inconsistency between action and metabelief to one of inconsistency between metabeliefs. Such a claim implies more than mere unavoidability of a certain kind of action if it assumes that a genuine metabelief must make *some* difference in practice—if it assumes, that is, that practice provides the only basis for thought (see 110: II,§7; 183-4: VI,§20; 489: VII,4). Moreover, I would argue that it is in such considerations that we find the implied rationale of Reid's view that the non-sceptical position has the benefit of the doubt, and that the burden of proof rests on the sceptic.[18] Reid's claim suggests that ingredient in the charge of inconsistency between theory

---

[18] Keith Lehrer proposes instead an 'agnoiological principle of impartiality' according to which the sceptical thesis is also innocent until proven guilty ('Why Not Scepticism?' in *Essays on Knowledge and Justification*, pp. 356-8). My entire chapter, however, argues that Reid's was not a dogmatic locating of the burden of proof, but one motivated by philosophical considerations about the relation between theory and practice. I thus take issue as well with Michele Federico Sciacca's claim that Reid's 'instinctive belief' or 'common sense' is a 'purely psychological datum, dogmatically accepted and related to ... the "pragmatic" use of sense data and not to their "epistemological" value' and that Reid is 'convinced that the proposition: "what all men think is true" is an irrefutable argument against Hume's scepticism, and that it can be so pragmatically just because dogmatically accepted ...' (*La Filosofia di Tommaso Reid*, 3rd ed., Milan, 1963), §38, p. 70. ('... dato puramente psicologico dogmaticamente accettato e riferito ... all'uso "pragmatico" dei dati sensoriali e non al loro valore "gnoseologico"'. 'Egli è convinto che la proposizione: "è vero ció che pensano tutti gli uomini" sia argomento inconfutabile contro lo scetticismo dello Hume; e puó esserlo pragmaticamente proprio perché dogmaticamente accettato ...')

and practice is a charge of inconsistency within the realm of theory, precisely because theory and practice are intrinsically and conceptually bound together. The following section will explore and develop this suggestion. In the process it will raise again from a different perspective some of the issues concerning tensions in Hume's thought, as those tensions were perceived by Reid.

B. THEORY *AND* PRACTICE — THE CONFLICT *WITHIN* THEORY

The charge of inconsistency within the realm of theory is raised in Reid's claim that

> We are born under a necessity of trusting to our reasoning and judging powers; and a real belief of their being fallacious cannot be maintained for any considerable time by the greatest sceptic, because it is doing violence to our constitution. It is like a man's walking upon his hands, a feat which some men upon occasion can exhibit; but no man ever made a long journey in this manner. (632)

'Some men upon occasion' can perform the feat—but not only could no man spend his entire life in such a way, no man 'ever made a long journey in this manner'. A 'real belief of their being fallacious cannot be maintained for any considerable time', though it can perhaps be held episodically, for heuristic purposes. One cannot, that is, extrapolate legitimately from the ability to do something on occasion the ability to do it always.[19]

Coupled with this is the argument from impossibility, 'ought implies can', to which he is explicitly committed. In a letter to Lord Kames, after expressing confidence that reason and the moral sense cannot 'differ on any point', he affirms that 'It is by the moral sense that I determine, in general, that it is unjust to require any duty of a man which it is not in his power to perform.'[20] Thus, one cannot be bound to do what one cannot do—this is a crucial addition to Reid's claim that even the avowed sceptic cannot maintain for any 'considerable time' a 'real belief' in the fallaciousness of our faculties.

Reid is here saying not only that we are under a necessity of trusting our faculties or treating them as reliable, but that we can-

---

[19] Note that Hume had Cleanthes express the same opinion in the *Dialogues Concerning Natural Religion*, ed. R. H. Popkin (Indianapolis, 1980), p. 5.

[20] Letter of 3 Dec. 1772, *Works*, p. 51.

not maintain for long 'a real belief of their being fallacious'. This is, I take it, more than the claim that the sceptic shares with the vulgar the unavoidable belief that our faculties are reliable, for the sceptic can admit he believes that, while believing it is unjustified to believe it. Reid, I suggest, is arguing that we cannot sustain the metabelief that such trust is unjustified. In other words, while we do not, admittedly, have a necessary positive belief that our trust in our faculties is justified, we cannot sustain the belief that such trust is *unjustified*. That is, we cannot sustain the theoretical conviction that the ground of doubt is a 'reasonable' one. Not only is it not in our power to abstain from the first-order belief, and not only is it not in our power not to act contrary to the metabelief— it is not in our power to sustain for any considerable time the metabelief.

A suggestion of this particular charge of inconsistency is present in Reid's claim that even Hume 'ingenuously acknowledges, that it was only in solitude and retirement that he could yield any assent to his own philosophy' (101-2: I,§5). That Reid is here referring quite strictly to Hume's failure to maintain assent to his own philosophy (except in solitude) as a lapse from the theoretical commitment (rather than a gap between theoretical and practical) is reinforced by the sentence immediately following which begins, '*Nor did I ever hear him charged with doing anything*, even in solitude, that argued such a degree of scepticism, as his principles maintain' (101-2, ital. mine). Only the second sentence concerns the conflict between theory and practice; the first concerns the conflict between theory and theory. Reid seems to be making a similar point about the lapse from the theoretical commitment when he, in the persona of the sceptic, criticizes the view that a man 'ought to have the same belief in solitude and in company, *or* that his principles ought to have any influence upon his practice' (110: II,§7, ital. mine). One could take these statements to refer to what he describes as the 'closet belief' of the sceptic, which can only be maintained 'in their most speculative hours', in 'some solitary moments'.[21] But Reid

---

[21] *Works*, 110: II,§§6, 7. That we cannot hold it without lapsing is also a way of understanding the claim in the *E.I.P.* that 'Of those who have professed scepticism, ... their scepticism lies in generals, while in particulars they are no less dogmatical than others' (448: VI,5). Although this charge of inconsistency between general and particular can be read as referring to the inconsistency between the general theoretical stance and the particular action (as in 416: VI,1), it could also refer to a lack of consistency between theory in general and theory in particular.

seems to go further in drawing out the implications of the relation between principles and practice, the implications of the suggestion that Hume did not even *do* anything, *even in solitude*, expressive of his theoretical commitment, for he continues:

It is probable the 'Treatise of Human Nature' was not written in company; yet it contains manifest indications, that the author every now and then relapsed into the faith of the vulgar, and could hardly, for half a dozen pages, keep up the sceptical character. (102: I,§5)

Reid's suggestion, then, is that though we can minimize our going out of the 'closet', we cannot avoid it entirely, and that, moreover, even inside the 'closet' we cannot maintain the sceptical metabelief. And not merely do such theoretical lapses occur, they are inevitable.

Before considering further warrant for this understanding of Reid's charge, it will prove useful to examine his suggestion that Hume himself acknowledges the conflict between explicit theory and implicit theory on the sceptic's part. At the very least, whether or not Reid is correct, the implication of inconsistency on Hume's part makes it possible to appreciate fully the 'naturalist' elements in Hume's thought (pointed to in Chapter 3 above) without rendering Reid's critique of Hume either implausible or otiose. If Reid is correct that Hume admits that the sceptic is unable to sustain even his theoretical commitment to the unjustifiability of natural beliefs, that says something about Hume's 'naturalist' response to scepticism. If Reid is not correct, it makes the differences between them more precise.

What claims does Hume make which would count in favour of Reid's reading? In an apparently quite straightforward passage Hume writes that

a Pyrrhonian cannot expect, that his philosophy will have any constant influence on the mind: or if it had, that its influence would be beneficial to society. On the contrary, he must acknowledge, if he will acknowledge anything, that all human life must perish, were his principles universally and steadily to prevail. All discourse, all action would immediately cease.[22]

He continues: 'the first and most trivial event in life will put to flight all his doubts and scruples, and leave him the same, in every point of action and speculation' with philosophers of other sects.

[22] *Enquiries Concerning Human Understanding*, p. 16c

The entire passage is important in illustrating a number of ambiguities in Hume's account of what mitigates the Pyrrhonist's demand for suspension of judgement because of lack of rational justification. It raises in particular the following kinds of question: (1) what in particular renders the influence 'on the mind' of Pyrrhonist 'principles' and 'philosophy' unable to be 'constant,' and (2) how far is the sceptic relapsing when '*all* his doubts and scruples' are put to flight and he becomes like others in '*every* point of action *and* speculation'?

The first ambiguity concerns the vacillation about the 'chief' objection to Pyrrhonism. He writes, for example, that 'the chief and most confounding objection' against such Pyrrhonism is that 'no durable good can ever result from it'.[23] This is explained in the passage noted above by saying that maintenance of Pyrrhonist 'philosophy' or 'principles' would lead to the cessation of 'all action'.[24] He goes on to say, however, that 'Nature is too strong for principle'. So it is not immediately clear whether the chief objection is Pyrrhonism's bad effect or its impossibility because natural beliefs are irresistible. Hume's lack of definitiveness is revealed in his formulation: the Pyrrhonist 'cannot expect that his philosophy will have any constant influence on the mind, *or if it had*, that its influence would be beneficial' (ital. mine).

Assuming that impossibility rather than undesirability is what he intends to argue, there is still a lack of clarity about the source of the irresistibility or necessity. On the one hand, there seems implied a connection between belief and action—maintaining Pyrrhonist principles would lead to cessation of all action. Hume seems, then, to mean that we cannot act as if *p* without believing that *p*. He implies that the sceptic misdescribes himself when he says he suspends judgement because in fact the non-cessation of all his action reveals the non-suspension of judgement. On the other hand, Hume sometimes seems to say that such suspension of judgement is impossible independently of any connection with action—Nature simply constrains us to believe particular things *and* to act in particular ways. A third option is the reconciling move of saying that Hume sees a connection between action and belief which coincides with the independent compulsion of the belief by Nature.

A further question can be raised about what is meant by 'philo-

<hr>

[23] *Enquiries Concerning Human Understanding*, p. 159.
[24] Ibid., p. 160.

sophy' and 'principles'—what precisely cannot be maintained in the face of Nature. Is Hume referring to a relapse into the vulgar beliefs that there is an external world, etc., or instead to a relapse from the philosophical principle that judgement ought to be suspended because it lacks rational justification? On the one hand, he speaks of the sceptic losing 'all his doubts and scruples' and of being rendered by Nature similar to other philosophers 'in every point of action and speculation'—Pyrrhonist 'philosophy' cannot have a 'constant' influence 'on the mind'. This parallels the impossibility of sustaining theoretical commitment suggested in the *Treatise*: he writes of sceptical reasonings—'were it possible for them to exist, and were they not destroy'd by their subtility'[25]—concluding that "Tis happy, therefore, that nature breaks the force of all sceptical arguments in time, and keeps them from having any considerable influence *on the understanding*'.[26] And he admits in the *Dialogues* that 'everyone is constrained to have more or less of this philosophy [which goes beyond the "absolute necessity" of the natural beliefs he spoke of earlier]'.[27]

On the other hand, he has Philo claim in the *Dialogues*:

if a man has accustomed himself to sceptical considerations on the uncertainty and narrow limits of reason, he will not entirely forget them when he turns his reflection on other subjects; but in all his philosophical principles and reasoning, I dare not say, in his common conduct, he will be found different from those who either never formed any opinions in the case or have entertained sentiments more favourable to human reason.[28]

This suggests that the inability to maintain Pyrrhonist principles refers only to the inability to suspend first-order beliefs.[29] It is, however, at least possible (and potentially fascinating) to see Philo as representing here, not Hume, but the extreme Pyrrhonist whose scepticism Hume wants to mitigate. This would explain the characterization of Philo at the outset of the *Dialogues* as the 'careless' sceptic.[30] If so, Philo's conclusion need not be inconsistent with the claims noted above.

---

[25] *Treatise*, p. 186.   [26] Ibid., p. 187, ital. mine.
[27] *Dialogues*, p. 7.   [28] Ibid., p. 6.
[29] See *Treatise*, p. 270: 'In all the incidents of life we ought still to preserve our scepticism.'
[30] *Dialogues*, p. 2. Note that this is even more plausible if Cleanthes's 'accurate philosophical turn' reflects, at least at times, a position Hume himself would espouse; Popkin suggests this when he says that 'As Cleanthes moderated his claims

In any case Reid may well have been referring to that variety or ambiguity in Hume's position when he suggested that even Hume admitted his point (that even the theoretical conviction could not be sustained). Hume certainly implies a connection between belief and action when he claims that maintaining Pyrrhonian principles will lead to the 'cessation of all action'. Moreover, this connection is stronger than can be defended in terms of logical connection— that is, one need not, except perhaps psychologically, believe that *p* in order to be able to act as if *p*—though Hume would be correct in pointing out that one does need some beliefs, perhaps beliefs about the possibility of *p*.[31] In other words, however Hume sees the strong connection between belief and action, he explicitly charges the Pyrrhonist with a conflict between theory and practice, and there is much to support the suggestion of a conflict at the level of theory as well.

It is appropriate to note here Reid's suggestion of another inconsistency in Hume's thought, one which has a direct bearing on the claim that it is impossible to sustain the theoretical conviction that doubt of the relevant beliefs is reasonable—namely, an inconsistency in Hume's thought on the relation between conceivability and possibility. In Chapter 3 of Essay IV on Conception, Reid quotes what he terms Hume's confession 'that in all cases where we dissent from any person, we conceive both sides of the question; but we can believe only one' (378: IV,3). From that, he goes on, it follows that we can conceive what is impossible,

and as Philo enlarged his, in a serious sense Cleanthes comes to represent a portion of what Hume really believed. In this case, Hume may be represented by different aspects of his characters, even by some bit of Demea's view' (*Dialogues*, Intro., p. xvi). I find support for Popkin's view in the following claim by Cleanthes: 'Our senses, you say, are fallacious; our understanding erroneous; ... You defy me to solve the difficulties or reconcile the repugnancies which you discover in them. I have not capacity for so great an undertaking ... I perceive it to be *superfluous*. Your own conduct, in every circumstance, refutes your principles' (p. 9, ital. mine). This calls to mind Hume's remark in the *Treatise*: 'Shou'd it here be ask'd me, ... whether I be really one of those sceptics, who hold that all is uncertain ... I shou'd reply, that this question is entirely *superfluous* ... Nature ... has determin'd us to judge as well as to breathe and feel' (p. 183, ital. mine). Moreover, Cleanthes, as we shall see, in Pt. IX explicitly holds Hume's standard position on conceivability. Cleanthes's espousal of the argument that one cannot extrapolate from the ability to do something on occasion to the ability to do it always (p. 6) might then be something that Hume would accept against the extreme Pyrrhonist.

[31] See Chap. 10 below for further discussion of these points.

yet I know no philosopher who has made so much use of the maxim, that whatever we conceive is possible, as Mr. Hume. A great part of his peculiar tenets is built upon it; and if it is true, they must be true. But he did not perceive, that in the passage now quoted, the truth of which is evident, he contradicts it himself.

Reid is correct that Hume explicitly depends on that maxim, both in the *Treatise* and the first *Enquiry*.[32] And we saw earlier how important the rejection of that maxim was for Reid. His case for an inconsistency in Hume is supported not only by the reference he cites, but also by the presence of other elements which counter the thrust of the one-to-one tie between conceivability and possibility. The most important was noted earlier in Chapter 3—namely, Hume's discussion of liberty and necessity,[33] which claimed explicitly that conceivability did not support 'the least possibility' of particular suppositions. Moreover, he seems to vacillate on the issue in the *Dialogues*. In Part IX he has Cleanthes offer the standard presentation of his conceivability thesis, claiming that

there is an evident absurdity in pretending to demonstrate a matter of fact, or to prove it by any arguments *a priori*. Nothing is demonstrable unless the contrary implies a contradiction. Nothing that is distinctly conceivable implies a contradiction.[34]

But in contrast, he has Philo (and it is significant that it is Philo[35]) join in the attack on Demea by means of an argument which presupposes just that view of conceivability which Cleanthes (and Hume usually) explicitly denies. Philo argues as follows:

Is it not probable ... that the whole economy of the universe is conducted by a like necessity [as is the case in mathematics] ... And instead of admiring the order of natural beings, may it not happen that, could we penetrate into the intimate nature of bodies, we should clearly see why it was absolutely impossible they could ever admit of any other disposition?[36]

In other words, Philo is here arguing against Cleanthes's denial of necessary existence and admitting that something can be 'absolutely impossible' even if the contrary does not imply a contradiction and so is conceivable. This is a denial that whatever we can conceive is

---

[32] *Treatise*, p. 89, and *Enquiries*, p. 26.
[33] *Enquiries*, Chap. VIII, Pt. I.
[34] *Dialogues*, p. 55.
[35] See n. 30 above.
[36] *Dialogues*, p. 57.

possible. Since Philo nowhere else expresses a less sceptical position than Hume's, it is plausible to see this as Hume too speaking, in contradiction with his more usual position on the relation between conceivability and possibility.[37]

Such a view of conceivability and possibility would complement Hume's discussion of unreasonable doubt in Section VIII of the *Enquiry* and warrant Reid's charge of Humean inconsistency on the issue. Moreover, such inconsistency would go far toward supporting the parallel inconsistency Reid notes in Hume's position on whether we can maintain even a theoretical commitment to the illegitimacy of common-sense beliefs. Whether or not it is implicit in Hume, however, the claim that we cannot sustain the metabelief—i.e. that we cannot sustain the conviction that the ground of doubt about first-order belief is a reasonable one—is, I shall continue to argue in what follows, implicit in Reid, and constitutes a mitigation of Pyrrhonism which is of philosophical relevance.

What, then, is the character of his response to scepticism? Is it a transcendental argument designed to show the legitimacy of particular beliefs (including non-sceptical metabeliefs) because of their necessity for the possibility of human experience?[38] At times he implies this, as when he says it is 'vain' to resist, and if we could resist we could not 'speak nor act like reasonable men' (455: VI,6). It is evident, moreover, that reliance on or trust in the senses is necessary for communication (445–6: VI,5)—without it the social fabric dissolves, '[e]very social tie is broken' (446). More strongly, his description of things illustrating universal agreement, evident as they are from the tenor of human conduct and the structure of language, shows that they are embedded in a socio-linguistic framework so as to make human experience impossible in their absence, without their guidance (236: I,3; 440: VI,4).

The sceptic will still argue, however, that such an argument only reinforces the claim that the beliefs are necessary—and that was never in question. Necessity, however, says nothing about the truth or the rationality of the beliefs. The experience they render possible is human experience as we know it, but that remains a hypothetical or conditional necessity. The only thing that would connect such

---

[37] Cf. D. C. Stove, 'Part IX of the *Dialogues*', *Philosophical Quarterly* 28 (1978).

[38] Reid clearly does not see it as the optional choice of a set of conventions in the way Rudolf Carnap suggests; see 'Empiricism, Semantics, Ontology', in *Meaning and Necessity*, 2nd enlarged edn. (Chicago, 1956).

necessity with truth is the notion of an unconditional necessity.[39] The sceptic, then, can easily accept a transcendental 'argument' to the necessity of the relevant beliefs. He can also accept a kind of 'naturalism' which appeals to a description of human nature and conduct (rather than an argument based on them) as supporting their necessity, because such 'naturalism' will remain a sceptical naturalism, rather than a response to scepticism, unless it somehow also manages to include considerations which challenge the sceptic's demand for justification.

What indications are there in Reid to suggest that he was attempting to offer more than what is achieved by a transcendental argument to the necessity of the beliefs in question—attempting, that is, to offer something which effectively undermined the sceptic's requirements? One preliminary consideration is his awareness of a distinction between a cause and a ground of belief (416: VI,1), between a ground and a 'just' ground (328: II,20). A more telling consideration (supporting the first) is a point he makes, noted earlier, about the status of 'evidence' for conclusions. He criticizes Descartes in the *Inquiry* for not realizing that in some cases the 'evidence' for a conclusion 'is no clearer, nor more immediate, than that of the proposition to be proved by it' (100: I,§3). He reiterates later: the evidence of sense, of memory, and for necessary relations are all 'equally grounded on our constitution'—what this means is that 'to reason against any of these kinds of evidence, is absurd; nay, to reason for them, is absurd' (108: II,§6). This general point— that doubt of the conclusion in such cases is unreasonable because anything that would count as evidence for (or against) it is no more sure than the conclusion itself—offers a philosophical challenge to the status of the sceptic's charge by suggesting the incoherence of the notion (and requirement) of a more unconditional necessity than the necessity of the human enterprise in which we are engaged. The necessity for which he argues goes beyond mere irresistibility or inability to doubt—it is the necessity implied by the impossibility of argument for or against because there is nothing more sure which could count as evidence, the necessity implied by the lack of reasonable ground for doubt.

Reid is concerned to argue that we cannot sustain the theoretical

[39] Barry Stroud, 'Transcendental Arguments', in *Kant on Pure Reason*, ed. Ralph Walker (Oxford, 1982); 'The Significance of Scepticism', in *Transcendental Arguments and Science*, ed. Peter Bieri (Dordrecht, 1979).

commitment that the doubt is not only possible but reasonable; this finds early expression in his second Philosophical Oration (1756), when he argues that the philosopher ought to refrain from 'overthrowing common notions' which 'snatch up assent from the very constitution of human nature' because 'in accordance with these axioms every principle of life revolves'.[40] He explains:

> If these common notions were removed, human plans, just like the dreams of a sick man, could have neither measure nor end and everything would of necessity be turned upside down. These common notions are both more ancient and more stable than the whole of philosophy; they have their deep roots fixed in human nature. So true is this that to tear these away by philosophical devices would be an insane and empty undertaking.

Validation, for Reid, is thus a function of the way in which our beliefs are interconnected and presupposed by all our activities. Without certain notions our plans 'could have neither measure nor end and everything would of necessity be turned upside down'. This theme finds later support in the *Essays'* discussion of the evidence of sense and memory. When, 'as a philosopher', he reflects on the beliefs challenged by the sceptic, he finds himself lacking 'that evidence which I can best comprehend, and which gives perfect satisfaction to an inquisitive mind' (330: II,20). None the less, he continues, 'It is ridiculous to doubt, *and* I find it is not in my power' (330, ital. mine). Whether he is also distinguishing between its being in his power to 'doubt' and its being in his power to 'throw off' the belief, it is at least quite clear that he distinguishes between the inability to doubt and the unreasonableness of doubting. If we could 'by a determined obstinacy, shake off the principles of our nature, this is not to act the philosopher, but the fool or the madman' because it is unreasonable to throw off a belief without being able to show 'how we come to deceive ourselves into the opinion' (111: II,§8)—that is, unless we can suggest a reasonable ground for doubting an irresistible belief. In summary, in the absence of a suggestion of reasonable ground for doubting an irresistible belief, it becomes even more unreasonable to shed it given the disastrous consequences that would ensue (184: VI,§20).

   This confirms the suggestion made earlier in this chapter that it is not belief in God which validates our natural beliefs. But it is not their irresistibility, either, which validates them; it is rather the

[40] Page C-5.

combination of their irresistibility *and* the lack of grounds for reasonable doubt of them. Paul Vernier, in a discussion of Reid's defence of first principles, argues similarly that Reid's answer to the sceptic is at the level of an epistemological or philosophical reply because Reid is not claiming that irresistibility or universality of first principles is the *ground* of their epistemic warrant or legitimacy.[41] These are marks or evidence, rather, of their status as authentic first principles. Their justification is not found in their necessity; rather Reid's reply to the sceptic, according to Vernier, is that

our self-evident beliefs are warranted because there are no reasonable grounds for doubting them. In light of their irresistibility, and the destructive practical consequences of their denial, absence of good reasons for doubt is adequate ground for denying the sceptic's challenge to their warrant.[42]

It should be noted here, moreover, that this validation is not for Reid a *guarantee* of their truth. He writes in the *Inquiry*, for example, concerning the constitution of our nature: 'If we are deceived in it, we are deceived by him that made us, and there is no remedy' (130: V,§7). In the same vein, he writes in response to the sceptic's question why he believes the existence of external objects:

The belief, sir, is none of my manufacture; it came from the mint of nature; it bears her image and superscription; and, if it is not right, the fault is not mine. (183: VI,§20)

That they are 'natural' provides no guarantee—it simply shows that we have no alternative. In sum, then, Reid is committed neither to a supernaturally-motivated trust in our constitution, nor to a guarantee (supernatural or otherwise).

What does Reid see as the heart of the unreasonableness of doubt in such cases? His answer begins with the striking concession that 'if a sceptic should build his scepticism upon this foundation, that all our reasoning, and judging powers are fallacious in their nature, or should resolve at least to withhold assent until it be proved that they are not; it would be impossible by argument to beat him out of this strong hold' (447: VI,5; cf. 434: VI,4). But the

---

[41] 'Thomas Reid on the Foundations of Knowledge and His Answer to Skepticism', in *Critical Interpretations of Reid*, pp. 14–24; my study elaborates and extends, with further analysis and defence, Vernier's excellent suggestion.

[42] Ibid., p. 20.

impasse is not absolutely final, for it ultimately leads to considerations which should count against the sceptic.

For example, he proposes elsewhere a converse advantage as a counterweight to this disadvantage—namely, the advantage implied in the claim that

> I confess I know not ... by what good argument he [a sceptic] can plead even for a hearing; for either his reasoning is sophistry, and so deserves contempt; or there is no truth in the human faculties, and then why should we reason? (104: I,§8)

That is, in terms of responses to the sceptic there is an important difference between the 'offensive' attempt to argue him out of his scepticism and the 'defensive' attempt to show that there is no reason to *become* a sceptic.[43]

Secondly, providing the rationale for the problem with the 'offensive' manœuvre, he notes that 'Every kind of reasoning for the veracity of our faculties, amounts to no more than taking their own testimony for their veracity' (447: VI,5). The circularity is clear:

> If a man's honesty were called in question, it would be ridiculous to refer it to the man's own word, whether he be honest or not. The same absurdity there is in attempting to prove, by any kind of reasoning, probable or demonstrative, that our reason is not fallacious, since the very point in question is, whether reasoning may be trusted. (447)

But it is crucial to note that the circularity is at the same time the rationale for the 'idleness' of the sceptic's question:

> If any truth can be said to be prior to all others in the order of nature, this seems to have the best claim; because in every instance of assent, whether upon intuitive, demonstrative, or probable evidence, the truth of our faculties is taken for granted, and is, as it were, one of the premises on which our assent is grounded. (447)[44]

Not only does every assent presuppose it, but so does every challenge. In other words, the sceptic's question about our faculties is

---

[43] Nicholas Rescher writes that it is 'critically important to distinguish between rather different sorts of "refutations of scepticism," namely: (1) arguments whose probative force is such as to dislodge the rational sceptic from his position, and (2) arguments whose probative force would impede "the reasonable man" from ever becoming a sceptic in the first place' (*Scepticism*, p. 8).

[44] Cf. Hamilton's footnote to this passage, *Works*.

not a genuine question because the attempt to answer it at all, or even frame it, presupposes an affirmative answer.[45]

The same point is also made in his variations on the theme that the sceptic is inconsistent because he gives one of the mental operations or faculties or some other element a privileged status for no obvious reason. That is, he charges the sceptic with the inconsistency of not treating equally things which are in fact on a par—accepting either reasoning (183: VI,§20; 447: VI,5), or consciousness (99: I,§2), or ideas and impressions (129: V,§7) as an *unvouched-for* standard.

Idleness based on circularity is also the heart of another consideration central to his account: namely, that doubting implies believing, that doubt is built on and only possible on the basis of accepting things without doubting. Offering a third reason for not attempting to distrust his faculties, he writes:

I gave implicit belief to the informations of nature by my senses, for a considerable part of my life, before I had learned so much logic as to be able to start a doubt concerning them ... I should not even have been able to acquire that logic which suggests those sceptical doubts with regard to my senses. (184: VI,§20)

This may, of course, be read as simply a point about temporal order. But it need not be. It can be quite straightforwardly read as a claim about a conceptual requirement, fitting in with the emphasis on the importance of the principle of 'credulity', so marked in the *Inquiry* and repeated in the *Essays*.[46] In the absence of a reasonable ground for doubting them, it is reasonable to continue to trust them.

In these chapters I have provided a detailed and comprehensive argument that what seems to the sceptic to be merely the unavoidability of our nature is interpreted by Reid in the context of a philosophical account whose main ingredient is a doctrine of unreasonable doubt. And I have argued that this holds true with respect to both his account of first principles and of

---

[45] Here Reid is indicating (and Newman will be even more specific) the particular way in which the sceptic's challenge is 'meaningless'—cf. Keith Lehrer, 'Why Not Scepticism?' pp. 354-5.

[46] *Works*, 184-5: VI,§20; 196-7: VI,§24; 450-1: VI,5. Note also that Credulity is not for Reid just an empirical generalization—it is explicitly paralleled with Induction, Memory, Consciousness, and Perception in the Birkwood manuscript 2131, 4/I/8.

probable reasoning. Thus, although his response to the sceptic is based at bottom on 'practice' and 'practices', it is not relegated to the level of a non-philosophical or antiphilosophical pragmatic response.

7

Newman: First Principles and Scepticism

THE influence of Reid lasted well into the first half of the nineteenth century, but it is not usual to connect him with Victorian
thinkers. It might seem particularly unlikely, moreover, that there
should be a connection between Reid and the controversial Victorian convert to Roman Catholicism, John Henry Newman
(1801-90), whose style of life and writings differed from Reid's so
markedly. In this chapter, however, I want to suggest and explore
a relation between them, one which will, I suggest, illuminate the
thought of both men.

Newman was first a student at Trinity College, Oxford, and then
a fellow of Oriel, where he had a very significant though temporary
relationship with Richard Whately, whose *Elements of Logic* maintained the reign of standard Aristotelian logic textbooks. Perhaps
the best introduction to his life then and after is his autobiography,
Apologia Pro Vita Sua (1864), in which he documents his part in
the Oxford Movement, initiating in 1833 his slow and agonizing
turn away from Anglicanism to Roman Catholicism (completed
with his reception into the Roman Church in 1845). He was a
leader in spite of himself, creating a stir which generated a variety
of polemical writings, including his *Apologia*. Unlike Reid, he was
a prolific author, often writing in the midst of considerable political
stress.[1] One of his most famous works, *The Idea of a University*,
was the result of the ill-fated attempt to found a Catholic university
in Dublin in the 1850s. He concentrated on explicitly theological
issues, one of which—the relation between faith and reason—was
the theme of many of the famous early sermons at St Mary's before
his conversion. This theme was explored again in the light of his
philosophical readings (including Reid) in the 1850s and 60s, finally

---

[1] In addition to the extensive list of works in the *Dictionary of National Biography*
account (Vol. XIV, pp. 340-51), the publication of thirty volumes of letters and
diaries is currently being completed.

reaching fullest expression in his *Essay in Aid of a Grammar of Assent* (1870), in which he addressed, he said, assent or belief in general, as a necessary prolegomena to discussion of religious belief. It is in the context of this concern with the relation between faith and reason, doubt and certainty, that we find the views most relevant to our concern with naturalist responses to scepticism.

In an 1895 article on Newman in a German encyclopaedia of Catholic theology, A. Bellesheim concluded that Newman's *Grammar of Assent* was 'not free from objection from an Aristotelian-Thomist standpoint', and that what was objectionable was due to the influence of Richard Whately's nominalist philosophy and Thomas Reid's 'common sense' theory.[2] Bellesheim did not explain the form he thought Reid's influence took, but what he apparently saw as obvious has remained an open question for many following him. For example, one of the two major studies of the sources of Newman's thought consigns the influence of Scottish Common Sense philosophy to the category of 'minor sources', concluding that there is 'no evidence to show that he ever made any extensive use of their ideas'.[3] The more recent survey of scholarship concerning Newman's sources suggests that neither 'the question of commonalities or influence, nor the question of the possible clarification of his own thinking through a give-and-take with Reid' is settled.[4]

It has long been known that Newman was familiar with Reid's works as early as 1822, for he wrote to his sister Jemima:

As to Reid, I used to know something of him some 12 years since, when I was preparing for standing at Oriel. He is a Scotch man, who pretends to set Plato to rights. I have no business to talk of writers I have not

---

[2] 'Newman', in *Wetzer und Welt's Kirchenlexicon: Encylopädie der Katholischen Theologie* (Freiberg, 1895), pp. 219–26. Present reference is to p. 224: 'Vom Standpunkte der aristotelisch-thomistischen Philosophie ist das Buch nicht frei von Einwänden, was jedenfalls dem Einflusse der nominalistischen Philosophie Whateley's [sic] und der Theorie des Gemeinsinnes von Reid zuzuschreiben ist.'

[3] Edward J. Sillem, *Philosophical Notebook*, Vol. I (Louvain, 1969), p. 221.

[4] Johannes Artz writes that 'Wenn er in der ersten Randbemerkung zur "Inquiry" Reid "seicht" nennt, so bedeutet das nicht eine Erledigung der Frage nach Gemeinsamkeiten oder Einflüssen, auch nicht der nach einer möglichen Klärung eigener Gedanken durch Auseinandersetzung mit Reid' ('Newman's Philosophische Leistung', *International Newman Studien* X, eds. H. Fries and W. Becker (Heroldsberg bei Nürnberg, 1978), p. 202).

studied, but your Scotch Metaphysicians seem to me singularly destitute of imagination.[5]

And it has been known that he studied them again beginning in 1859—in the years, therefore, when the *Grammar* was beginning to take shape in his mind. The clearest documentation is found not only in his collected *Philosophical Notebook*, and the occasional pieces collected under the title, *Theological Papers on Faith and Certainty*,[6] but also in the fact that he annotated his copy of Reid's works extensively—nearly seventy-five per cent of the pages of the *Inquiry* bear some kind of marking and the *Essays* bear fewer but more significant comments.

Newman's negative comments on Reid have been duly noted: Reid was not only unimaginative, but 'shallow' (i.e. he 'mistakes others').[7] What has not been sufficiently appreciated, however, is that before his close study of Reid began in 1859, Newman had already given evidence of holding Reid in significant esteem. In an 1854 essay printed in his *Idea of a University*, Newman severely indicted a number of the foremost standardbearers of the British empirical tradition (e.g. Locke he judged to be of 'unsatisfactory repute', while Hobbes, Hume, and Bentham were 'simply a disgrace').[8] He added, however, that by way of 'compensation', philosophy could boast of Clarke, Berkeley, Butler, Reid, and Bacon. Newman's commendation of Reid is significant because it places Reid in the company of at least two sources of influence on him whose importance Newman explicitly admitted (i.e. Butler and Bacon). It is also significant because it occurs before he took up Reid seriously in 1859—it therefore shows that on the basis of his early acquaintance with Reid, contrary to his explicit estimate, he took Reid to be worthy of being placed in the company of men he openly admired and expressly followed in important ways. By this commendation then Newman himself raises the question how far his thought is similar to and influenced by Reid's thought. Whether or not reliance by Newman on Reid can be established, however,

---

[5] *Letters and Diaries of John Henry Newman* IV, 253, (18 May 1834); (hereafter *L.D.*).

[6] Eds. Hugo de Achaval, SJ and J. Derek Holmes (Oxford, 1976); (hereafter *T.P.*).

[7] Newman writes this on the opening page of Reid's *Inquiry* in his copy of Reid's *Works* (1858); this is also noted by Sillem, *Philosophical Notebook* I, p.223.

[8] Ed. Ian T. Ker (Oxford, 1976), Pt. II, University Subjects III, 'English Catholic Literature', Sect. 3, p. 263.

comparison of their responses to scepticism can contribute to an enhanced understanding of both figures.

There is much in Reid, I shall argue in the following chapters, which Newman could have found congenial—much to warrant his commendation. Perhaps the most likely object of Newman's appreciation of Reid lies in his model of non-demonstrative certainty, to which Newman's own account bears striking similarity both in imagery and strategy. This locates them both, I shall argue, in the tradition of 'proof' discussed in earlier chapters. Grounding that understanding of proof, however—thus at the same time less obvious than it, but more fundamental—is their similar position on the 'sanction of the natural'. Newman's position is indicated in a letter to Charles Meynell, who was painstakingly commenting on the final draft of the *Grammar* as it was being completed. Newman anticipated difficulty with an upcoming and possibly 'decisive' section on the 'dictate of conscience' and in his description of that section he makes the following claims:

(*a*) 'the *belief* in an external world is an *instinct* on the apprehension of sensible phenomena',

(*b*) 'to *deny* those instincts is an absurdity, *because* they are the voice of nature',

(*c*) 'it is a duty to trust, or rather to use our nature—and not to do so is an absurdity',

(*d*) 'to recognize our nature is really to *recognize God* ... those *instincts* come from *God*.'[9]

Those claims are at least at first glance strikingly similar to claims made by Reid a century earlier. I want to argue in the following chapters that Newman's response to scepticism, like Reid's, was fundamentally constituted by an appeal to the 'sanction of the natural', and that an important element in that appeal was the distinction between doubt that was reasonable and doubt that was possible, but none the less unreasonable. By putting them both in a line of similar naturalist responses to scepticism, that appeal emerges as a shared theme of far more significance than their no less real differences on other points.

Though both responses depend on the same rationale, however, they express themselves in different ways. Both deal with the category of first principles and its relevant faculty as well as with the category of 'probable' or non-demonstrative reasoning, but their

[9] *L.D.*, XXIV, 294 (25 July 1869).

emphases are, at the very least, in inverse proportions. As is clear from the preceding chapters, first principles and the faculty of 'common sense' which picks them out are front and centre in Reid's response to scepticism. I have argued, however, that his attempt to expose a framework of universally accepted first principles, to codify a set of universal beliefs, is fundamentally based on the sanction of universal agreement in 'what we do'—it is that which ultimately affords the legitimation of his claim for certainty in non-demonstrative reasoning. In other words, his view of first principles and 'common sense' depends radically on his view of the sanction of 'the natural', and the category of certainty in non-demonstrative reasoning is an instantiation of that appeal to 'the natural'. To anticipate the following chapters, for Newman the category of the certainty possible to non-demonstrative reasoning and the 'illative sense' lie front and centre. I shall argue that they make a direct appeal to the sanction of 'the natural', and allow an indirect role for first principles. Comparison of their views will, therefore, illustrate two different, perhaps contrasting, forms a naturalist response to scepticism can assume. Moreover, I will argue that Newman's response at times makes explicit what remains implicit in Reid's account, and makes specific what remains merely suggestive in it.

This chapter and those following will address Newman's response to scepticism, examining his claims in the letter to Meynell noted above, analysing first of all Newman's view of first principles, since both Newman and Reid agree that belief in an external world is a universally accepted first principle. Though first principles as such are not at the heart of Newman's programme in the way they are in Reid's, such an analysis provides a fruitful starting-point for examination of Newman's response as a whole because his understanding of first principles directly points to the role and importance of probable reasoning, and to the fundamental reliance of his entire programme on the sanction of 'the natural'. Analysis of first principles thus provides an appropriate way to initiate comparison and contrast between their respective responses.

A. FIRST PRINCIPLES

To determine Newman's mature position on 'first principles' we need to examine at least five separate discussions in his *Grammar of Assent*, all but one of which explicitly use the term 'first princi-

ple'.[10] All the discussions reveal that the term 'first principle' has
a variety of kinds of referent, but two of the discussions are particularly interesting because they are explicit and detailed attempts
to address the question of the character of 'first principles' and
there is, at the very least, a striking contrast in emphasis between
them. I suggest that if the two discussions do not actually put
forward conflicting models of 'first principles', the contrast between
them highlights important aspects of his position. Until this contrast is explored it is impossible to make any critical appraisal (and
a fortiori, any comparative analysis) of the role 'first principles'
play in his response to scepticism.

Although Newman discusses 'first principles' in earlier works,
most importantly in *The Present Position of Catholics*,[11] concen-
trating on his presentation in the *Grammar* will give us the benefit
of his mature thought on the subject, and will avoid obscuring the
issue with possible discrepancies between the *Grammar* and earlier
works. The aim of this section will be to reveal a significant difference between Newman and Reid on the character of 'first principles', but at the same time to reveal an important similarity between
them in the character of their anti-sceptical response concerning
non-mental objects existing external to us. The first principle concerning an external world, moreover, serves a twofold purpose: it
is an especially apt example not only for highlighting Newman's
view of the character of first principles in general, but also indirectly for illuminating his position on perception.

Before considering in detail the two contrasting discussions of
first principles, however, I want to put, briefly and in general terms,
all the discussions in context. The first major discussion is found
early on in the *Grammar*, in the section on 'Presumptions' (or
'assents to first principles'), where a definition of first principles as
starting-points of reasoning is followed by lengthy analyses of a
number of examples (60–72). First principles are then described, in
a chapter on the 'indefectibility of certitude', as 'initial truths' (237),
'primary principles, the general, fundamental, cardinal truths'
(239), and 'primary truths' (240). Later Newman considers 'first
principles' (269) as initial assumptions, in relation to which the
limits of formal inferences or syllogism are most apparent. Still

[10] London, 1901. Page references in parentheses in what follows will refer to the
Grammar unless otherwise noted.
[11] London, 1908; (hereafter *P.P.C.*).

later the question of first principles is reintroduced in a treatment of the action of informal reasoning in relation to 'principles ... taken for granted' (360-1), 'first elements of thought' (361), and 'elementary premises' (363). This same discussion of 'first principles' (371) is resumed and elaborated when Newman directs his attention to 'the implicit assumption of definite propositions in the first start of a course of reasoning' (375), and equates first principles with 'assumptions' and 'principles' (375-81). In the midst of these explicit discussions of first principles is an implicit reference—a long illustrative list of beliefs characterized only as 'unconditional assents' (177-8), including both beliefs which Newman elsewhere explicitly calls 'first principles' and beliefs which are comparable to other examples he gives of 'first principles'.

Even a cursory reading of these discussions reveals that Newman had in mind a variety of kinds of referent for the term 'first principle'. First principles can be divided on the basis of degree of shared acceptance (60, 177-8, 269-70, to be discussed later). A second contrast is immediately apparent. He describes 'first principles' as 'certain' or 'certainties' (237, 239), 'clear and immutable' starting-points (238), and 'immutable' truths (239). This is perhaps not surprising in the context of a discussion of certitudes. The later discussion of 'first principles' in relation to informal reasoning at the beginning of inquiries or disputes (360-81) emphasizes, on the other hand, the 'intensely personal' variety of 'first principles' (373). And it is not merely variety, but 'elementary contrarieties' (371) which are being pointed out—the result of 'essential and irremediable variance' of personal characteristics (362), and the cause of the lack of a 'common measure' between 'first principles' (362, 367). The emphasis on contrariety contrasts with the emphasis on 'clear and immutable' truths, and the emphasis on 'personal' variety is striking, given Reid's emphasis on consensus.

It is clear, then, that Newman does not understand 'first principles' exclusively as certain, clear, and immutable truths, universally accepted. His response to scepticism, then, whatever else it is, cannot be the kind of response which attempts to silence the sceptic by appeal to 'first principles' as a codified set of putatively unchallengeable propositions.

I want now to turn to the two major attempts in the *Grammar* to address the question of the status of 'first principles' which I suggested at the outset might be significant because they offer, at the very least, a contrast which can illuminate Newman's position. The first of the two attempts, that in the section on 'Presumptions', contains Newman's most explicit definition—'first principles' are 'the propositions with which we start in reasoning on any given subject-matter' (60). He continues immediately:

> They are in consequence very numerous, and vary in great measure with the persons who reason, according to their judgment and power of assent, being received by some minds, not by others, and only a few of them received universally.

They are, moreover, 'notions ... because they express what is abstract, not what is individual and from direct experience'. Two points can be made at the outset concerning this characterization. First, Newman is explicitly considering first principles as propositions, and he maintains this usage; where he does not specifically refer to them as propositional, he does not characterize them in any other way (as tendencies, for example, as Reid did). Secondly, the characterization is putatively descriptive, but the examples which follow are not merely the recording of a few of Newman's own first principles, more or less widely shared. Rather, he discriminates among putative first principles, and attempts to defend the claim of some to the title of first principle. Descriptively, if someone holds a proposition as (in the manner of) a first principle, it is for that person a first principle. But the exercise in which Newman is engaged is not one of simply reporting empirical generalizations (although it depends importantly on such reporting); it is, rather, one of giving examples of some propositions which, whether they are so held or not, ought to be judged to be first principles.[12]

He gives the following examples: first, 'that there are things existing external to ourselves' (which is a first principle 'of universal reception'—61); second, that '"there is a right and a wrong", "a true and a false", "a just and an unjust", a "beautiful and a deformed"' (64); third, 'that nothing happens without a cause' (66); fourth, that there is 'an ordinary succession of antecedents and consequents, or what is called the Order of Nature' (i.e. uniformity of nature, or induction—68). These examples immediately bring to mind Reid's enunciation of unproblematically generally accepted truths:

[12] Cf. *T.P.*, p. 68 ('Assent and Intuition', 1860?).

Who can doubt whether men have universally believed the existence of a material world? Who can doubt whether men have universally believed that every change that happens in nature must have a cause? Who can doubt whether men have universally believed, that there is a right and a wrong in human conduct?[13]

These examples are most plausibly considered framework principles, or conditions for reasoning in general, in any subject-matter. But Newman's admission of the large number of first principles and their extreme person-variance, in conjunction with his emphasis noted earlier on the differences between first principles (the result of the 'essential and irremediable variance' of personal characteristics—362, 367, 371), imply that the definition is meant to cover more than just the kind of framework first principle used in illustration. And that implication is confirmed by his explicit sensitivity to different kinds of first principles. He distinguishes, for example, between 'those assumptions ... which resolve themselves into the conditions of human nature' and those 'directly arising out of these primary conditions, but ... traceable to the sentiments of the age, country, religion, social habits and ideas of the particular inquirers or disputants' (270); these latter, however, are not noticed as being thus circumscribed because they are 'admitted equally on all hands'. He summarizes this discussion in terms of those 'pre-existent beliefs ... which are hidden deep in our nature, or, it may be, in our personal peculiarities' (277). This twofold distinction between kinds is a refinement of the threefold one in the *Present Position of Catholics*, where in the lecture, 'Assumed Principles the Intellectual Ground of the Protestant View', he notes that some first principles 'are common to the great mass of mankind', 'others are peculiar to individuals', and still others are 'common to extended localities'.[14] At the end of the lecture he opposes mere 'opinions' to 'instincts' which 'range through time and space' (303), and contrasts principles which are 'innate and necessary' with those which are 'local, national or temporary'.[15] Through the entire lecture he gives examples which fit·all three kinds, and notes that 'in many cases it is very difficult to draw the line, and to decide what principles are, and what are not, independent of individuals, times, places'.[16]

[13] *Works*, 440: VI,4; see 233: I,2.   [14] Page 287.
[15] Ibid., pp. 303, 314.   [16] Ibid., p. 293.

Although Newman is not at all careful to call attention to differences in the kinds of examples he uses, or to keep discussion of one kind separate from another kind, it is clear that he does distinguish between three importantly different kinds of first principles. Some propositions serve as purely idiosyncratic or individual initial premisses in particular chains of reasoning. His descriptions of first principles as 'conditions of our mental life' and as things without which we could not 'think at all' are actually references to such personal principles, because he qualifies his summary of them by saying that they 'constitute the difference between man and man'.[17] Other propositions are used as initial premisses in inquiries or ways of reasoning common to larger groups; these are less easy, because of their commonality, to detect as ungrounded. Finally, some propositions 'resolve themselves into the conditions of human nature' and 'range through time and space', being 'innate and necessary'. Although he does not address the question how the distinction between those first principles which are 'certain' and 'immutable' and those which are not relates to the degree of shared acceptance and integralness to human nature, he does seem to connect universal or general acceptance with necessity, innateness, or integralness to human nature.

First principles are thus propositional starting-points at a variety of levels. The character of such starting-points is elucidated when Newman takes up another discussion of first principles in the *Grammar* with the aim of showing that they play a decisive and often insufficiently appreciated role in reasoning. Noting that premisses of inferences are assumed, rather than proven, Newman uses an infinite regress argument to defend the existence of first principles. He claims that in any attempt to justify the premiss of an inference we are 'thrown back' upon some previous reasoning, and then 'still farther back, we are thrown upon others again ... Where is this process to stop?' (269). 'It would', he continues,

be something to arrive at length at premisses which are undeniable, however long we might be in arriving at them; but in this case the long retrospection lodges us at length at what are called first principles, the recondite sources of all knowledge, as to which logic provides no common measure of minds,—which are accepted by some, rejected by others ... and which are called self-evident by their respective advocates because they are evident in no other way. (269-70)

[17] *Works*, pp. 284, 279, 284.

Newman is clear, however, that not only are they 'called' self-evident—there *are* self-evident propositions ('of course I hold there are'). However, 'logic' can neither 'determine' nor 'prove' them (270).

The *Present Position of Catholics*, though much earlier and not to be taken as definitive on the issue, supports and elaborates this model of 'self-evident' first principles, and shows the importance of infinite regress arguments to it. Newman writes:

> [T]here must be such things as First Principles—that is, opinions which are held without proof as if self-evident,—and, moreover, that every one must have some or other, who thinks at all, is evident from the nature of the case. If you trace back your reasons for holding an opinion, you must stop somewhere; the process cannot go on for ever; you must at last come to something you cannot prove. (279)

He is thus 'but illustrating what is meant by a First Principle, and how it is that all reasoning ultimately rests upon such' (280). First principles are 'means of proof, and not themselves proved' (283); 'they are a man's elementary points of thinking, and the ideas which he has prior to other ideas' (284). Moreover, First Principles are to be distinguished from 'prejudices' because the latter are formed upon 'grounds' which the agent refuses to examine; First Principles, on the contrary, 'do not depend on previous grounds, ... are not drawn from facts ... have from the first no grounds at all, but are simple persuasions or sentiments, which came to the holder he cannot tell how, and which apparently he cannot help holding' (278).

To review quickly up to this point: (1) Newman sees first principles exclusively in terms of propositions or beliefs (rather than propensities or dispositions as Reid sometimes does); (2) first principles include for him both propositions which constitute part of a framework for reasoning at all and propositions which serve as initial premisses of particular arguments or inquiries; (3) first principles are implicitly distinguished into those which are properly first principles (because ungroundable) and those which are merely taken in the manner of first principles (ungrounded); (4) his rationale or defence of first principles is the same as Reid's—an infinite regress must be stopped, and it is stopped only at self-evident propositions. Thus far, even if Newman parts company with Reid in some ways, the similarity on the fourth point seems to outweigh the differences, and the account seems unproblematical on Newman's own terms. But the explication in the *Grammar* of what were for Reid paradigmatic examples of self-evident first principles (external world, causality, right and wrong) presents, at first sight at least, a striking contrast to the discussion of self-evident principles to which we are forced back on pain of infinite regress. Such first principles as that there is a right and a wrong are, he writes, 'abstractions to which we give a notional assent in consequence of particular experiences of qualities in the concrete, to which we give a real assent' (64)—they are 'really conclusions or abstractions from particular experiences ... in themselves they are abstractions from facts, not elementary truths prior to reasoning' (65). They are, in fact, *inferences*: we 'abstract and generalize; and thus the abstract proposition "There is a right and a wrong", as representing an act of *inference*, is received by the mind with a notional, not a real assent' (65, ital. mine). The first principle that 'nothing happens without a cause, is derived, in the first instance, from what we know about ourselves; and we argue analogously from what is within us [experiences of "willing and doing"] to what is external to us' (66).[18]

Newman's position is clearest in his discussion of the character of the first principle of belief in an external world, as that occurs in the *Grammar*. The proposition 'that there are things existing external to ourselves' is considered by Newman to be a first principle of universal reception and equivalent to the proposition 'that there is an external world, and that all the phenomena of sense proceed from it' (62). It is equivalent as well to the proposition that there is a 'vast external world' or a 'multiform and vast world, material and mental' (63). In explaining the character of this first principle, however, Newman makes very clear he is being literal-minded and speaking strictly. He is referring to a proposition quite literally about *things*—not about one thing. The phrase 'external world' used in a response to scepticism is ambiguous. For Newman, the first principle refers to a *plurality* of non-mental objects beyond our personal, individual experience; it does not refer, as it might have, to what has quite a different status for Newman, namely, to the proposition that there is 'something' (at least one thing) external to me.

The first principle about an external world is based on and

---

[18] Reid's similar view of the relation between 'cause' and 'will' is expressed in his letters to James Gregory (*Works*, pp. 75, 77).

abstracted 'by an inductive process' from 'particulars' or 'individual' experiences (62). These particulars themselves are 'instinctive' moves via particular experiences of 'phenomena of sense' to particular perceptions of a 'something distinct from and beyond those phenomena' (62). The primary data for the inductive generalization are a set of particular acts of instinct (62),[19] each of which in the face of sense phenomena is a perception of a particular beyond the sense phenomena—an image on the retina, for example, is the 'means' of a perception of something real beyond it (63). From those experiences 'we go on to draw the general conclusion that there is a vast external world' (63). Newman sums it up quite effectively by saying later that 'from a multitude of instinctive perceptions, acting in particular instances, of something beyond the senses, we generalize the notion of an external world' (104). Newman thus distinguishes sharply between the initial data which are 'instinctive perceptions' of a 'something' beyond the sense phenomena (presumably the sensations) and the 'first principle' concerning a plurality of objects beyond our experience which is the result of an inference or inductive generalization.

These examples of starting-points of reasoning are not merely 'abstract' propositions—they are abstracted propositions. Quite simply, they are not what others have claimed first principles to be—he claims they are not 'elementary truths prior to reasoning'. If the claims that first principles are abstractions, generalizations, and inferences are not to belie the claim to their self-evidence, however, it must either be the case that Newman is referring to two different kinds of first principles—some inductive generalizations, and some self-evident—or that he is attempting to show that both kinds of characterization can be meaningfully applied at the same time.

Something similar to the first suggestion has been offered by J. H. Walgrave, with respect to a similar problem in a different context. In an unpublished set of lectures, he attempts to reconcile what he calls the 'face-value' contradiction between the claim in the *Grammar* that first principles are abstractions from facts and the claim in the *Present Position of Catholics* that they are not drawn from facts.[20] His strategy is to suggest that because of dif-

---

[19] Cf. *L.D.*, XXIV, 309 (17 Aug. 1869).

[20] Unpublished lectures, 'J. H. Newman, His Personality, His Principles, His Fundamental Doctrines' (Katholieke Universiteit, Leuven, 1975-7), pp. 48-9. The whole of Pt. II, 'Newman's First Principles', is nevertheless a most useful discussion.

ferences in the purposes of the two works, Newman is actually referring to different kinds of first principles in each discussion. In particular he suggests that the opposition between the two discussions can be resolved by the recognition that in the latter Newman is referring to historically conditioned assumptions of a group, nation, or culture, while in the *Grammar* he is referring instead to assumptions which are universally or generally shared because they are integral to human nature. The point is, I take it, that because the 'facts' of human nature are 'ever-recurring'. they sustain the first principles in question (so it could be said that they were drawn from facts) while the 'facts' giving rise to more localized or contingent assumptions do not sustain them in the same way (so it could be said that they were not drawn from facts). Walgrave admits a certain 'subtlety' in his reconciliation, and I find it neither clear why, nor convincing that, less contingent facts should count as facts while more contingent or more historically conditioned ones should not.

It is in fact quite interesting that those propositions which are most plausibly said to be generally accepted are considered by Newman to be inferences, because if there were a connection one might at first glance expect it to go the other way round. That is, one might expect that those propositions which are most necessary (and hence most generally or universally received) would be precisely those that are not the result of an inference. The emphasis on inference and inductive generalization (in contrast to 'instinctive perceptions') on which Newman's early *Grammar* discussion of first principles so crucially depends, seems, at first glance, to run counter to his usual sensitivity to and resistance against intellectual élitism. It is just such élitism which other accounts explicitly seek to avoid precisely by refusing to see first principles as inferences.

The suggestion that Newman is simply considering two kinds of first principles—some reasoned, and some self-evident—is problematical, however, in two respects. First, such a reading assumes that the word 'abstract' in the initial characterization is only coincidentally similar to the 'abstractions' he cites as examples. If it is only an accident that Newman uses those two particular words, and they are not related, then he need not be seen as giving examples which are in any way normative of first principles, and the definition need not claim that first principles are necessarily inductive abstractions. But if the two words are used intentionally by Newman to refer to the same characteristic of first principles (as seems likely given the apposition of the term 'abstract' with 'not what is individual and from direct experience'), then it seems the claim is that by definition first principles are inductive abstractions. And one needs then to ask whether the 'self-evident' propositions we are thrown back on to avoid an infinite regress can be seen as inductive generalizations.

A second problem for such a reading concerns the implications of Newman's own rationale for self-evident first principles, namely, the infinite regress argument. Whether or not he needed to fear such an infinite regress,[21] he did, and if such an argument is applicable in general it would seem that first principles *as such* must be propositions which come at the end of our attempts to provide reasons for our conclusions—i.e. self-evident in some meaningful sense. One needs then to ask in what meaningful sense the early examples of inductive generalizations could be seen as 'self-evident'.

In other words, if either (1) 'abstract' is meant to be equivalent to or imply abstractive generalization, as illustrated in the examples, or (2) the infinite regress argument is a general rationale for first principles, there is at least a prima-facie contradiction between the two accounts of first principles. The first (1) results in the view that first principles are by definition inductive generalizations, and so seems to conflict with examples of self-evident propositions we are forced to admit on pain of accepting an infinite regress. The second (2) results in the view that first principles are by definition self-evident—in some sense having no 'reasons'—and the early examples of inductive generalizations need either to be discarded or radically reinterpreted.

The question then is whether Newman sees first principles as (*a*) by definition inferential, (*b*) by definition self-evident, (*c*) able to be either, or (*d*) having at the same time characteristics which are appropriately called attention to by both the terms 'inferential' and 'self-evident'. I have argued above that a commitment on Newman's part to (1) implies (*a*) that first principles are by definition inferential, and that a commitment to (2) implies (*b*) that first principles are by definition self-evident. Only if he was committed neither to (1) nor (2) could he hold position (*c*) that some first

---

[21] Cf. Ernest Sosa's discussion of a variety of issues relevant to the notion of an infinite regress, 'The Raft and the Pryamid', in *Midwestern Studies in Philosophy* V, eds. P. French *et al.* (Minneapolis, 1980), pp. 9–13.

principles could be inferential while others were self-evident. Even if that could be shown, however, there would remain the problem of explaining how those particular first principles called inductive inferences by Newman could plausibly be seen as inferential since they are usually considered paradigmatically self-evident. If either (1) or (2) holds, or both, reconciliation of the two accounts would have to take the form of showing how a single proposition could at the same time be considered *both* self-evident and inferential in any meaningful sense of either term. These questions are not settled by showing that Newman distinguishes between different kinds of first principles in terms of acceptance or necessity or certainty. Rather we need to examine both the contrast between 'self-evident' and 'inductive inference', and the contrast between the 'inductive inference' which constitutes at least some first principles, and the 'instinctive perceptions' on which they are, according to Newman, based. Fortunately, the attempt at reconciliation of the first contrast can shed light on the second.

B. SELF-EVIDENCE

If the term 'self-evident' meant for Newman that the proposition is not the result of any reasoning at all, there would result a blatant and unresolvable conflict between the later and earlier discussions of first principles in the *Grammar*,[22] and it seems unlikely that he would have allowed such a contradiction to go unnoticed or unresolved in a work he complains he wrote and rewrote ten to fifteen times.[23] But 'self-evident' could mean several other things as well, and it is possible that his references to self-evidence were intended to express his recognition of, and call our attention to, characteristics which first principles as such have, even while they are appropriately called abstractions or inferences.

Self-evidence might mean, for Newman, simply that the proposition was not provable by formal inference or logic. He does after all characterize self-evident propositions negatively most of the time—they cannot be 'proved' and they cannot be proved by 'logic'. A proposition could then be both the result of inference

---

[22] Note his claim that while perception is 'direct', reasoning is 'indirect': 'by means of reasoning we gain [knowledge] indirectly, that is, by virtue of a previous knowledge' (p. 260).

[23] *L.D.*, XXIV, 389 (14 Dec. 1869).

and yet not be provable by logic. Newman might simply mean in that case that such propositions were not provable by formal inference, but were justifiable by a more nuanced kind of reasoning. Such an attempt to show the illegitimacy of a purportedly exhaustive dichotomy between logically-reasoned and non-reasoned fits in well with the general impulse at the heart of his programme. On such a reading 'self-evident' would mean 'self-evident' with respect to logic or formal inference. But that seems to stretch unduly our ordinary sense of the word 'self-evident' (a sense of the word shared, at least at times, by Newman).[24]

Related to this would be a reading of self-evidence as meaning that there were no conscious mediating factors. A proposition could be said to be self-evident with respect to conscious argumentation or mediation. Such psychological immediacy, however, does not rule out epistemological dependence on other propositions.

Other views of self-evidence go beyond psychological immediacy to the claim of epistemological independence. For example, self-evidence might mean that the proposition in question is not deducible or otherwise derivable from propositions which are more evident than itself. A proposition would therefore be self-evident, or as Newman says, 'evident in no other way', because it is not derived from propositions which are more established, more certain, less open to doubt than itself. A first principle would then not only not be derived deductively from any proposition—it would not be derived even inductively from propositions more certain than itself. In this way there could be a 'basis' for the conclusion or generalization which did not constitute 'argument' (either formal or informal) for the conclusion because the 'basis' itself was not more firmly established than the conclusion—they would be in that sense on a par. The first principle could be derived from other propositions, but the latter would not constitute 'evidence' or 'reasons' for the conclusion, which could then be said to be 'self-evident'.[25]

An alternative reading of self-evidence which goes beyond the

---

[24] *Philosophical Notebook* II (Louvain, 1970), p. 73.

[25] Cf. *On Certainty* (§1), where Wittgenstein refers to Newman in precisely this connection (though it is unclear whether he realized that Newman was making his point) when he writes: 'When one says that such and such a proposition can't be proved, of course that does not mean that it can't be derived from other propositions; any proposition can be derived from other ones. But they may be no more certain than it is itself. (On this a curious [komische] remark by H. Newman.)'

claim of psychological immediacy involves the claim that, although the 'basis' is more certain than the conclusion from it, the 'basis' consists of experiences which are not the sort of thing that can count as 'reasons' or 'grounds' to justify a conclusion. That is, we can go back in our regress from tertiary principles to secondary principles, and from those to primary principles—but beyond that we have no *principles*, only discrete experiences.[26]

Any of the last three readings of self-evidence would allow both the characterization of 'self-evident' and of 'abstractive generalization' to be meaningfully applied to the same proposition. The discussion of self-evidence and the need to halt an infinite regress can then be seen as a way of emphasizing that first principles have no 'reasons' or 'grounds' in the sense of *premisses* which *justify* their acceptance. Nothing would count as 'justification' for them because either (1) there are no recognizable premisses, (2) there are no premisses more certain than the conclusion, or (3) there is nothing appropriately called a 'premiss' at all. The discussion of first principles as abstractions, inferences, or generalizations would be a way of emphasizing how some conclusions have a 'basis' which must be taken into account (a basis which is for Newman common to animals and humans) even though it cannot plausibly be construed as providing 'justification' or 'reasons'. The use of the word 'inference', both in its ordinary sense and in the light of his claim that all inference has the same form as logical inference (292), seems to limit his position to (1), self-evident with respect to conscious psychological mediation. If (2) or (3) in his intention, however, the use of the term 'inference' is misleading in the absence of further elucidation of the word.[27]

It is appropriate at this point to consider a possible implication of his use of the word 'inference' to characterize first principles, for he might well have used it precisely in order to confine the self-evidence to psychological immediacy. If so, one might hazard

[26] He writes later in the *Grammar* that 'What is called reasoning is often only a peculiar and personal mode of abstraction, and so far, like memory, may be said to exist without antecedents' (p. 337). To exist without antecedents, he admits, is not to exist without 'previous conditions' on which the abstraction depends.

[27] It is possible that the retention of the word 'inference' is a foreshadow of the main point in the *Grammar*—namely, the unrecognized potential and subtlety of 'inference'. Such a foreshadow is, however, somewhat misleading when it occurs before that point is made much later in the *Grammar*. Cf. *T.P.*, p. 53 ('Lecture on Logic', Jan. or Feb. 1859).

a few guesses as to why he might have thought it necessary to do so.

One option is simply that he thought anything less than an inferential conclusion does not deserve to be called a 'principle' of any sort, because it does not provide a promising substantive basis for further development. Supporting this interpretation is the interesting fact that Newman is not concerned, as others have been, with first principles as primitive propositions of logic—e.g. the principle of non-contradiction.[28] His marginal comments on Reid's sections on first principles show that he considers certain of them to be 'truisms' or 'tautologies'.[29] First principles, it is implied, should be substantive foundations for further reasoning; in this he would seem to agree with Locke that such principles of logic are not the foundations of knowledge.[30]

Newman's emphasis on first principles as inferential conclusions, however, might instead be thought to result from his anxiety to have assent supported by prior inference. Inference, he insists, is a necessary, though not sufficient, condition of assent:

though acts of assent require previous acts of inference, they require them, not as adequate causes, but as *sine qua non* conditions.[31]

If then we are rightly to assent to first principles there must be a supporting inference, but if first principles are propositions we assent to prior to reasoning, as a basis for reasoning, then assent cannot be supported in such cases by 'previous acts of inference'. Obviously this problem is eliminated if we see first principles as reached by inductive inference. So the question is whether Newman's commitment to the legitimation of assent by reasoning, in particular by 'previous acts of inference', commits him as well to the position of having putatively 'first' principles depend on premisses from which they derive their evidence.

It is of course possible that reasoning can support acceptance of a proposition even when the proposition is not itself the result of reasoning; a conclusion can be inferentially justified even when it is itself neither reached nor capable of being reached by inference. As noted earlier (Chapter 5), such 'retrospective' justification can

---

[28] But cf. *T.P.*, p. 68 ('Assent and Intuition', 1860?).

[29] *Works* (1858), pp. 644, 683; cf. p. 620.

[30] Locke, *Essay Concerning Human Understanding*, IV, vii, 10–11.

[31] *Grammar*, p. 41.

occur in two ways. First, the acceptance of a conclusion which is not actually, or cannot be, reached by reasoning can nevertheless be justified retrospectively by inference *directly* supporting the conclusion—i.e. counting as evidence for the substantive content of the proposition. But that Newman recognizes the asymmetry of justification—that retrospective justification might be possible even when prospective justification is not—is clear from his own distinction in the University sermon, 'Faith and Reason Contrasted as Habits of Mind', between the 'creative' and the 'critical' role of reason with respect to faith.[32] Since he allows that retrospective inference can equally justify assents, he need not have assumed that the inference he required to justify the assent had to be temporally prior to the assent (as his reference in the *Grammar* to 'previous' implies). But if such retrospective justification is of the sort which evidentially supports the substantive content of the conclusion, the justification would be logically prior even if not temporally prior. So retrospective justification of this sort would not preclude the possibility that the putatively 'first' principle depended on logically prior premises and so was not logically a first principle at all (though it was psychologically a first principle). That is, a requirement of the temporal priority of reasoning is not as such the source of any problem Newman might have with first principles, for direct retrospective justification provides logically prior premisses as much as direct prospective justification does.

There is, however, another way in which justification of assents can be considered. The acceptance of a proposition not capable of being reached by reasoning can be justified by reference to reasons which do not bear directly on the substantive content of the proposition—e.g. justification for accepting a conclusion of a particular type or a conclusion with particular characteristics. Consider, for example, the justification of a proposition because of a particular kind of desirability or necessity, such as one might find advocated by William James, or by Kantian (or other) transcendental arguments. Presumably such pragmatic justification in terms of desirability or necessity would fall short of the theoretical justification Newman sought, but it is possible that other indirect justification might be relevantly theoretical. For example, one might consider the question of justification in terms of a combination of

[32] *Fifteen Sermons Preached Before the University of Oxford* (London, 1892), pp. 182–4; (hereafter *U.S.*).

necessity and some more standardly theoretical factor such as is found in a variety of 'no reasonable doubt' strategies—i.e. a proposition which we necessarily hold, *and* whose only challengers are not more certain than itself, can be considered justified (or at least not unjustified).

Newman could then in principle have satisfied his requirement (that inference legitimate assent to first principles) by means of a supporting inference which was neither temporally prior nor *directly* evidential. Since he was aware of the first possibility (though it did not qualify his formulation of the requirement in the *Grammar*), the question is whether he required direct justification (either prospective or retrospective) to legitimate assents to first principles and so was led to a view of first principles as epistemologically dependent on premisses (though psychologically primary) or whether he recognized the possibility of indirect justification for them and so could allow more than psychological immediacy. A look at his position on the truth and corrigibility of first principles can be helpful in suggesting his position on the indirect justification of them.

In the *Present Position of Catholics* he says explicitly that 'it is plain that First Principles may be false or true ... Certainly they are not necessarily true' (279). He even provides criteria or marks for the determination of their truth or falsity when he writes that those 'common to the great mass of mankind' are 'therefore true, as having been imprinted on the human mind by its Maker' (287). We can judge that the first principles of morals, for example, are true because they are 'not peculiar or proper to the individual, but the rule of the world, because they come from the Author of our being, and from no private factory of man' (292). True first principles come 'from heaven, or from the nature of things, or from the nature of man' (293). Newman seems, then, to be connecting the truth of first principles with their commonness or universality.

He claims, nevertheless, that being held by the multitude does not itself guarantee the truth of the first principles in question. He recognizes both (*a*) that 'the consequence of a First Principle being held in common by many at once' is that 'it ceases to be an opinion; it is taken at once for truth; it is looked upon as plain common sense; the opposite opinions are thought impossible; they are absurdities and nonentities, and have not rights whatever' (288), and (*b*) that it is possible 'for our First Principles to be but the opinions of a multitude, not truths' (289). I suggest that these two claims can be reconciled by appeal to the same strategy as was used by the seventeenth-century figures and Reid—namely, that a principle held by the multitude is given the benefit of the doubt *unless* some cause can be shown why the multitude should have gone wrong. And Newman seems to recognize the possible causes of error in ways not unlike theirs. He comments in the *Grammar*, for example, on how 'the perception of its first principles which is natural to us is enfeebled, obstructed, perverted, by allurements of sense and the supremacy of self...' (311).[33] Newman thus distinguishes proper or genuine first principles (ungroundable) from those that are merely taken without grounds; he also distinguishes genuine first principles from true ones.

Finally, Newman claims in the *Present Position of Catholics* that first principles are corrigible: 'certainly there *are* ways of unlearning them when they are false' (279). This claim is also made, though much less explicitly, when he writes in the *Grammar*:

[I]f anyone starts from any other principles but ours, I have not the power to change his principles, or the conclusions which he draws from them, any more than I can make a crooked man straight. Whether his mind will ever grow straight, *whether I can do anything toward its becoming straight* ... is another matter. (413, ital. mine)

The *Grammar*, however, also contains the specification that 'first elements of thought' may be illustrated, established, and eliminated by the mind (361); more explicitly, reasoning has a role in 'discovering them ["first principles"], following them out, defending or resisting them' (371).[34]

---

[33] It is interesting to note that in the previous lecture in the *P.P.C.*, namely, 'Prejudice the Life of the Protestant View', the distinction between true and false 'prejudices' centres on the same issue—true prejudices are those found 'in all times and places, with exceptions too rare or inconsiderable to be worth noting'; whereas prejudices are false if they are marked by '*not* being common to all' and '*not* being found in the mind from the first' (p. 230). It is difficult to make sense of his claim that 'prejudice' is based on grounds (as opposed to first principles), and yet that false prejudice is marked by *not* coming thither no one knows how' and '*not* being found in the mind from the first' (p. 230). This seems to make true prejudices groundless, like first principles, and seems to be the same way he later uses to distinguish first principles from prejudices (pp. 278, 280). That is, Newman's attempt radically to distinguish prejudice from first principles in relation to having and not having grounds ends up sounding like a case of making first principles equal true prejudices.

[34] See his suggestion that 'it may be true that a continuous meditation may bring out to a particular mind a truth in the way of intuition, I mean as something

Thus, Newman allows indirect justification of first principles—though he gives no indication of methods for correcting or adjudicating in the way that Reid does. The allowance of indirect justification of first principles at least precludes the need to read the inference supporting first principles as direct justification, and so precludes the need to see inferential first principles as epistemologically dependent on prior premises. One can, therefore, read the inferential character of first principles as compatible with their self-evidence in any of the ways noted earlier—i.e. in ways which allow a 'basis' which is not strictly speaking a 'justification'.

How, then, does Newman's account of first principles compare with Reid's? First principles as such are clearly important to both. Indeed, Newman, as we have seen, went so far as to say that in 'first principles, the recondite sources of all knowledge ... and not in the syllogistic exhibitions, lies the whole problem of attaining to truth' (269), adding:

Syllogism, then, though of course it has its use, still does only the minutest and easiest part of the work, in the investigation of truth, for when there is any difficulty, that difficulty commonly lies in determining first principles, not in the arrangement of proofs. (270)

Since probably no other thinker since Aristotle and Buffier[35] gave so much detailed attention to the necessity and character of the starting-points of reasoning as did Reid, his attention to that wherein 'lies the whole problem of attaining to truth' would clearly be cause for Newman's commendation of Reid despite other differences. Before considering those differences further, however, I want to examine briefly another ground for Newman's commendation of Reid, namely, their substantive agreement on an anti-sceptical theory of perception.

In notes for a lecture on logic written in 1859 Newman concludes that 'No one whatever doubts that what the mind contemplates, at least in corporeal objects, is not the object itself, but a representation of it, which we call an idea.'[36] This would seem to be a perfect object for Reid's attack on the notion of an 'idea' as the direct

perceived without reason or middle term—as eyes long accustomed to gaze upon darkness see objects for which others would require more light' (*Philosophical Notebook* II, p. 29).

[35] Cf. Marcil-Lacoste for a detailed study of Buffier's thought on first principles, *Claude Buffier and Thomas Reid*, pp. 11–71.

[36] The passage is an interlinear addition, *T.P.*, p. 56.

object of perception. Moreover, Newman's use of the Lockean language of 'impression' seems to support further a representationalist theory of perception, bearing the sceptical implications against which Reid so assiduously warned. I would argue, however, (1) that Newman and Reid were in substantive agreement on the status of perception of objects existing external to ourselves, and (2) that despite some ambiguities in both their positions, they held a direct, though critical, perceptual realism.

That their theories of perception, whatever their status, were similar is suggested by Charles Meynell's explicit comparisons of Newman's theory with Reid's. Reviewing the final draft of the *Grammar* for Newman, Meynell wrote that 'Reid wavers between two views of sensible perception, one of direct immediate perception, and another which is precisely your own'.[37] The view which he attributes to Newman he calls 'hypothetical realistic', and he distinguishes as follows: whereas the hypothetical realist 'postulates' as a 'hypothesis' that there is an external object, and admits that he 'cannot *prove* the existence of such object [*sic*], ... the natural realist believes that we can immediately perceive the object, and therefore it requires no proof'.[38] The real danger in Newman's account, according to Meynell, was the problem he seemed to share with Reid—the problem inherent in any theory 'of a natural suggestion which refers, by instinct, our sensations to an external object'.[39]

Reid's introduction of the notion of 'suggestion' in the *Inquiry* (II,§7) has seemed to some to counteract its express intention and to imply the very representationalism or indirect perception which it was meant by Reid to attack,[40] and Meynell's reference suggests that Newman's 'instinctive perception' failed for similar reasons to guarantee sufficient immediacy. In what follows I will merely

[37] *L.D.*, XXIV, 306 (16 Aug. 1869); the entire correspondence between Newman and Meynell from 16 Aug. 1869 to 27 Nov. 1869 is relevant to this issue.

[38] Ibid., p. 306. William Hamilton takes Reid's claim, for example, that he is led by his nature 'to conclude some quality to be in the rose, which is the cause of the sensation' (*Works*, 310: II,16) to be a disavowal of a theory of immediate perception; no doubt similar remarks led to Meynell's charge of vacillation.

[39] *L.D.*, XXIV, 306 (16 Aug. 1869).

[40] See Timothy Duggan's 'Introduction' to his edition of Reid's *Inquiry* (Chicago, 1970), especially pp. xxx–li for a discussion of the criticisms made by Peter Winch ('The Notion of "Suggestion" in Thomas Reid's Theory of Perception', *Philosophical Quarterly* 3 (1953)) and A. D. Woozley ('Introduction' to his edition of Reid's *Essays on the Intellectual Powers of Man* (London, 1941), pp. xix–xxiv).

indicate what I have argued elsewhere at greater length,[41] namely, that Newman's defence of his theory, explaining his distinction between mediate and immediate perception, supports a direct, though critical, realism, and can shed some light on Reid's view as well.

Responding to Meynell, Newman wrote that 'perception comes to me *through* my senses—therefore I cannot call it *immediate*'.[42] He continues: 'If it were not for my senses, nothing would excite me to perceive—but ... I perceive by instinct (as I call it) without *argumentative* media, *through* my senses, but not logically *by* my senses.'[43] The point of such passages is that what precludes the attribution of unqualified immediacy to perception is the instrumental role of the senses. Reid makes a similar kind of remark in his *Inquiry* when he writes that 'Although there is no reasoning in perception, yet there are certain means and instruments, which, by the appointment of nature, must intervene between the object and our perception of it' (VI,§21), and I take his point to be the same as Newman's: it is a way of distinguishing between ontological conditions (causal and instrumental mediation) and epistemological intermediation. Images on the retina are, for Newman, examples of the 'means of our perceiving something real beyond them',[44] but we are not directly aware of the 'means'. Reid, too, emphasizes this point when he says 'we are not conscious of this impression' on the retina; 'it is not an impression on the mind but on the body' (VI, §8). The notion of X 'suggesting' Y does not therefore necessarily imply an epistemological intermediary.[45]

Indications of a representationalist theory of perception in Newman can also be accounted for, I suggest, by his combining two related but quite different issues—namely, directness of perception and metaphysical agnosticism. An agnosticism about real essences

---

[41] See my 'Newman's Theory of Perception: Realism or Representationalism', forthcoming in *Philosophical Studies*.

[42] *L.D.*, XXIV, 314 (20 Aug. 1869).

[43] Ibid.

[44] *Grammar*, p. 63.

[45] It may be read as an adverbial theory of perception (according to which we are 'appeared to redly'), given Reid's view that the appearance or 'idea' is a 'kind of thought' (137: VI,§4) and that a thought is a manner of thinking (277: II,9), or, as Timothy Duggan suggests, as the converse of a 'perceptual taking' ('Introduction' to *Inquiry* (1970), pp. xxxviii–xl). It is also interesting in this respect that, commenting in the margins of his edition of Reid's *Works*, Newman at least five times corrects the word 'suggests' to 'logically implies'—one could read this as an attempt to avoid any notion of mediation which might be read into 'suggests'.

or ultimate natures is found in both Reid and Newman,[46] but this does not imply a claim that we indirectly perceive objects. The gap for Newman is between the external object and its real or ultimate nature, not between a sensation or idea and an external object. The same can be said for Reid. Thus, Newman's self-conscious and determined attempt to avoid a perceptual theory which would give support to scepticism would no doubt also be able to account for his commendation of Reid, despite terminological differences about an 'inferential' first principle concerning an external world.

But there are differences between them—at least prima-facie ones—concerning the status of first principles. For Reid the self-evidence of first principles is clearly seen in terms of *intuitive* apprehension. Newman had, before the *Grammar*, written in just that way as well:

If we are to advance to conclusions of any kind and extend the range of our knowledge, we are obliged to recognize certain assents as the primary premisses of our investigations and their results, and as self evident neither requiring nor admitting of proof ... This is the obvious argument for the existence of Intuition.[47]

But later in the *Grammar* the self-evidence of first principles, at least of the ones seen by Reid as paradigmatic, is understood in terms of inductive generalization or inference. The possibility that this contrast may be one of style and emphasis rather than of substance is, however, suggested by two considerations: (1) Reid's admission that where reasoning has only a single step it may be difficult to distinguish from intuitive judgement,[48] and (2) Newman's admission that 'What is called reasoning is often only a peculiar and personal mode of abstraction, and so far, like memory, may be said to exist without antecedents.'[49] The relation

---

[46] For Newman such agnosticism is apparent in his claims that representations are inadequate (*Grammar*, p. 103; *Apologia Pro Vita Sua*, ed. Martin J. Svaglic (Oxford, 1967), pp. 15-16, 18, 23, 29; *L.D.*, XXI, 473-4 (23 May 1865). Reid's agnosticism is seen, for example, in his claim that our conceptions of things are 'inadequate and lame' for they 'have a real essence, or constitution of nature, from which all their qualities flow; but this essence our faculties do not comprehend' (364: IV,1), and in his innumerable references to our inability to give ultimate explanations or reasons, except 'the will of our Maker'; cf. M. F. Sciacca's discussion of the empiricist basis of Reid's agnosticism and its difference from Locke's (*La Filosofia di Tommaso Reid*, esp. §§39, 40).

[47] *T.P.*, p. 67 ('Assent and Intuition', 1860?).

[48] *Works*, 475: VII,1.

[49] *Grammar*, p. 337.

between Newman and Reid on this question will be explored further in the following chapter.

They differ about first principles in another way as well, and that has implications for the way the rest of their response to scepticism is carried out. For Reid agreement in first principles is emphasized: such agreement points indirectly to the 'sanction of the natural', and it is directly intended by Reid to reveal to the sceptic the existence and importance of intuitive judgement and 'common sense'. Newman, on the other hand, emphasizes disagreement about first principles. Presaging his emphasis in the *Grammar* on variety and contrariety among first principles, he had written earlier:

there is very little agreement in the world or among philosophers what these truths are, whether they are many or few, and what their characteristics ... while I maintain that there are such, I also maintain that there is nothing like a consensus among men what they are.[50]

I shall argue in the next chapter that he highlights disagreement about first principles in order (1) to reveal the need for a more nuanced understanding of reasoning, and (2) to reveal the understanding we implicitly rely on concerning the status and implications of descriptions of 'what we do'.

[50] *T.P.*, p. 67 ('Assent and Intuition', 1860?).

8

Newman: Proof, Probable
Reasoning, and Practice

INSTEAD of turning, as does Reid, to a codified set of putatively universally-held first principles to answer the sceptic, Newman turns to the 'illative sense'—'a grand word for a common thing', he admits, for it just is the ratiocinative faculty.[1] In other words, Newman does not turn, as does Reid, to another use of reason in contrast to 'reasoning'. In this chapter I will consider the 'illative sense', by comparison and contrast with 'common sense' as Reid understands it, as well as Newman's view of the achievement of the illative sense—the category of 'proof' and non-demonstrative certainty.[2] I want to argue that Newman's very explicit challenge to Locke's dichotomy between knowledge and probability puts him in a direct line with a tradition preceding him in which a certainty equal to that of demonstration can result from a converging, probabilistic process of reasoning in which the conclusion is secured 'beyond reasonable doubt'. In particular I want to argue that Newman's view of the certainty possible to non-demonstrative reason-

[1] L.D., XXIV, 375 (17 November 1869).
[2] A word of explanation is needed for my use of the word 'certainty' here. Newman makes a distinction between 'certitude' as a property of minds and 'certainty' as a property of propositions (*Grammar*, pp. 344, 196; *Apologia*, p. 31), but he does not maintain it in his writings—in the papers in preparation for the *Grammar* (1865) he uses 'certainty' to refer to assurance or conviction at least nine times in the space of six pages (*T.P.*, pp. 125–31), and earlier had defined 'certainty' as 'an act or habit of intellect' (*T.P.*, p. 31 (1853)). Even in the *Grammar* itself several passages are ambiguous (e.g. pp. 242, 326, 412). More importantly, while making the distinction in the *Grammar* he explains: 'Those propositions I call certain, which are such that I am certain of them' (p. 344); similarly he writes that 'the certainty of a proposition does properly consist in the certitude of the mind which contemplates it' (p. 293). I suggest, then, that for Newman the word 'certainty' can be used as equivalent to justified certitude. This accords with the standard account in the *Encyclopaedia of Philosophy*: 'Usage follows the rule ... that for certainty of a proposition to obtain, someone must have made sure or become justifiably certain of the proposition. Thus, certainty of propositions requires psychological certainty plus its justification.'

ing bears striking similarities to Reid's, both in its imagery and its strategy. Whether or not Newman derived it from Reid, the ity in their views goes far to explain Newman's marked appreciation of Reid. Moreover, this shared ingredient in their responses to scepticism provides a way in which the prima-facie critical difference between 'common sense' and the 'illative sense' can be mitigated. Finally, and this will be the concern of the following chapter, the category of proof exemplifies an understanding of the sanction of 'the natural' which is similar in important respects to that which grounds Reid's response to scepticism.

A. THE 'ILLATIVE SENSE' AND 'COMMON SENSE'

The limits of formal inference or logic are most clearly and forcibly revealed, for Newman, in the differences of opinion about first principles 'as to which logic provides no common measure of minds,—which are accepted by some, and rejected by others'.[3] How can 'reasoning by rule', which was supposed to 'establish a standard of truth, and to supersede the *ipse dixit* of authority' manage to fulfil this purpose 'if it only leads us back to first principles, about which there is interminable controversy' (270). We can neither prove that there are any self-evident first principles, or determine by logic which they are, so, he says provocatively, 'logic does not really prove':

for genuine proof in concrete matters we require an *organon* more delicate, versatile, and elastic than verbal argumentation. (271)

'Inference', he writes later, 'considered in the sense of verbal argumentation, determines neither our principles, nor our ultimate judgments ... it is neither the test of truth, nor the adequate basis of assent' (287). The initial search for a 'common measure' between minds (262, 264) leads to formal inference, but the limits of such inference reveal the need for a more subtle understanding of the potential of reasoning—which turns out to be an understanding of our most natural mode of reasoning. The limits of logic, highlighted by the problem of disagreement about first principles and compounded by the necessary abstraction of formal inference, point

---

[3] *Grammar*, p. 269. Unless otherwise noted further page references in parentheses will be to this work.

to the operation of the ratiocinative faculty in concrete matters—
namely, the 'illative sense'.

The illative sense is at the heart of Newman's response to scepticism in just the way that common sense is at the heart of Reid's—
how then do they compare? The most decisive similarity is that the
word 'sense' is used in each case in its popular, as opposed to
philosophical, meaning—namely, judgement. Despite Reid's proclaimed concern with common language, the word 'sense' stands
out as an instance in which he really does maintain a popular
usage.[4] That Newman too uses the word in that way has been
noted, but its importance has not been duly appreciated.[5]

Newman defines the illative sense as the 'power of judging and
concluding, when in its perfection' (352). The claim that 'judgment
in all concrete matter is an architectonic faculty and what may be
called the Illative Sense, or right judgment in ratiocination, is one
branch of it' (342) reinforces this definition of sense as judgement.
The most explicit association of illative sense with the common
notion of sense is found in his claim that

the sole and final judgment on the validity of an inference in concrete
matters is committed to the personal action of the ratiocinative faculty,
the perfection or virtue of which I have called the Illative Sense, a use of
the word 'sense' parallel to our use of it in 'good sense,' 'common sense,'
a 'sense of beauty,' &tc. (345)

The latter phrase implies that 'common sense' is a parallel, rather
than equivalent, notion—but Newman's attitude to the concept
'common sense' is ambivalent. He sometimes equates 'common
sense' with illative reasoning (282) and summarizes the action of
the illative sense in terms of 'good sense' and 'common sense' (296,
277, 300). On the other hand, he writes that whereas Locke ap-
pealed to 'common sense', for him 'that supra-logical judgment,
which is the warrant for our certitude about them, is not mere
common sense, but the true healthy action of our ratiocinative
powers' (317). (Other uses of 'common sense' are ambiguous (261)
or can support the equivalence of common sense and illative sense.[6])
The question of the relation between common sense and illative

---

[4] See *Works* 223: I,1, and 336: II,22 for Reid's position on the limits of the
normativity of ordinary usage; see also the remaining references in Chap. 5, n. 31,
above.

[5] Cf. Sillem, *Philosophical Notebook* I, p. 102n.

[6] *Grammar*, pp. 303, 378, 380; see also *T.P.*, p. 24 (16 Dec. 1853), p. 121 (1865).

sense cannot, however, be decided by reference to such passages in any case since what is at issue here is the relation of the illative sense to Reid's particular notion of common sense, and, as I noted earlier, although Reid uses the word 'sense' in its popular meaning, he uses 'common sense' as a technical term with stipulative characteristics which do not necessarily coincide with popular usage. The question then is how does common sense as Reid sees it substantively relate to the illative sense.

For Reid, common sense is a 'gift of heaven' and cannot be acquired. Newman spoke similarly of the illative sense—it comes to us 'by nature' and 'to all of us in a measure' (331). It is sometimes totally 'gift'—'natural uncultivated habit'—and sometimes 'improved by practice and habit' (334, 333). Thus, although it is present in all, it is not the same in all (334). Despite Newman's reference to it as 'sometimes an acquired habit' (331), his gloss on that—'*nascitur, non fit*'—makes clear that he does not think the capacity can be acquired by any effort of ours, though we can acquire the habit as 'second nature' by practice. Moreover, although 'reasoning by rule and in words' is also 'natural' to us (286), 'ratiocination, in what may be called a state of nature, as it is found in the uneducated,—nay, in all men, in its ordinary exercise' (260) is unscientific and informal. Natural reasoning is exemplified in both the uneducated and the genius (331), and, as for Reid, it distinguishes us from 'brutes' (61-2).[7]

Newman illustrates the illative sense by suggesting it is parallel to Aristotle's notion of *phronesis* with respect to moral duty. By such *phronesis*—an 'authoritative oracle' which comes first from nature but can be improved by experience—we apply general rules to particular cases (353-4). Newman notes that although in principle Aristotle allowed *phronesis* to be relevant to theoretical matters, he nevertheless in fact treated of it only as a guide 'in matters of conduct' (354)—Newman attempts then to fulfil the original potential of the notion of *phronesis*, translating it from the field of conduct to that of truth and falsity. Common sense, Reid had insisted, was likewise addressed to the theoretical determination of truth and falsity as well as matters of conduct.

The illative sense is, in addition, made more specific by Newman in that it is attached to particular subject-matters in the way, for example, that memory is (338-9)—we can be better at right reason-

[7] Cf. however *Grammar*, p. 282, for a contrasting view.

ing in some areas than others. In this way too it parallels *phronesis* (356–7).

Although common sense and the illative sense have some features in common, there is at bottom a prima-facie critical difference—namely, that while common sense has jurisdiction only over the determination of self-evident truths (though it can judge whether reasoned conclusions conflict with self-evident truths) and does not guide reasoning processes, the illative sense is equated by Newman with 'right judgment in ratiocination' (342) and with the 'ratiocinative' faculty (330). It is, as the word illation (taken from Locke) suggests, concerned with inference. Though in some respects it might be thought that the illative sense informs or guides all reasoning processes, including logical or formal inference (because even logical inference is directed ultimately though inadequately at the concrete (262) and because all inference, however informal, has the form of logical inference (292)), his use of the term is explicitly reserved for the most natural mode of reasoning— the 'personal action of the ratiocinative faculty', reasoning about particulars. At times he even restricts it to the 'perfection' of such natural reasoning (345, 353). Moreover, 'the Illative Sense, that is, the reasoning faculty, as exercised by gifted, or by educated, or otherwise well-prepared minds, has its function in the beginning, middle, and end of all verbal discussion and inquiry, and in every step of the process' (361). The crucial difference thus seems to be that for Reid the turn to common sense was a turn away from reasoning, while for Newman the illative sense just is the ratiocinative faculty applied both to first principles and to processes of reasoning. For Reid the central contrast is between intuitive and discursive judgement, with the former the domain of common sense—for Newman the central contrast is between formal and informal inference, both within the realm of (discursive) reasoning, with informal inference being the domain of the illative sense.

The illative sense, nevertheless, addresses the question of first principles. Controversies, Newman argues, are carried on from 'starting points, and with collateral aids, not formally proved, but more or less assumed, the process of assumption lying in the action of the Illative Sense' (371). In addition, we deal with 'those first elements of thought which in all reasoning are assumptions' in terms of detection, illustration, elimination, and resolution into simpler ideas (361). Reasoning is relevant to 'discovering them, following them out, defending or resisting them' (371). Thus, the illative sense is directed both to the assumption of first principles and to what appears to be equivalent to Reid's legitimation of indirect reasoning about first principles. Reid, like Newman, allows indirect reasoning to be relevant to first principles, and even specifies possibilities in detail—the difference is that such reasoning is not the role of common sense.

The question whether common sense substantively differs from the illative sense is most obviously raised, however, by the role of the illative sense with which Newman was most concerned in the *Grammar*—namely, its role 'in the final determination of concrete questions' (362)—for the crowning achievement of the illative sense is the determination of 'the limits of converging probabilities and the reasons sufficient for a *proof*' (360, ital. mine). So while the illative sense, like common sense, addresses itself to first principles, its scope is more extensive. Reid's discussion of non-demonstrative reasoning is not at the same time an illustration of the action of common sense—he radically separates common sense from reasoning of any kind. Newman's discussion of non-demonstrative reasoning is, however, precisely an illustration of the action of the illative sense—'proof' or certainty in probable reasoning is the paradigm example of the illative sense in action.

Thus, although Reid allows both reasoning about first principles and certainty in non-demonstrative reasoning, he excludes both from the task of common sense. Both are tasks, however, of the illative sense, so we still need to determine whether the difference is substantive, whether common sense and illative sense play different roles in their respective responses to scepticism. The suggestion that they differ because 'common sense can easily become the protective formula for unscrupulous assumption of opinions in vogue, whereas the illative sense operates from personal vindication of the truth' is naïve in two respects.[8] First, it ignores the technical nature of Reid's notion of common sense—it is not whatever any one thinks, nor is it what every one thinks. It is restricted to apprehension of self-evident truths, and Reid admits that that requires both 'a sound mind and freedom from prejudice'. Secondly,

---

[8] Johannes Artz writes that 'Der Common Sense kann leicht zue Schutzformel für bedenkenlose Übernahme von Modemeinungen werden, während der Illative Sense aus personaler Verantwortung vor der Wahrheit wirkt' ('Newman's Philosophische Leistung', *International Newman Studien* X, p. 203).

the suggestion expresses a naïve optimism about the illative sense which Newman did not share—for like Reid, he realized that prejudice, ignorance, and incapacity can obscure our perception of first principles and legitimate conclusions (311, 331). If there is a substantive difference between the two, it will lie instead in the relation or contrast between Reid's notion of intuition and Newman's notion of informal reasoning.

The question of the relation between common sense and the illative sense is thus best addressed by examining Newman's notion of 'proof' in non-demonstrative reasoning. Such an examination will serve two purposes. First, it will suggest a remarkable similarity between his and Reid's model of certainty in non-demonstrative reasoning. Secondly, it will clarify the kind of reasoning he depends on in his response to scepticism (and thus further the comparison and contrast with Reid's view of intuition). The categories of informal reasoning and intuition are integral to their respective responses—Newman's determination to work within the rubric of reasoning and Reid's resolute contrast between intuition and reasoning are expressions of their respective fundamental commitments. It is important to determine just what about intuition Newman felt obliged to reject, and what about reasoning Reid felt obliged to reject, in what was at heart the shared purpose of undermining the sceptical challenge. Nevertheless, I suggest that the understanding of certainty in non-demonstrative reasoning which Reid and Newman shared allows the prima-facie critical difference between their responses to scepticism to be mitigated from both directions.

B. PROOF

Whatever the status of his individual achievement, Newman followed in the footsteps of Wilkins, Hume, and Reid in criticizing 'the pretentious axiom that probable reasoning can never lead to certainty' (160). In particular, whether or not he was aware of it, Newman echoed Hume's explicit criticism of Locke. Just as Hume challenged Locke's stark and uncompromising dichotomy between demonstration and probability as failing to do justice to the intermediate category of 'proof', so Newman criticized Locke and his followers for holding a doctrine which had as a logical consequence that absolute assent has no legitimate exercise, except as ratifying acts of intuition or demonstration. What is thus brought home to us is indeed to be accepted unconditionally; but, as to reasonings in concrete matters, they are never more than probabilities. (159)[9]

On the contrary, Newman suggests, 'the common voice of mankind' protests 'that there are many truths in concrete matters, which no one can demonstrate, yet every one unconditionally accepts' (160).

Newman not only points to the same dichotomy, but uses Hume's own example to make the same point:

how is it that a proposition which is not, and cannot be, demonstrated, which at the highest can only be proved to be truth-like, not true, such as 'I shall die', nevertheless claims and receives our unqualified adhesion. (157-8)

That proposition, which to Newman's mind was a telling example for he gave it extended treatment later in the *Grammar* (298-301), not only 'receives' but 'claims' unqualified adhesion. It thus illustrates, I shall argue, the category of non-demonstrative argument which for Newman, as for Wilkins, Hume, and Reid, leaves 'no room for doubt'. It puts him in the tradition of 'proof', 'moral certainty', or a substantive equivalent. More particularly, as will become clear, Newman's argument bears striking similarities to specific elements which are peculiar to Reid's account.

1. 'Probable'

The claim that non-demonstrative reasoning can generate certainty is embodied in the particular use of the word 'probable' employed by Newman. As early as 1846 he was self-consciously preoccupied with the same philosophical sense of the term that Reid used, in contrast to the popular usage. It is not surprising that he annotated the two chapters in Reid's *Essays* which directly address 'probable'

---

[9] Although it is true that there is much in Locke's work, especially in the *Essay* IV, xvii and 'Of the Conduct of the Understanding', which Newman could have found congenial (as he admits in the *Grammar*, p. 162), he explicitly criticizes Locke on his view of reasoning. He seemed to see apparent points of agreement as emptied of their force by Locke's other conclusions with which they were inconsistent (this appears to be his charge, *Grammar*, p. 163). This might be true as well of Locke's claim that the logic of the schools was inadequate or that 'natural reason' was a touchstone vs. his claim that 'in all sorts of reasoning, every single argument should be managed as a mathematical demonstration ...' ('Conduct', pp. 188, 193 vs. 203).

reasoning, as well as a third (on conception) which bears on it. Where Reid had written that 'Philosophers consider probable evidence, not as a degree, but as a species of evidence which is opposed, not to certainty, but to another species of evidence called demonsration' (730), Newman wrote in a letter:

I find the *Essay* [*On Development of Doctrine*] is accused of denying moral certainty and holding with *Hermes* we cannot get beyond probability in religious questions. This is far from my meaning. I use 'probable' in opposition to 'demonstrative'.[10]

A few days later he was again contrasting the philosophical with the popular understanding:

The chief thing which I think is original is one which I have worked on a great deal ... viz that antecedent probability is the great instrument of conviction in religious (nay in all) matters. Here persons at first misunderstood me, and because I talked of 'probable arguments', they thought I meant that we could not get beyond a probable conclusion in opposition to a moral certainty ... but I hope they understand me better now. I use probable as opposed to demonstrative, not to certainty.[11]

Not only did they agree on their adoption of the philosophical sense of the term 'probable', but their examples and contrasts were similar. Newman scored, in his edition of Reid's works, the passage beginning 'That there is such a city as Rome, I am as certain as of any proposition in Euclid', and then illustrated such certainty himself in his *Grammar* by reference to the example that 'there are really existing cities on definite sites which go by the name of London, Paris, Florence and Madrid' (177). A few pages later Newman berates those philosophers who warn us that we believe 'at our peril' those truths which have 'no proof of the fact, in mode and figure equal to the proof of a proposition of Euclid' (181). As if to show how crucial this theme was to him, Newman double-scored *and* underlined Reid's conclusion to the chapter on probable reasoning: '*many things are certain* for which we have only that kind of evidence which philosophers call probable'.[12]

---

[10] *L.D.*, XI, 289 (8 Dec. 1846). Sillem refers to this, repeating C. S. Dessain's observation (*L.D.*, XI, 288–9n.), in his discussion of Butler (*Philosophical Notebook* I, pp. 178–9 n. 68), but, as at p. 102 n., he seems not to see its full import for the relation between Newman and Reid.

[11] *L.D.*, XI, 293 (13 Dec. 1846).

[12] Reid's *Works* (1858), p. 484.

Newman, like Reid, operates with a model of probabilistic, convergent, and reinforcing reasoning. Reid had argued that the strength of probable reasoning depended 'not upon any one argument, but upon many, which unite their force' so that while 'any one of them by itself would be insufficient to convince ... the whole taken together may have a force that is irresistible, so that to desire more evidence is absurd' (730). For Newman the 'real and necessary method', he writes, 'by which we are enabled to become certain of what is concrete' is as follows:

the cumulation of probabilities, independent of each other, ... too fine to avail separately, too subtle and circuitous to be convertible into syllogisms, too numerous and various for such conversion, even were they convertible. (288)

The 'principle of concrete reasoning is parallel to the method of proof' put forward by Newton—the conclusion in a concrete case is compared to a polygon inscribed in a circle whose sides continue to increase in number until it 'tends to become that circle, as its limit', for the conclusion is

foreseen in the number and direction of accumulated premisses, which all converge to it, and as the result of their combination, approach it more nearly than any assignable difference, yet they do not touch it logically (though only not touching it), on account of the nature of its subject matter, and the delicate and implicit character of at least part of the reasonings on which it depends. (321)

The reinforcing character of the convergence, he continues, is due to the 'strength, variety or multiplicity of premisses' as well as to 'objections overcome', 'adverse theories neutralized', 'difficulties gradually clearing up', and 'unlooked for correlations found with received truths'; in this manner we can with practice see reasons '"amounting to a proof"', for a proof is the limit of converging probabilities' (321).

The achievement of such 'probable reasons viewed in their convergence and combination' is 'a proved or certain conclusion' (327)—and the force of such conviction is expressed in terms of a lack of doubt. He writes that in cases of concrete reasoning the evidence can warrant the conclusion that 'it is impossible to doubt, ... we should be idiots if we did not believe' (317). Moreover, and here the echo of the earlier tradition is made explicit, even in non-demonstrative cases the evidence can lead us to 'see there is no room, no corner, for a doubt, we have no fear at all that we can be mistaken in maintaining it'.[13]

Quite strikingly, Newman uses an image almost identical to Reid's to illustrate such certainty. Just as for Reid probable evidence 'may be compared to a rope made up of many slender filaments twisted together' such that 'the rope has strength more than sufficient to bear the stress laid upon it, though no one of the filaments of which it is composed would be sufficient for that purpose' (482: VII,3), Newman suggests that

The best illustration of what I hold is that of a *cable* which is made up of a number of separate threads, each feeble, yet taken together as sufficient as an iron rod.

An iron rod represents mathematical or strict demonstration; a cable represents moral demonstration, which is an assemblage of probabilities, separately insufficient for certainty, but, when put together, irrefragable.[14]

It is noteworthy that the image shared by Newman and Reid is not found in Butler or Wilkins, and I suggest that it makes more significant the similarity between their uses of the word 'probable'.[15] Moreover, Newman's assessment of the force of such 'proof' makes clear that he sees it not only as equal in assurance to demonstration, but equal in legitimacy as well, for he continues, 'A man who said "I cannot trust a cable, I must have an iron bar"', would, *in certain cases*, be irrational and unreasonable.' Newman wanted to differentiate himself from theologians who depended on 'the *greater* probability' or 'the more probable'—for him, in particular cases of 'the highest probability' an appropriate 'assemblage and accumulation of probabilities ... *rationally demanded* to be considered sufficient for certitude'.[16]

Before considering further the question of the rationality or legitimacy of such certitude, I want to present in more detail Newman's understanding of the assurance generated by that particular

---

[13] *T.P.*, p. 127 (25 Sept. 1865).

[14] *L.D.*, XXI, 146 (6 July 1864); cf. *Philosophical Notebook* II, p. 133 ('Sundries', March 21/61 ⟨13⟩).

[15] It should be noted that Newman first read Butler in 1825, three years after reading Reid. See Walker's defence of Newman, *L.D.*, XXI, 146 n. (4 July 1864): Walker writes that 'Newman is not talking about probability in the popular sense in which it has *always* some uncertainty or misgiving about it, but in the philosophical sense in which it rises to the highest certainty in given cases equal to but differing from demonstration.' Such certainty, he continues, is 'not a jot inferior to the other'.

[16] Cf. *Grammar*, p. 412.

'assemblage and accumulation of probabilities' which he goes on to argue it would be 'irrational and unreasonable' not to accept. In other words, I want to abstract for the moment from the question of legitimacy in order to consider, as I did earlier with Reid, just what the content of the claimed certainty is.

2. 'Practical' vs. 'Speculative'

Newman's position on the descriptive character of the assurance generated by converging probabilities is unambiguous—it is certainty-that-*p*-is-true (which he calls 'theoretical' or 'speculative') rather than assurance sufficient for acting-as-if-*p*-is-true without certainty that it is (which he calls 'practical'). In response to a review of the *Grammar* by R. H. Hutton, he objects to the latter's use of the word 'practical' to describe his position and clarifies it as follows:

The Article uses the word 'practical' throughout. There is a sense in which I should admit the word, but also a sense in which I should not. We commonly use the word in opposition to speculative, when we use it of arguments, that is, of what is sufficient, not for belief, or assurance of truth, but for action. But I mean to assert that probable arguments may lead to a conclusion which is not only safe to act upon, but is to be embraced as true.[17]

Whatever his achievement, his intention should at least have been obvious from the distinction made in the *Grammar*'s discussion of the certainty generated in the 'summation and coalescence of the evidence into a proof' which is possible in particular concrete cases (e.g. jurisprudential cases). The certitude possible (and necessary) is not 'merely that which is sometimes called a "practical certitude", that is, a certitude indeed, but a certitude, that it was a "duty", "expedient", "safe", to bring in a verdict of guilt' (325-6). What is required and possible is rather a ' "speculative certitude", that is, a certitude of the fact that the man was guilty'. Moreover, his earlier criticism of Locke makes the point as well by highlighting Locke's inconsistency in allowing that not only do we 'act according' to the assent, but we 'assent as firmly' as if they were demonstrated, and not only do they 'influence all our actions' but they 'govern our thoughts as absolutely' as demonstrations. He

[17] *L.D.*, XXV, 114 (27 Apr. 1870).

makes the point doubly emphatic by both putting the relevant words in italics and then repeating them in his summary (161).

Although he at times seems to argue only for practical certitude,[18] his position had long been the stronger one. In 1853 he had asked rhetorically why 'the result of converging probabilities, and a cumulative proof' could not yield a 'conclusive' argument, for

> it seems to be most clear, and in the experience of every day, that we are positively and absolutely and speculativé (not practicé only) certain of a thing by a combination of arguments, each of which is only probable.[19]

Likewise he had contrasted practical certainty—which was present when we 'know enough, at a given moment ... to decide our actions'—with 'certainty as a conviction that a thing is actually true':

> Thus a man may be certain, as a practical point, that he ought to accept Scripture as the Word of God, though he be not certain, as a speculative matter, that it is such; and again he may [be] certain of its being his duty to perform acts of religion, whatever becomes of his doubts about the existence of a God. But speculative certainty, to be really such, must have a truth for its subject, and it must be a conviction of that truth.[20]

Practical certainty, then, as contrasted with speculative, is 'an opinion which it is safe and wise to take as true'.[21]

He admits that certainty 'has a bearing upon practice', as he had always done,[22] but he is not arguing simply for certainty in terms of expedience, safety, or connection with duty. So as to leave no doubt about his position, he contrasts it over and over again with Butler's. For example, he writes that Butler

> thought it enough for religion to attain to a certainty of safeness, or what theologians call '*practical* certainty.' He tends to say 'I do not say I have proved my point, but at least I have made it so probable that (without deciding absolutely that it is true) to believe is the safer side, *or rather*, to act as if you believe is the safer side.[23]

---

[18] *Grammar*, pp. 326, 412.

[19] *L.D.*, XV, 457 (7 Oct. 1853).

[20] *T.P.*, p. 128 (25 Sept. 1865); note his use of 'certainty' to refer to 'conviction'.

[21] Ibid., p. 35 (16 Dec. 1853). The shift between this and the *Grammar* centres on the view that such certainty is uncommon, p. 36.

[22] Ibid., p. 160 (letter of 1859 to Charles Meynell, not sent).

[23] *L.D.*, XV, 456 (7 Oct. 1853).

He continues: 'Hence moral certainty with him is only the highest step of mounting probabilities, not differing from probability in kind but only in degree.' This makes it clear that Newman is arguing for a qualitative distinction between probabilities which are sufficient for a 'proof' and those which are not.

Again, showing his disagreement with Butler he writes:

> Bishop Butler stopped the evil (of scepticism) only by lowering by many pegs the pretensions of Christianity ... it does seem to me as if the practical effect of his work was to make faith a mere *practical certainty*, i.e. a taking of certain statements of doctrine, not as true, but as safest to act upon.[24]

Such criticisms of Butler on this point are present elsewhere in his writings as well.[25]

Though he much admired both John Keble and Butler, their views were similar and inadequate in that both implied 'little more than *practical* certainty' whereas Newman's theory by contrast 'was intended to show how we could be *certain* on probabilities'.[26] Consequently, although Newman shared much with Butler—admittedly influenced quite early on by his view that 'Probability is the guide of life'[27] and referring explicitly to his claim that ' "probable proofs ... by being added, not only increase the evidence, but multiply it" '[28]—he nevertheless quite clearly did not agree with Butler's view of the achievement of such probable reasoning. Butler, he concluded, 'treats of probability, doubt, expedience and duty, whereas in these pages, without excluding, far from it, the question of duty, I would confine myself to the truth of things, and to the mind's certitude of that truth' (344).[29]

It is interesting in this connection to notice that in the margin near Reid's claim that 'the man who makes the best use he can of the faculties which God has given him, without thinking them more perfect than they really are, may have all the belief necessary in the conduct of life, and all that is necessary to the acceptance of his

[24] *L.D.*, XIX, 480 (8 Mar. 1861).
[25] *T.P.*, p. 3 (1853); *L.D.*, XXI, 270 (24 Oct. 1864).
[26] *L.D.*, XXI, 129 (24 June 1864); cf. *L.D.*, XV, 457 (7 Oct. 1853).
[27] *Apologia*, pp. 23, 29.
[28] *Grammar*, p. 319; cf. *Philosophical Notebook II*, p. 133.
[29] See *Apologia*, p. 30; John L. Murphy, 'The Influence of Bishop Butler on Religious Thought', *Theological Studies* (1963), p. 385; J. Robinson, 'Newman's Use of Butler's Arguments', *Downside Review* (1958), p. 170; Revd. James W. Lyons, 'A Philosophical Critique of Certitude According to Newman', Ph.D. dissertation (Loyola University, 1975), p. 62; Sillem, *Philosophical Notebook I*, p. 176.

Maker' (485: VII,4), Newman queries 'Is "speculative certainty" included' and underlines the phrase 'in the conduct of life'. At the very least then Newman is concerned to claim that probable evidence can generate speculative certainty—total certainty that *p*. Referring to examples which clearly call to mind the developments preceding him—namely, 'that there is a country called India, that England is an island, that we must all die'—he writes:

> Now you may say we *ought* not to feel speculative certainty in such cases, but *we do*. Not only do we think it safe to act as if there was a country called India, but *we do* think and hold it without doubt *or fear* that there *is* such a country.[30]

But he has more than this in mind. His rejection of 'practical' certainty is more than a *descriptive* qualification—it is also a rejection of the view that such assurance, however total and unavoidable, is none the less unjustified. Another criticism of Butler makes this clear:

> Butler *tends* to reduce the certainty to a *practical* certainty, viz that it is *safer to act, as if* the conclusion were true; I maintain that probabilities lead to a speculative certainty legitimately; so that it is quite *rational* to come to that conviction.[31]

Such a criticism shows that for Newman the category of 'proof' and certainty resulting from convergent probabilities not only describes an assurance equal to that of demonstration, but claims for it legitimacy as well. It also shows that as Newman saw it, nothing in Butler's notion of convergence of probabilities implied more than 'practical' certainty, either in terms of assurance or legitimacy. So what is distinctive about Newman's position cannot derive from Butler's influence.

3. *Convergence and Threshold*

An understanding of convergence which is not found in Butler but is especially suited to make the points Newman considers decisive— namely, that the achievement of reinforcing probable reasoning be both certainty that *p* and legitimate certainty (as opposed to inevitable but unjustified)—is embodied in the model of the cable which Newman shared with Reid. I argued earlier that for Reid the image

[30] *T.P.*, pp. 89–90 (13 Mar. 1860).
[31] *L.D.*, XXI, 270 (24 Oct. 1864).

of the rope and filaments was an implicit recognition that certainty was a 'threshold' concept and consequently at the very least implied that non-demonstrative certainty could be descriptively equal to that of demonstration. Newman reinforces and elaborates the image by making more explicit the notion of a threshold concept so as to suggest more clearly why non-demonstrative certainty can be as legitimate as demonstrative certainty. In what follows I shall be arguing that what Newman peculiarly shared with Reid, over and above what they both shared with Butler, was the locus of what he considered distinctive about his position on certainty and probable reasoning.

Newman's paper of 20 July 1865 in preparation for the *Grammar* elaborates, whether self-consciously or not, the implications of the cable image as a threshold category. He writes explicitly that 'certitude does not admit of more or less—but is a state of mind, definite and complete, admitting only of being and not-being. To fancy that it may be strengthened, is to imply that it has never been attained.'[32] His essay 'Faith and Doubt' had made the same point:

conviction may be felt as strongly in consequence of a clear conclusion, as of one which is clearer. A man may be so sure upon six reasons, that he does not need a seventh, nor would feel surer if he had it.[33]

An understanding of certainty as a threshold concept at least implies the *descriptive* equivalence of the assurance generated by converging probabilities and that generated by demonstration. Newman also wanted to claim, however, that in particular non-demonstrative cases the assurance could be as legitimate as that arising from demonstration: as noted earlier he insisted that 'A man who said "I cannot trust a cable, I must have an iron bar", would, *in certain given cases*, be irrational and unreasonable.'

He makes explicit the implications of the cable image (as a threshold concept) and begins to suggest its relevance for the legitimacy of such assurance when, in the same 20 July 1865 paper, he explains:

If there were twelve witnesses to an occurrence, a thirteenth makes the fact that it took place more evident to the reasoning faculty ⟨(i.e. the evidentia greater)⟩; but, on the other hand, if twelve have been in matter of fact

[32] *T.P.*, p. 124 (20 July 1865).
[33] *Discourses Addressed to Mixed Congregations* (London, 1892), pp. 234-5.

sufficient to lead me to be certain, the thirteenth is simply superfluous, because inoperative, in that respect.[34]

And he considers the question of any 'encouragement' I might feel to be distinct from this 'intellectual consideration' of superfluity. The *Grammar* makes clear that from 'probable reasons viewed in their convergence and combination', from 'various details accumulating and of deductions fitting into each other' there can result a 'real' proof, 'which of course might have been ten times stronger than it was, but was still a proof for all that, and sufficient for its conclusion' (327).

Newman's repeated references to the *sufficiency* of the evidence for its conclusion and the consequent 'superfluous' nature of additional evidence is precisely the point of the cable/rope image (as was argued in Reid's case), and points to crucial elements of his position on the legitimating implications of the cable image. Though none of the individual components could bear the weight of a stipulated burden, together they can. Even though an iron bar could *also* lift the weight, the cable can be *sufficient* to do so. The important question is whether there is sufficient evidence to bear the weight—not whether there could have been more evidence. So, the iron bar cannot be used as a standard with respect to which the cable can be said to be inadequate to the task.

Newman reinforces this suggestion with another image of a threshold category when he writes:

You cease walking when you have got home ... *Inquiry* ends, when you at length *know* what you were inquiring about. When the water boils you take the kettle off the fire.[35]

The boiling point of the water is a critical threshold—a need for boiling water is satisfied when it has reached that temperature. Though it could have become hotter, there is nothing lacking to it at that point. The extra is, as Newman says, 'superfluous'—it cannot legitimately be used to constitute a standard with respect to which the actual achievement is said to be insufficient or unjustified.

A threshold notion of certainty thus implies a claim that all certainty is equal in terms of descriptive assurance, but it also suggests a claim that there is nothing lacking to non-demonstrative

---

[34] *T.P.*, p. 124 (20 July 1865).
[35] *L.D.*, XXVII, 161–2 (27 Nov. 1874).

certainty to render it unjustified. If this suggestion can be supported philosophically, the threshold notion of certainty can be of philosophical and not merely psychological relevance for non-demonstrative reasoning. And I shall argue in the following section that Newman attempts to do just that.

4. Legitimacy and Unreasonable Doubt

Certainty is constituted, for Newman, by there being 'no room for doubt' (i.e. doubt is unreasonable). Unreasonable doubt is, therefore, as the source of the assurance, seen as a threshold concept too. When doubt is unreasonable, it is unreasonable, full stop. If so, once the critical threshold is reached, the assurance is legitimated. Newman's task then is to argue that neither fallibility nor the lack of entailment constitute reasonable ground for doubt. Put in terms of the cable image, his task is to show that even if infallibility or logical entailment could *also* generate the unreasonableness of doubt in a given case, they cannot be legitimately set up as the standard in terms of which the descriptively equal assurance of concrete reasoning can be judged illegitimate.

Newman's view of the distinction between reasonable and unreasonable doubt begins to emerge in his stated understanding of the relevance of fallibility. Newman begins, like Reid, by suggesting that the requirement of infallibility is too strict a condition for certainty:

It is very common, doubtless, especially in religious controversy, to confuse infallibility with certitude, and to argue that, since we have not the one, we have not the other, for that no one can claim to be certain on any point, who is not infallible about all; but the two words stand for things quite distinct from each other. (224)[36]

For example, he continues, 'I am quite clear that two and two make four, but I often make mistakes in long addition sums'.

Our fallibility is known to us because we have in the past made mistakes, and Newman's strategy is similar to Reid's for defending

---

[36] This point—that we cannot require infallibility for certainty—is, interestingly enough, made by William Chillingworth (*Works*, pp. 203-4) as part of his attack on the Catholic position in the seventeenth-century controversy over the rule of faith; Chillingworth uses the point to argue against the need for an infallible authority. Newman refers to Chillingworth (*Grammar*, p. 226) in this context (and in the *Development of Doctrine*, p. 71), but he fails to appreciate this important point of agreement.

the possibility of certainty even though we have made mistakes in the past. He considers the objection that 'What happened once, may happen again. All my certitudes before and after are henceforth destroyed by the introduction of a reasonable doubt, underlying them all' (228). His response, like Reid's, depends on two related requirements: (1) an accurate assessment of the relevance and import of past mistakes, and (2) the recognition that the past mistakes which enter into the argument are by definition subsequently *discovered* as such.

First, he offers a candid avowal of the prima-facie relevance of past mistakes: 'Certainly, the experience of mistakes in the assents which we have made are to the prejudice of subsequent ones' (228). In particular, 'we are bound of course to take the fact of this mistake into account, in making up our minds on any new question, before we proceed to decide upon it' (230). But the import of this must be carefully qualified, and Newman expresses this in just the same way that Reid did:

[I]f, while weighing the arguments on one side and the other and drawing our conclusion, that old mistake has already been allowed for, or has been, to use a familiar mode of speaking, discounted, then it has no outstanding claim against our acceptance of that conclusion, after it has actually been drawn. Whatever be the legitimate weight of the fact of that mistake in our inquiry, justice has been done to it, before we have allowed ourselves to be certain again. (230-1)

That is, our past error takes its toll once and thereby exhausts its power; it cannot be used over and over again to render the new conclusion insecure. It is, as Reid has noted, unfair to use the same objection at subsequent stages as if it were a new objection each time.

Newman illustrates the second point—that past mistakes are by definition discovered as such—as follows:

Suppose I am walking out in the moonlight, and see dimly the outlines of some figure among the trees;—it is a man. I draw nearer,—it is still a man; nearer still, and all hesitation is at an end,—I am certain it is a man. But he neither moves, nor speaks when I address him; and then I ask myself what can be his purpose in hiding among the trees at such an hour. I come quite close to him, and put out my arm. Then I find for certain that what I took for a man is but a singular shadow, formed by the falling of moonlight on the interstices of some branches or their foliage. (231)

The question: 'Am I not to indulge my second certitude, because I was wrong in my first?' The answer: 'may I not at least be certain that I have been mistaken?' (231). In other words, it is only by trusting our senses and faculties that we can even charge ourselves with error.

According to Newman, a past mistake, even one relevant to the instance in question, need not introduce in the given instance more than an 'abstract argument' against the claimed certitude, for 'the antecedent objection to my admission of a truth which was brought home to me second, drawn from a hallucination which came first, is a mere abstract argument, impotent when directed against good evidence lying in the concrete' (232). Although the possibility of a ground for doubt is generated by our fallibility or past errors, no actual ground for doubt need be provided by it. All that can be rightly inferred to follow necessarily from the fact of either fallibility or past mistakes is that we ought to be more careful than before. Although it is obviously true that 'There is an antecedent difficulty in our allowing ourselves to be certain of something today, if yesterday we had to give up our belief of something else, of which we had up to that time professed ourselves to be certain,' nevertheless

Antecedent objections to an act are not sufficient of themselves to prohibit its exercise; they may demand of us an increased circumspection before committing ourselves to it, but may be met with reasons more than sufficient to overcome them. (228–9)

Hence, although a sufficiently poor record in similar instances could well provide reasonable ground for doubt in a given case, neither fallibility in itself nor past mistakes necessarily introduces reasonable ground for doubt.

Newman's illustration noted above concerned fallibility with respect to concrete matters. Although his point is that fallibility in itself does not introduce reasonable grounds for doubt into any case, it is important to his defence of certainty in concrete cases that he make clear that our fallibility extends to demonstrative reasoning. Accordingly he writes: 'Argument is not always able to command our Assent, even though it be demonstrative' (169–70). In 'long and intricate mathematical investigations' even when 'every step may be indisputable, it still requires a specially sustained attention and effort of memory to have in the mind all at once all the steps of the proof, with their bearings on each other, and the antecedents which they severally involve' (170). He notes, as did Reid, that even expert mathematicians, when working in 'new and difficult ground' or with 'abstruse calculations', look for the corroboration of others (171).[37]

Like Reid, Newman had the precarious project of trying to show the limits of demonstrative argument without at the same time undermining the possibility that even probable reasoning could issue in total certainty. His point: 'There is a vast difference between argument in the abstract and concrete.'[38] To show that doubt can be unreasonable even in a non-demonstrative case, he has to show that demonstration or entailment cannot be set up as the unquestioned standard with respect to which all other reasoning is judged inadequate or illegitimate. His understanding of our fallibility even in demonstrative cases has brought to light one way in which he attempts to challenge that demonstrative standard: while demonstration in the abtract seems to 'prove' more than probable reasoning does, demonstration in the concrete (i.e. doing justice to the inescapable element of personal appropriation) is itself a realm in which doubt of the conclusion can be either reasonable or unreasonable. A sufficiently poor track record in a given kind of demonstrative exercise could well provide reasonable ground for doubt of the conclusion. Because of that the reasonableness of doubt is not excludable in cases of demonstration—i.e. it is a function of context of appropriation, not form of argument. Newman's point is that for the same reason the reasonableness of doubt is not necessarily present in non-demonstrative cases.

He makes this even more emphatic when he claims that *all* reasoning is a matter of personal appropriation, because even when 'the reasoning is abstract, the mind which judges of it is concrete' (344–5). That is why even what is 'in itself demonstrably true ... is not therefore true irresistibly' (410). He explains:

Truth certainly, as such, rests upon grounds intrinsically and objectively and abstractedly demonstrative, but it does not follow from this that the arguments producible in its favor are unanswerable and irresistible. (410)

Rather, he continues, 'these latter epithets are relative, and bear upon matters of fact; arguments in themselves ought to do, what perhaps in the particular case they cannot do'. As we saw earlier,

---

[37] See *T.P.*, p. 125 (20 July 1865).
[38] Ibid., p. 88 (26 Jan. 1860).

'Argument is not always able to command our Assent, even though it be demonstrative' because at the very least some demonstrations require 'a specially sustained attention and effort of memory'.[39]

Not only the limits of our intelligence as such, but our moral limits are at issue. Like Reid before him (and like Aristotle and Berkeley before them both) Newman stresses the moral conditioning necessary for right reasoning: 'Truth there is, and attainable it is, but ... its rays stream in upon us through the medium of our moral as well as our intellectual being' (311). There is obviously no question for any of these thinkers whether even evil people can see that two and two make four—rather they are referring to those biases and prejudices which make it difficult, if not impossible, to separate the two factors in all cases. But even if we restrict consideration as much as possible to obviously intellectual issues, it is still the case that even demonstration is inescapably personal.

The reasonableness of doubt of a conclusion cannot then be tied to the question of the abstract form of the argument or the possible falsity of the conclusion, since doubt may well be reasonable even in a case of demonstration.[40] The sceptical implication of Newman's admission concerning demonstration is avoided because by taking the emphasis away from the abstract form of argument and attaching it to context, he guaranteed that the fact that an argument is not demonstrative is not in itself an actual ground for doubt. The critical line between reasonable and unreasonable doubt depends on actual rather than possible grounds for doubt. So conclusions in either kind of reasoning can be subject to either determination—doubt of either kind of conclusion can be either reasonable or unreasonable. The absence of logical entailment would not then necessarily provide reasonable ground for doubt because judgements of reasonableness or unreasonableness of doubt are a function of context, not form of argument. The point is that *sufficiency* of evidence for total assurance can only be determined in context—and if, as a matter of fact, the assurance is total, there is no reason to regard that assurance as illegitimate simply because demonstration rules out some kinds of possibility of error *in addition* to those ruled out in a given concrete case. Demonstration can ideally provide 'extra' in that sense—but Newman suggests that the

[39] This qualifies his claim that 'proof, except in abstract demonstration, has always in it, more or less, an element of the personal' (*Grammar*, p. 317).

[40] Cf. Chap 4, n. 31, above.

'extra' is 'superfluous', and cannot be used as the standard for rendering illegitimate the total assurance possible to particular cases of non-demonstrative reasoning.

That this point needed to be made in Newman's time is clear from his friend Meynell's estimate of what Newman had taught him. He wrote humbly: 'well, I have learnt a great deal from you: I had no notion that an inference was such a leaky sort of thing!'[41] A few weeks later he repeated:

> I said *my mind* was lopsided. I thought the form of all reasoning was the Barbara, Celarent; and now a larger view was put before me... [Y]ou showed me that all reasoning wasn't shut up in the logical forms. This opened a new world to me.[42]

It was precisely the lack of such sensitivity which led to the holding of a demonstrative paradigm of certainty with which Reid too had done battle. Though with Reid its hold began to be broken, it obviously maintained itself well into Newman's time.[43] R. H. Hutton wrote in 1872 to Newman:

> The more I think of it the less can I understand how any accumulation of mere probabilities is to amount to the mathematical certainty, or how moral certainty, short of mathematical, can be in the *strictest sense*, certainty at all... This is why I falsely assumed that you relied, in religious matters, on some divine *supplement* to the weight of mere practical probability, rather than that you thought that the accumulation of probability itself amounts to certainty when it passes a given point.[44]

It was in fact T. H. Huxley's 'principle' as expressed nearly two decades later: 'in matters of the intellect, do not pretend that conclusions are certain which are not demonstrated or demonstrable.'[45]

That logical 'dubitability' is not in itself a reasonable ground for

---

[41] *L.D.*, XXIV, 384 (18 Nov. 1869).

[42] Ibid., XXIV, 387 (11 Dec. 1869).

[43] Wilbur Samuel Howell, *Eighteenth-Century British Logic and Rhetoric*, pp. 58–60, 700–3, 706.

[44] Letter of 20 Feb. 1872, cited in A. J. Boekraad and H. Tristram's *The Argument from Conscience to the Existence of God According to Newman* (Louvain, 1961), p. 195.

[45] 'Agnosticism', *The Nineteenth Century* XXV (Feb. 1889), p. 187; see also his alternate statement of the 'principle': 'it is wrong for a man to say that he is certain of the objective truth of any proposition unless he can produce evidence which logically justifies that certainty' ('Agnosticism and Christianity', ibid., (June 1889), pp. 937–8).

doubt is also made clear by Newman's view of the implications of conceivability. That he writes critically of philosophers who 'warn us, that an issue which can never come to pass in matter of fact, is nevertheless in theory a possible supposition' simply because 'there is no proof of the fact, in mode and figure equal to the proof of a proposition of Euclid' (181) suggests that he agrees with Reid's distinction between the 'supposition that such a thing is possible' and 'good evidence that it is possible'. His scoring of Reid's passages in Essay IV, Chapter 3, implies that he agrees with Reid's rejection of conceivability as the test of possibility.[46] Moreover, his 1871 emendation to the sermon, 'The Nature of Faith in Relation to Reason', asserts that we never in concrete matters get 'proofs such as absolutely to make doubt impossible', but what is an 'abstract possibility' need not be 'assumed', for 'to be just able to doubt is no warrant for disbelieving'.[47] Finally, he reminds us, emphasizing common language as Reid did, that if we require absolute indubitability for the use of the word 'certain', we would have no more use for it in our language—indeed, if we require demonstrative grounds for such ascriptions, 'the words *infallibility*, *necessity*, *truth*, and *certainty* ought all of them to be banished from the language'.[48]

But Newman, like Reid, is arguing for something stronger, as his examples make clear. In cases of *concrete* reasoning the evidence can warrant the conclusion that 'it is impossible to doubt, ... we should be idiots, if we did not believe' (317). There is, he admits, 'the *possibility* of the conclusion not being true' even in cases where *phronesis* tells us 'It is a duty to receive it', but it is against 'common sense' to dwell on that possibility—it generates a state parallel to 'the wild unhealthy state of mind which says "Perhaps there is poison in my breakfast, poison in my dinner"—or "perhaps if I go out walking, I shall break my leg" '.[49] What is particularly noteworthy is his appeal, similar to Reid's, to jurisprudential analogies. Although Reid's references are more frequent, Newman's are lengthier and more detailed. The 'courts of law' provide a particularly

---

[46] There are a number of other references in the *Theological Papers* to this issue, some rather difficult to interpret; cf. p. 42 n. 2; 'Lecture on Logic', p. 59; papers on 'Conception' (1863), pp. 104–19; cf. *Philosophical Notebook* II, pp. 152–4 (July 7/63 ⟨18⟩; Sept. 7, 1861 ⟨19⟩).

[47] *U.S.*, p. 215; *Development of Doctrine*, 'Introduction' (1845 edn.), p. 71.

[48] *Development of Doctrine*, Chap. II, Sect. 2 (1845 edn.), p. 170.

[49] *Philosophical Notebook* II, p. 195 ('Sundries', 7 Nov. 1877).

good example of the kind of reasoning he thinks can issue in 'proof' (323-8), and such conclusions are more than merely logically dubitable. The evidence against the criminal 'must bear with it, along with the palpable arguments for that guilt, such a reasonableness, or body of implicit reasons for it in addition, as may exclude any possibility, *really such*, that he is not guilty' (324). It must exclude anything which 'would hinder that summation and coalescence of the evidence into a proof' (325) which is possible in particular cases. The achievement of such 'probable reasons viewed in their convergence and combination' is 'a proved or certain conclusion, that is, a conclusion of the truth of the allegation against the prisoner'—'a real, though only a reasonable, not an argumentive [i.e. demonstrative], proof' (327). It is with reference to a legal example that he makes the claim, noted earlier, that the resulting proof 'might have been ten times stronger than it was, but was still a proof for all that, and sufficient for its conclusion' (327). 'Lawbooks tell us', he concludes, 'that the principle of circumstantial evidence is the *reductio ad absurdum*' (321-2)—and it is precisely that principle (important to both Butler and Reid)[50] which he explicitly says again and again is at the heart of proof in concrete matters (295, 300, 319).

The 'mental process in concrete reasoning' (322) of which legal reasoning is one illustration, is evident also, urges Newman, in the sciences and in literary disputes. In all such cases it is possible for the evidence to result in a conclusion which 'is as good as proved, and a man would be irrational who did not take it to be virtually proved' (323). To repeat, the evidence for some non-demonstrative conclusions can lead us to 'see there is no room, no corner, for a doubt, we have no fear at all that we can be mistaken in maintaining it'.[51] Though doubt is logically possible, and even more than logically possible, there remains 'no room' for doubt.

The unreasonableness of doubt is further explained in ways that remind one of Reid's claim that the result of removing certain kinds of notions would be that 'everything would of necessity be turned upside down',[52] for Newman writes quite clearly of the import of the way things 'hang together'. In an early piece, he writes:

[50] See Reid, *Works*, 439: VI,4.
[51] *T.P.*, p. 127 (25 Sept. 1865).
[52] Philosophical Oration of 1756, Page C-5.

By evidentia then is meant the witness of existing or ascertained truths, to a certain further proposition that is their correlative, or hangs together with them.[53]

He continues to elaborate the importance of the 'web' of our beliefs by emphasizing coherence as follows:

We see a proposition to be true, when we can make it dovetail closely into our existing knowledge, and when nothing else but it will so dovetail, that is, when we have proofs for it.

Later he gives an example:

I am sure that Great Britain is an island; I have no reserve of doubt in the matter ... yet what is my and their real, substantial proof that it is an island? There may perhaps be cogent arguments at bottom; it may be said, for instance, that all our knowledge of the earth, of men, of history, of present politics, would come to pieces and be nought, if it was not an island; and that this vague, implicit, latent argument is felt indirectly, though it is not consciously before us; I am not denying this, but if so, there may be the like circuitous, impalpable demonstration leading to certainty, of many other things too.[54]

Newman is not denying that these are 'cogent arguments'; he is merely wanting to extend the range of things legitimated by that kind of argument.

Finally, he explains in the *Grammar* that the reason, given a particular assemblage of evidence, 'a man would be irrational who did not take it to be virtually proved' is that 'when the conclusion is assumed as an hypothesis, it throws light upon a multitude of collateral facts, accounting for them, and uniting them together in one whole' (323). Admitting that such 'consistency is not always the guarantee of truth,' he goes on, 'but there may be a consistency in a theory so variously tried and exemplified as to lead to belief in it, as reasonably as a witness in a court of law may, after a severe cross-examination, satisfy and assure the judge, jury and the whole court, of his simple veracity'. Consistency or coherence may not 'guarantee' truth, but in our attempt to determine truth what we count as validating is what hangs together in a particular way with the other things we already hold. What puts it beyond reasonable doubt is just that particular way it hangs together, such that there is nothing more sure on the basis of which to challenge it.

[53] *T.P.*, p. 18 (16 Dec. 1853).
[54] Ibid., pp. 129-30 (25 Sept. 1865).

C. NEWMAN AND THE ARISTOTELIAN PARADIGM

In addition to highlighting the importance of context of appropriation, Newman also argued for the radical priority of non-demonstrative reasoning as a way of undermining an analytic paradigm
of certainty. That argument involved a selective appropriation of
Aristotle, and begins mildly enough with an affirmation of a central
Aristotelian claim. Newman's conclusion that we can in concrete
matters sometimes reach total certainty that *p* is true, that we need
not resign ourselves to less simply because the evidence is not
demonstrative, depends for him in great part on the argument
(specifically attributed by him to Aristotle) that evidential requirements must be suited to subject-matter. The *Grammar*'s claim,
putting him in a direct line with Wilkins, Chillingworth, Tillotson,
and Glanvill by using the identical reference and example, is the
following:

Speaking of the variations which are found in the logical perfection of
proof in various subject-matters, Aristotle says, 'A well-educated man will
expect exactness in every class of subject, according as the nature of the
thing admits; for it is much the same mistake to put up with a mathematician using probabilities, and to require demonstration of an orator
…' (414)

This is just a repetition of the same point made earlier in his *Essay
on Development*.[55] He speaks equivalently of how God 'varies the
way according to the subject-matter' (351) and how the 'dictate of
nature' yields different evidential requirements in different subject-
matters (412). Though he denies that we 'reason in one way in
chemistry or law, in another in morals or religion', it is nevertheless
true that reasoning is employed 'in different measures'—that is, the
'logic of language' is supplemented to a greater or lesser extent by
less formal reasoning (358–9). His point is always the same—namely,
that the 'general law which attaches to the intellectual exercises
of the mind' is that there is no single formula for determining
'every sort of truth' (358). The point is not that there are different
senses of 'truth'—only that determination of truth in all topics is
not subject to a single all-encompassing rule, calculus, or method.
   The legitimacy of this move, however, is premised on the inap-
propriateness of a syllogistic paradigm of certainty, which inappro-

[55] Page 105.

priateness is the result of the *inherent* limits of syllogistic reasoning. Without this additional claim of the inherent limits of syllogistic reasoning, the sensitivity of suiting proof to subject-matter is innocent of legitimating implications—it leads only to resignation to less than the best in non-demonstrative reasoning. Newman, however, wants to defend that legitimacy and he does so by arguing the radical priority of non-demonstrative reasoning over demonstrative.

The cable image suggests that an objector might phrase his criticism this way: 'non-demonstrative certainty, though total assurance, is not legitimate because if there *had been* a demonstration there *would* have been greater evidence; without the greatest possible evidence, the resulting assurance is illegitimate.' In its crudest form a response to this is as follows: 'demonstration of matters of fact is not possible; what is impossible to matter of fact reasoning cannot be a legitimate requirement for such reasoning (ought implies can), so matter of fact reasoning cannot be faulted for not meeting a requirement which is actually inapplicable.'[56] Sometimes Newman seems to mean just this when he speaks of the limits of demonstration in terms of abstractness vs. concreteness (277 ff.).

But it is still open to someone to object that entailment is a requirement that *can* be met by *some* conclusions, so matter of fact reasoning fails to meet an intelligible and possible standard for certainty. To this Newman's response is not simply to say that there could not have been a demonstration of a particular *p*, but rather that there cannot in principle *ultimately* be demonstration—i.e. that demonstration itself cannot be ultimate. In other words, he points to the radical priority of the non-demonstrative reasoning on which demonstration depends, and here his claim takes the form of a critique of Aristotle.

Reid's critique of Aristotelian logic had been reprinted in Britain five times between 1812 and 1837, so its influence reached well into Newman's formative period.[57] Though Newman does not undertake a similar explicit critical study of Aristotle's logic, he reiterates often enough his rejection of what he takes to be the Aristotelian

---

[56] This seems to be the point of Nicholas Rescher's use of the maxim *Ultra posse nemo obligatur*, at the heart of his response to scepticism (*Scepticism*, pp. 49, 56 and *passim*).

[57] Howell, *Eighteenth-Century British Logic and Rhetoric*, p. 397; the reference is to the 'Brief Account of Aristotle's Logic'.

view of reasoning. His conclusion is uncompromising: 'In spite of Aristotle, I will not allow that genuine reasoning is an instrumental art' (338). The reference to 'instrumental' is at least to be understood in terms of the earlier contrast in the *Grammar* between genuine reasoning and the 'conscious adoption of an artificial instrument or expedient' (331). But the problem with Aristotle's 'instrumental art' is made explicit in his earlier unpublished papers. There he sees it in terms of its 'hypothetical' character—it is 'not concerned with any definitive subject-matter' and hence 'not concerned with the truth or falsity' of the premisses or terms.[58] Reasoning as an instrumental art, therefore, is a common denominator 'equalizing all men and all discoveries'.[59] The general claim is made specific when the limits of demonstration are detailed at length by Newman.

Though he does not, as did earlier anti-sceptics, point to the radical circularity of demonstration—its inability to surpass or transcend its own premisses—he does highlight the inherent limits of demonstration as follows. 'As to Logic', he writes

Its chain of conclusions hangs loose at both ends; both the point from which the proof should start, and the points at which it should arrive, are beyond its reach; it comes short both of first principles and of concrete issues. (172; see also 269, 271)

Logical inference, syllogism, or demonstration (all of which terms he uses interchangeably) is limited first and most importantly, he writes, because its premisses are 'assumed, not proved' (269). Logic, he writes, cannot really 'prove' (271) because

Inference is always inference; even if demonstrative, it is still conditional; it establishes an incontrovertible conclusion on the condition of incontrovertible premisses. (172)

Moreover, major premisses are sometimes 'more difficult to accept than the conclusion' (304). Thirdly, abstract arguments cannot 'reach the particular' (278)—and this is sometimes phrased in the idiom of the problem of the open-endedness of rule-application ('who is to apply them to a particular case? whither can we go, except to the living intellect'—354). Thus, 'in concrete reasonings we are in great measure thrown back into that condition, from which logic proposed to rescue us. We judge for ourselves, by our own

[58] *T.P.*, pp. 53, 58 (1859).   [59] Ibid., p. 92 (12 Oct. 1861).

lights' (302). For Newman, the fact that demonstration cannot be employed at all except in dependence on non-demonstrative reasoning means that demonstration and its certainty can hardly be used as a standard.

Such a recognition of the limits of syllogistic reasoning led some to strident critiques of Aristotle, mitigated only now and then by weak defences or strained appreciations.[60] Heavily influenced as he was by his early and serious study of the *Nicomachean Ethics*, the *Rhetoric*, and the *Poetics*, however, Newman was led instead to develop and extend Aristotle's thought. It was as if he recognized before others did that Aristotle's theory concerning demonstrative syllogism (in the *Posterior Analytics*) was not practised in his other works,[61] and so was able to appreciate Aristotelian insights. For example, the very point he was making about the limits of demonstration can be found in the *Nicomachean Ethics* itself. Aristotle writes:

induction is the starting-point which knowledge even of the universal presupposes, while syllogism proceeds *from* universals. There are therefore starting-points from which syllogism proceeds, which are not reached by syllogism; it is therefore by induction that they are acquired.[62]

The *Nicomachean Ethics* was in fact full of important insights with which Newman agreed.[63] He explicitly recognized the potential bearing of Aristotle's notion of *phronesis* on speculative questions

---

[60] See Reid's letter to Gregory (1783), *Works*, p. 75: 'I humbly think you are too severe against Aristotle and Plato, especially the former. Two hundred years ago, it was proper to pull him down from the high seat he held; but now he is sufficiently humbled, and I would not have him trampled upon'. In 1774 he clearly felt less sympathetic.

[61] See Jonathan Barnes, 'Aristotle's Theory of Demonstration' (see Chap. 4, n. 40). See also Gérard Verbeke, 'Aristotelian Roots of Newman's Illative Sense', in *Newman and Gladstone: Centennial Essays*, ed. James D. Bastable (Dublin, 1978), p. 186.

[62] VI, 3, pp. 140–1; cf. also I, 7 (trans. Sir David Ross (London, 1945)).

[63] Verbeke (n. 61) argues that it would be 'exaggerated to maintain that Newman borrowed his teaching on the illative sense from Aristotle' because 'the context and background of the Aristotelian phronesis and of Newman's illative sense are in many respects different' (p. 191); moreover, Newman's Aristotelianism is qualified by his rejection of the model of knowing in the *De Anima* (179). Franz M. Willam, on the other hand, argues for a much stronger Aristotelianism in Newman (*Aristotelische Erkenntnislehre bei Whately und Newman* (Freiburg, 1960)), while Jan Walgrave claims that though Newman 'was indeed a Platonist in his way of feeling and experiencing the world', nevertheless, 'his method of reasoning was that of a disciple of Aristotle' (unpubl. lectures, Katholieke Universiteit, Leuven, 1975–7, p. 17).

of truth and falsity, though Aristotle himself limited it to 'τα
πρακτα' (353 n. 1). He saw that Aristotle's sensitivity to the open-
endedness of rules—the necessity and difficulty of applying general
rules to particular cases—was as relevant in the theoretical as in
the moral domain, and he appreciated his suggestion that training
and experience cultivate right judgement in applying rules (354–5,
360). He agreed that our insight into truth similarly depends on
'practice and experience more than on reasoning' (342), referring
explicitly to Aristotle's prescription that we trust those who have
'the eye of experience' (341), those who 'by long acquaintance with
their subject have a right to judge' (342). And, as we saw earlier,
he agreed wholeheartedly with Aristotle's prescriptions concerning
sensitivity to context and suiting evidence to subject-matter (414).
Out of six explicit references to Aristotle in the *Grammar*, five
express praise and/or agreement, justifying his description of Aristotle as his intellectual 'master' (430).[64]

There was, then, in the centuries just preceding Newman a selective appropriation of Aristotle's thought. The seventeenth-century
thinkers considered earlier appropriated the Aristotelian notion of
suiting proof to subject-matter, though it is not clear, except in
Wilkins's case, that they thought it bore legitimating implications.
Without an admission of the inherent limits of syllogism, the doctrine of suiting proof to subject-matter, as I suggested earlier, leads
only to resignation to less than total justified certainty in non-
demonstrative cases. Eighteenth-century thinkers, in particular
Reid, focused attention on the limits of the syllogistic paradigm,
with little if any appreciation of the potential in Aristotle's thought
for precisely the sort of case they wanted to make. For example, as
noted earlier, Reid refers to Aristotle mainly to criticize the doctrine of intelligible species, and either fails to give Aristotle credit
for obviously Aristotelian insights or gives the credit to others, as
when he attributes to Locke the 'seasonable' and clearly Aristotelian counsel of improving our reasoning power by 'intimate acquaintance with the authors who reason the best [rather] than from

    [64] *Grammar*, pp. 338, 341–2, 353–5, 414, 430, 498. Newman's 'Lecture on Logic',
1859, expands on the critical reference to Aristotle (*T.P.*, pp. 53, 58) as does a
remark in a paper of 12 Oct. 1861 (*T.P.*, p. 92), but elsewhere he speaks apprecia-
tively ('Assent and Intuition', *T.P.*, p. 74; revised version of reply to A. M. Fairbairn,
Stray Essays on Controversial Points (Birmingham, 1890), pp. 97–8 (reprinted in
T.P., pp. 152–3)). See Sillem, *Philosophical Notebook* I, pp. 151–63, on Newman's
references to Aristotle in earlier works.

study of voluminous systems of logic'.[65] Newman, however, picked up in Aristotle the recognition of the importance of non-syllogistic reasoning embodied in the *Nicomachean Ethics*, freeing it from the constraints imposed on it by the Aristotelian claim that reasoning was an instrumental art. Like Reid, he combined the appreciation of the limits of syllogism with the doctrine of suiting proof to subject-matter in order to argue that syllogism could not constitute a standard with respect to which non-syllogistic reasoning could be said to lack something essential to its justification. Newman, however, was far more appreciative of the 'naturalist' potential already ingredient in Aristotle's work (as will become even clearer in the following chapter).

D. THE 'ILLATIVE SENSE' AND INTUITION

Having examined Newman's understanding of the 'proof' achievable by informal reasoning, and seen his comparison of the illative sense with *phronesis*, we are in a position to face again the question of the substantive relation between the illative sense and Reid's 'common sense'. In particular, how does illative reasoning relate to or contrast with intuitive judgement. That determination will, I suggest, reveal a (perhaps fruitful) tension in Newman's thought.

Newman's understanding of informal inference is usually phrased in psychological terms—namely, lack of conscious awareness of the process of reasoning to something on the basis of something else (260). He speaks of a process 'without the direct and full advertance of the mind' (292), a process altogether unconscious (330), an inference in which the process and the antecedents are ignored (331), and which is 'without assignable media of perception' (334). These claims all fit together with his claim that all reasoning has the same form (292), that reasoning involves antecedents and mediation 'in its very idea' (337), and that there is always a 'method', however 'implicit' (331).

His point is introduced with a set of images—namely, a contrast between a sketch, provided by formal inference, and a portrait, with the details filled in by informal reasoning (288). Informal reasoning is seen as a supplement to verbal, formal, propositional reasoning, and all reasoning includes the former to a greater or lesser extent (359). Reasoning is thus radically implicit in that it

[65] 'Brief Account of Aristotle's Logic', in Reid's *Works* (1852), p. 709.

can never be adequately analysed or put under a rule, calculus, or method (292, 301, 303, 316, 371).

Informal reasoning is the 'tacit dimension' in all reasoning; it is what fleshes out the formal analysis which is only possible to a certain extent. Reasoning in a concrete case is made up of considerations which function as

parts of a great complex argument, which so far can be put into propositions, but which, even between, and around, and behind these, still is implicit and secret, and cannot by any ingenuity be imprisoned in a formula, and packed into a nut-shell. (307)

Even in its 'most elaborate exhibitions' formal inference fails to represent 'adequately' all the considerations by which our judgement is determined (284). Again, formal and informal inference do not constitute an either/or, but rather supplement each other:

methodical processes of inference, useful as they are, as far as they go, are only instruments of the mind, and need, in order to their due exercise, that real ratiocination and present imagination which gives them a sense beyond their letter, and which, while acting through them, reaches to conclusions beyond and above them. Such a living *organon* is a personal gift, and not a mere method or calculus. (316)

What is at issue then is the complexity of reasoning—a 'multiplicity of premisses' (321), a 'sum-total' of considerations which cannot be adequately analysed (284), 'minute reasonings too subtle' for analysis (264).

Where the reasoning is most informal the multiplicity of premisses is not only not consciously recognized, but it is not 'assignable' or recognizable either. Not only do people not go by rule or method, but the reasoning cannot ever be adequately reconstructed even in retrospect. (Newman's assumption is clearly that if the process could be made fully explicit, it would at least in principle generate logical compulsion (313).) The emphasis is on the impossibility in principle of adequate or total reconstruction or analysis. It remains 'reasoning', however, because the form of inference—premisses and conclusion—is always present. The in-principle impossibility of *adequately* analysing does not render vacuous the claim that the formal structure remains. Even when he argues that it is a case of seeing the conclusion 'per modum unius' in the premisses, it is still *in* and *through* the premisses in such a way that juxtaposition of propositions remains 'useful ... both to direct and verify' (301-2).

There is, then, for Newman a continuum in which less and less is able to be analysed—until the reasoning is 'altogether unconscious and implicit' (330). But where altogether implicit means altogether unanalysable the claim that the form of inference remains loses its force, and he writes instead that

what is called reasoning is often only a peculiar and personal mode of abstraction, and so far, like memory, may be said to exist without antecedents. (337)

To exist without antecedents, he admits, is not to exist without 'previous conditions' on which the abstraction depends, but the lack of antecedents constitutes a lack of anything appropriately called premisses—and so it constitutes a lack of the form of inference.[66]

The distinction between reasoning and 'what is called reasoning' begins to blur, and with it the line between natural instinctive reasoning and intuition. Newman argues that sometimes we have only the indirect argument from 'success' to show that in reasoning which is a 'simple divination or prediction' there is nevertheless 'a method ... though it be implicit' (331). But earlier he had not been as confident or committed to the claim that however implicit there was still a process. Using the same example he later used in the *Grammar* (333, 336), he wrote in 1860:

On calculating boys, not *really* reasoning by *methods*, but by instinct. This will not easily be granted me. I was reading some one the other day, who said *of course* the boys *did* go by method, though they could not bring it out—but I do not think it matters for my purpose, whether we say that the logic is implicit, or that there is no *real* logic except as symbolical.[67]

The fragments in his *Philosophical Notebook* reveal his self-conscious questioning of the relation between discursive and non-discursive uses of reason. He writes:

I doubt whether what is called reasoning be in its essence a process. When I look at a page of print, & say one line is less than the whole type, I do not make ⟨two⟩ syllogisms, 'The whole is greater than its part, the paper is a whole, therefore it is greater than its part. Again The page is greater

---

[66] See Chapter 7's discussion of first principles as abstractions.
[67] *T.P.*, p. 90 (27 Mar. 1860).

than its part, a line is a part, therefore a page is greater than a line—' there is no recurrence to general ideas ... I mean it is self-evident. In like manner to a mathematical mind, the truth flashes at once that vertical angles are equal.[68]

On the following page he sees it as 'a kind of intuition':

there is no reason to say that every one need, or does, certainly not mathematical minds, go through this process. They see the truth all of a heap, by one act ... It is a kind of intuition, and hence it is very difficult to separate what is called reasoning from intuition.[69]

This tension between 'process' and 'intuition' may well be an expression of a more general tension in Newman's thought between Aristotelian and Platonic inclinations (which some might say is the tension within Aristotelian thought itself).[70] It leads us to see, at any rate, that from Newman's side the contrast between common-sense and the illative sense is mitigated by his understanding of the radical implicitness of informal reasoning for at its extreme the implicitness of informal reasoning renders it nearly indistinguishable from intuition. From Reid's side the contrast is mitigated by the understanding he shares of non-demonstrative certainty—that is, allowing reasoning to be subtle enough to generate certainty from converging probabilities might lessen the need to contrast it radically with intuition. And from both sides it is mitigated, as the following chapter will show, by the relation between their understanding of certainty in non-demonstrative reasoning and their more radical commitment to the sanction of 'the natural'.

---

[68] *Philosophical Notebook* II, p. 73.

[69] Ibid., p. 75. Newman refers to footnotes to both passages to Stewart's work, citing relevant pages, and makes explicit in the note to the first passage that Locke and he are in agreement on the matter.

[70] Cf. Jan Walgrave (n. 63 above) calls attention to this 'dialectical tension' and 'polarity' which 'accounts for the curious blending of Platonism and Aristotelianism in his way of thinking'. He continues: 'He was indeed a Platonist in his way of feeling and experiencing the world. But his method of reasoning was that of a disciple of Aristotle. The *Grammar of Assent* is a masterpiece within the tradition of Aristotelian thought.' (p. 17)' I would argue that even within the *Grammar* this tension is expressed. See David Newsome's *Two Classes of Men* (London, 1974) for a suggestive study of the two tendencies of thought and Newman's relation to them. Andrew Louth in *Discerning the Mystery* (Oxford, 1983) implies that Newman's insight here is 'in some part the fruit of his deep knowledge of the Fathers (especially the Greek fathers)', p. 138.

9

Newman: The Sanction of the Natural

FOR Newman the legitimation of non-demonstrative certainty is based on the sanction of the natural. 'None of us', he writes in his *Grammar*

can think or act without the acceptance of truths, not intuitive, not demonstrated, yet sovereign. If our nature has any constitution, any laws, one of them is this absolute reception of propositions as true, which lie outside the narrow range of conclusions to which logic, formal or virtual, is tethered; nor has any philosophical theory the power to force on us a rule which will not work for a day.[1]

Newman's response to scepticism is in crucial respects like Reid's: an appeal to the constitution of our nature, a claim that the dictates of our nature override conflicting philosophical theory, and an emphasis on the centrality of practice in theoretical commitments. He is, however, usually much more explicit about his arguments.

The appeal to the constitution of our nature is the point of his repeated criticisms in the *Grammar* of what he calls the 'a priori' method of considering the human mind (64, 164, 166, 176, 216, 247). He replies to his friend R. H. Hutton's characterization of the *Grammar* by clarifying his sense of 'a priori':

I ought to have explained my use of the words 'a priori'. I accuse Locke and others of judging of human nature, not from facts, but from a self-created vision of an optimism by the rule of 'what they think it ought to be'. This is arguing, not from experience, but from pure imagination.[2]

Locke, he had argued in the *Grammar*, was guilty of trying to impose an ideal on human nature, but 'the practice of mankind is too strong for the antecedent theorem, to which he is desirous to

---

[1] Grammar of Assent, p. 179. Unless otherwise noted, further references in parantheses will be to this work.

[2] *L.D.*, XXV, 114 (28 Apr. 1870).

subject it' (160). Locke's theory shows that 'abstract argument is always dangerous'; Newman, on the contrary, writes:

I prefer to go by facts. The theory to which I have referred [Locke's] cannot be carried out in practice. It may be rightly said to prove too much; for it debars us from unconditional assent in cases in which the common voice of mankind, the advocates of this theory included, would protest against the prohibition. (160)

'We must', he insists, 'take the constitution of the human mind as we find it, and not as we may judge it ought to be' (216). The 'a priori' method adopted by Locke, he says, leads to a 'view of the human mind . . . which to me seems theoretical and unreal':

Reasonings and convictions which I deem natural and legitimate, he apparently would call irrational, enthusiastic, perverse, and immoral; and that, as I think, because he consults his own ideal of how the mind ought to act, instead of interrogating human nature, as an existing thing, as it is found in the world. (164)

Such a criticism is similar to Reid's charge that knowledge is not 'confined within the narrow limits which Mr. Locke assigns to it; because the far greatest part of what all men call human knowledge, is in things which neither admit of intuitive nor of demonstrative proof'[3]—it is similar both as regards Locke's mistake and the source of it.

It might seem, however, that such a criticism is misplaced for in his *Essay*'s 'Epistle to the Reader' Locke prided himself precisely on addressing just that hitherto neglected descriptive task.[4] Moreover, he wrote to the Bishop of Worcester:

If I have done anything new, it has been to describe to others more particularly than had been done before, what it is their minds do, when they perform that action which they call knowing.[5]

What kind of description then is Newman proposing? He wants to describe the 'laws of our nature', our 'constitution'. He talks about 'laws' both in the sense of regularities (85) and as rules which can be violated (6–7, 170, 229). His point, however, in so far as it relates to laws of the human mind is made in terms of the latter— the laws of our intellectual nature are 'rules' which are revealed in 'the natural'.

---

[3] *Works*, 426: VI,3.   [4] Page 7.
[5] *Works*, 11th edn., Vol. IV (London, 1812), pp. 143–4.

Newman has two main tenets about 'the natural'. The first is that what is natural cannot be faulted (7, 348). There may be errors in the particular exercise of any natural faculty, but that 'cannot avail to forfeit [a] natural right' to the exercise of our mental faculties (7). It is, he says, 'a general law that, whatever is found as a function or an attribute of any class of beings, or is natural to it, is in its substance suitable to it, and subserves its existence, and cannot be rightly regarded as a fault or enormity' (348). The reason is that 'no being could endure, of which the constituent parts were at war with each other'. Another formulation of this central point is his claim that

My only business is to ascertain what I am, in order to put it to use. It is enough for the proof of the value and authority of any function which I possess, to be able to pronounce that it is natural. (347)

The difficult question, however, is 'what is natural?' Newman's second tenet is that the natural is determined by what we have seen called an appeal to the 'common voice of mankind'; he explains:

That is to be accounted a normal operation of our nature, which men in general do actually instance. That is a law of our minds, which is exemplified in action on a large scale, whether *a priori* it ought to be a law or no. (344)[6]

The natural is what is instanced in large-scale action, and it is natural or a law of our mind 'whether *a priori* it ought to be a law or no'. This crucial passage raises two different questions—one about practice and one about the function and justification of such 'rules'. I will consider each in turn.

A. PRACTICE

It is interesting that it is in the process of indicating what is 'natural' in the preceding quotation that Newman makes the claim that his is a 'practical' aim, such as was Butler's. Here Newman is endorsing the 'practical' as opposed to the metaphysical or

[6] After referring to Reid on natural acts of the mind, Newman recognizes the problem with the notion of 'natural'. He writes: 'Is what is natural, true? Yes, when it is proved to be natural; but we may be fairly asked not to confound what is idiosyncratic or arising from the weakness of childhood with what is natural; at the same time, if what is *universal* and belongs to all ages is not natural, what is? Yet, I suppose the positive school wd try to make out that our own minds were warped thro' life by the weak impressions of the nursery' (*Philosophical Notebook* II, p. 24).

abstractly theoretical, at the same time as he, as we saw earlier, rejects the achievement of 'practical' as opposed to speculative. The sign that Locke's theory is incorrect is that 'it cannot be carried out in practice', for 'the practice of mankind is too strong for the antecedent theorem' (160). 'None of us can think or act' without adopting particular stances (179), and this legitimates them. The general charge is the same as Reid's—practice belies sceptical theory, or renders such theory in conflict with itself. Just as Reid writes that 'the immediate dictates of our natural faculties are of higher authority than any theory',[7] Newman denies that any 'philosophical theory [has] the power to force on us a rule which will not work for a day' (179). Newman would clearly agree with Reid that with respect to particular convictions 'even those who reject [them] in speculation, find themselves under a necessity of being governed by [them] in their practice; and thus it will always happen when philosophy contradicts first principles'.[8] Like Reid, Newman agrees that scepticism cannot be maintained—it is illegitimate to extrapolate from what we can sometimes do to a claim about what we can always do.

B. LEGITIMATION OF 'RULES'

The second question raised by Newman's view of the natural concerns the status, function, and justification of such 'rules' or 'laws of the mind'. What is the import of the claim that such action on a large scale is a law 'whether *a priori* it ought to be a law or no'?

Newman makes an interesting claim in one of the early papers in preparation for the *Grammar* when he suggests that the objection that speculative certainty cannot ever be attained in concrete matters is 'overset by the common sense and universal practice of men, that is, by the laws of the human mind'.[9] It is not immediately obvious, however, whether he is suggesting that the laws of the mind are constituted by the universal practice and common sense of men (as is implied in the qualification 'whether *a priori* it ought to be a law or no'), or that such laws, revealed in the universal practice and common sense of men, conform to norms which are not themselves generated by practice? In other words, do the laws

---

[7] *Works*, 431: VI,3.
[8] Ibid., 447: VI,5.
[9] *T.P.*, p. 129 (25 Sept. 1865).

of the mind which we describe *generate* norms or do they *reveal* norms to which they conform?

The tension or ambiguity in Newman's thought is present in a single discussion found in the *Grammar*. The discussion begins by claiming that we gain knowledge of the laws of the mind, in particular the law of progress, not 'by any *a priori* view of man, but by looking at it as the interpretation which is provided by himself on a large scale in the ordinary action of his intellectual nature' (349). He looks explicitly to the maxims of Bacon for support. We must

sternly destroy all idols of the intellect, and subdue nature by cooperating with her. Knowledge is power, for it enables us to use eternal principles which we cannot alter. (350-1)

He goes on: 'so also in that microcosm, the human mind. Let us follow Bacon more closely than to distort its faculties according to the demands of an ideal optimism, instead of looking out for modes of thought proper to our nature, and faithfully observing them in our intellectual exercises' (350-1).

The suggestion that the laws of the mind parallel the laws of nature, which are 'eternal principles which we cannot alter', supports the claim that such laws reveal norms to which we conform. On the other hand, Newman's claim that 'as the structure of the universe speaks to us of Him who made it, so the laws of the mind are the expression, not of mere constituted order, but of His will' is immediately qualified by the important counterfactual 'I should be bound by them even were they not His laws' (351). The implication of this latter qualification, coupled with the earlier claim that a law of the mind was a law 'whether *a priori* it ought to be a law or no', is that the justification of the norms is not a function of their revealing God's will, or revealing norms which exist independently of our human practices. Moreover, the insistence just prior to the reference to Bacon that nothing is 'left to us but to take things as they are, and to resign ourselves to what we find ... to confess that there is no ultimate test of truth besides the testimony borne to truth by the mind itself' emphasizes the determination (as opposed to the definition) of truth in such a way as to preclude the need for something beyond our rule-generating practices to justify the rules.

In what follows I want to consider more closely Newman's

understanding of the status of the sanction of the dictates of our nature. This will allow further contrast and comparison of his naturalist response with Reid's.

C. 'TRUST' IN OUR FACULTIES

In the *Grammar* Newman makes a claim at first sight quite at odds with one of Reid's fundamental tenets when he writes: 'I cannot call the trustworthiness of the faculties of memory and reasoning one of our first principles' (61). However differently he may have spoken or felt earlier, this is his considered judgement, and as such the position that deserves most attention. But as late as 25 July 1869 Newman could write to Charles Meynell that 'It is a duty to trust, or rather to use our nature'.[10] That is, it still seemed natural to him to use the language of 'trust'—it was deeply engrained in him though he wanted finally to reject it. An understanding of the *Grammar*'s claim and its relation to Reid's view on the matter can be improved by looking at least briefly at some of the earlier for- mulations of Newman's earlier position, for I suggest that although the shift away from 'trust' seems to distance him from Reid, it is actually his earlier position in which he did speak of 'trust' which differed radically from Reid's. The shift away from the language of 'trust' is in any case an important indicator of his response to scepticism; moreover, I shall argue that it is just when he is reading Reid again that his position assumes a good deal of the shape of Reid's position, and by the time of the *Grammar* can be said to be even a little bolder or more Reidian than Reid's, despite the con- trast concerning 'trust'. Examining the development of Newman's thought on 'trust' can, therefore, shed light on his anti-scepticism, as well as suggest how close he and Reid are on an issue which is perhaps more fundamental than anything which divides them.

Consider his early position. The 1829 sermon, 'Religious Faith Rational', is in great part a sermon on 'trust'. Before dealing with trust in testimony, Newman spends time showing that 'we trust to our *memory*', have 'faith in our memory', and 'we trust the general soundness of our reasoning powers'.[11] His point: 'our memory and

---

[10] *L.D.*, XXIV, 294.
[11] *Parochial and Plain Sermons*, Vol. I (London, 1894), pp. 191, 191-2; (hereafter *P.P.S.*).

reason often deceive us, yet no one says it is therefore absurd and irrational to continue to trust them ... because on the whole they are true and faithful witnesses.[12] To trust them is admittedly only 'to trust ourselves', and this is appropriate because the senses and reason 'are so continually about us, and so at command, that we can use them to correct each other; so that on the whole we gain from these the truth of things quite well enough to act upon'[13].

In 1843 he offered this further comment in his University sermon on 'The Theory of Development in Religious Doctrine':

We have an instinct within us, impelling us, we have external necessity forcing us, to trust our senses, and we may leave the question of their substantial truth for another world.[14]

The suggestion is that all we can know is that we *necessarily* trust— the question whether we *rightly* trust is another, and for us on this side of the grave, insoluble question.

An uneasiness about speaking of 'trust' in our faculties begins to emerge, however, in the 1859 paper 'Proof of Theism'.[15] Here Newman comments directly on Ward's attempt to counter scepticism by appeal to 'intuitive' judgements which go beyond the claims of consciousness—e.g. judgements of memory and sense— and obliquely comments as well on the positions of Reid and Stewart as presented through Hamilton's eyes. It is possible to speak of our faculties in two ways, however, and Newman's rejection of the notion of 'trust' is initially directed only to the first. At this stage he and Reid are opposed. Eventually it will be directed to both ways of speaking, and at that stage his position will come to resemble Reid's.

One can, and Newman does, talk about the faculties in terms of (1) their operations as such, as well as in terms of (2) their performance. In this 1859 paper Newman is expressing on the one hand a position on the status of the operations of reasoning, memory, and sense as such—their status *vis-à-vis* consciousness and existence. On the other hand, he is expressing a position on what is more appro-

[12] *P.P.S.*, p. 192.
[13] Ibid., pp. 193-4.
[14] *U.S.*, p. 349.
[15] *Philosophical Notebook* II, pp. 30-77. Further references in parentheses unless otherwise noted will be to this piece; angle brackets indicate interlinear additions by Newman. Note that Boekraad's *Argument from Conscience to the Existence of God* is essentially a commentary on this piece.

priately called their 'trustworthiness'—that is, the accuracy of their performance. Newman has a different position on each of these ways of talking about the faculties, and they result from a division central to his thought at the time—namely, a division between inner/outer, or internal/external to us.

His general position on the status of the faculties as such is an attempt to enlarge what he considers an unduly restricted Cartesian starting-point for consideration of the whole question of a response to scepticism. He sums up his 'main point' as 'the implication of certain mental acts with the act of existence—e.g. of memory, sensation, ratiocination' (69). That is, he denies that we 'believe' or have 'faith' in our being or existence, and consequently denies that we have 'faith' or 'trust' or 'belief' in the 'faculties' or 'operations' through which our existence is manifested to us: 'I am conscious that I am; as I have not faith in my existence ... [I have not] faith in my consciousness, which is the faculty ... through which I know that I exist' (33). For the same reason, he continues, 'it is improper, and (strictly speaking) absurd, to say that I have faith in my sensation. I feel pain. I have not faith in the feeling, but the feeling is part of me, or bound up in my "I am".' And in parallel fashion with the other faculties.

But the parallel must be understood precisely. What is too close to us to need 'faith' (too near to us to have 'faith' in (79))—what we, on the contrary, intuit—is the *fact* of the exercise of these faculties, not what they witness to. 'The faculty of reason, or that I reason, is as much a fact as my existence'; 'I do reason' parallels 'I do exist' (47). Similarly with sensation in general:

I have a sensation of colours and forms—this is one thing. I have a persuasion that these colours and forms convey to me the presence &c. of external objects—this is a second thing. I have said that the sensation is not an object of faith, but of consciousness—but the second *is* an object of faith. Its ⟨truth⟩ is not bound up in that act of consciousness, by which I know I am. Though those colours & forms meant nothing beyond themselves, my consciousness of my existence would not be affected. (37–9)

What is intuited is the fact of the sensation—that the sensaton has an external referent is not intuited.

Thus, implicated with the recognition of existence and consciousness, for Newman, is the recognition of the fact of the exercise of other operations—memory, reasoning, sensation. The fact of their exercise is intuited with or in the intuition of existence and consciousness. The division on which he relies is that between internal and external: 'I would draw a broad line between what is within us and without us, and apply the word "faith" to our reliance ⟨certainty⟩ of things without and not within us' (71, cf. 37, 75). His division then is not the division made by others to whom he refers—it is not the division either of (a) consciousness vs. the other faculties (70-1) or (b) consciousness, memory, reason vs. the senses. His division between inner and outer is rather the division between inner facts of consciousness and its implicated operations vs. the testimony of those inner facts or exercises concerning things beyond themselves, things external to us. It is therefore the division between the equal status of consciousness with its implicated operations and the reliability or trustworthiness of the operations. The question of the ontological status of the faculties is settled by the argument that implicated in the recognition of consciousness are all its 'primary modes', all those operations through which it manifests itself to us. The question of their trustworthiness is another question altogether.[16]

The question of the status of the fact of the exercise of a faculty illustrates one aspect of what Newman claims is a 'two-fold sense of memory and reason' (45)—that is, there is no faith in the acknowledgement of the exercise of the faculties since the fact that they are exercised is brought home to us in one complex act of intuition. The second aspect of the 'two-fold' sense is their manner or accuracy of performance, as contrasted with their exercise, for

The act of ⟨my⟩ thinking, remembering, reasoning is one with my existing; but it admits, which existing does not, of well or ill. (45)

But he hurriedly counters that this does not mean that we have 'faith' in the accuracy of their performance, because 'it depends on the particular case'—'whether I exercise it rightly or wrongly in a particular case is not a matter of faith, but of opinion, judgement &c' (47). That the faculties perform accurately is not intuited, but it does not require 'faith' either. He sums up the whole as follows: there is no faith in recognizing *that* I exist or reason or sense; 'nor

---

[16] Newman's clear distinction between inner facts and testimony highlights the same distinction in Reid's formulation of his first principles in the list in Essay I, and suggests that the first in Essay VI, 5 should be read similarly (which obviates Newman's marginal criticism of it, *Works*, p. 442).

is there implicit faith, or *foi aveugle*, in the particular exercise—but a judgement or opinion about it. So that *foi aveugle* comes in nowhere' (47). The question of their trustworthiness—do they tell truly? are they reliable, accurate?—is a question about considered judgement as to their testimony in 'the particular case' before us. Thus, Newman's inner/outer distinction does not coincide exhaustively with the intuition/faith distinction—faith applies to the external *in general*, judgement to the external *in particulars*.

Newman speaks specifically of reasoning and memory, and presumably the same would hold true of sensation. But the case of sensation reveals more clearly the distinction within the realm of the external. Newman says, as noted above, that although the fact of sensation is 'not an object of faith, but of consciousness', the 'persuasion' that the sensation has an external referent *is* an object of 'faith' (37).[17] Thus, the claim that we do not have faith in the performance of the faculties must be qualified in the case of sensation, as must the earlier claim that we do not have faith in 'those faculties, their exercise, and their dictates' (33), for presumably one of the 'dictates' of the senses is the claim that there is an external referent to the sensations. (He also says we have 'faith' in the existence of an 'external world' (71).) In other words, in one sense we are required to have faith in the 'dictates' of the senses—namely, with respect to the dictate that there are external referents (or external world)—but not the respect to any particular beliefs we hold on the basis of the senses. The unspecific dictate or belief that there is an external referent to sensation requires 'faith', but specific dictates or beliefs about those referents require considered 'judgments', rather than 'faith', as to their accuracy. Again, the realm of the external is itself divided so as to correspond to both faith (in general) and judgement (in particulars).

Newman, then, is speaking quite literally when he says that he disagrees with those who put 'faith in the fidelity of the senses on a level of intimacy and necessity with consciousness of our being or its primary modes' (39). (Though this as a criticism of Ward is contradicted by the later criticism that Ward separates consciousness off as the single indubitable of its kind (71).) 'Fidelity' here is presumably meant in the sense of reliability as to external claims, either general or specific. He is not, however, speaking strictly when he distinguishes himself from those who 'make the case of the

[17] *Philosophical Notebook* II, pp. 41, 71, 75.

senses and the case of memory one and the same' (43), for he too makes the case of the memory and the case of the senses the same in so far as he treats their status as acts and their reliability as to external claims in parallel fashion. Both memory and sense have inner and outer dimensions. Similarly, he seems to conflate at times the 'broad' line between inner and outer (71) with the 'broad & deep' line between 'reliance on reason and conscience' and 'trust-worthiness' of the impressions of sense or the existence of matter (41)—reliance on, or the reliability of, reason is a matter of judge-ment (as opposed to intuition or faith) and so lies on the same side of the divide as the reliability of the senses.

Newman admits that he has not proven that the trustworthiness of the senses is not on a par with consciousness and its modes (63), but the divide between inner and outer which is central to his thought seems to preclude the possibility that they could be on a par. (Moreover, his position at this stage seems congruent with or even called for by his lengthy discussion in an unpublished paper on 'Intuition' (1860?) concerning the conditions of the putative intuition that 'what the universal human nature assents to' or 'what the mind naturally assents to' is 'true'.[18]) In spite of the sharpness of the divide, however, he sees the reliability of the testimony of the faculties as providentially generated—'those instincts come from God'.[19] This is not a guarantee of infallibility, however, because Newman continues to believe what his early sermon 'Re-ligious Faith Rational' made clear—namely, that the faculties do deceive us on occasion. The guarantee is rather that in particular cases we can in principle, by using them, discover and correct our errors. Judgements as to the accuracy of the performance of our faculties are 'blessed' by the Author of our nature (169). That God *'means* me to *use* the senses', he says, 'forms a basis for the belief in the senses' (66), and this is complemented by the repetition of the University sermon claim that we are bidden by God to trust the information we gain through our natural faculties, so it *must* be sufficient for our needs (67). Newman's rather surprising refer-ence to believing things (which others take for granted on the basis of the senses) only because 'the Church tells me' (39) is muted into the claim that the awareness of the being of a God gives him a 'guiding truth, which gives a practical direction to my judgement

[18] *T.P.*, pp. 65–7.
[19] *L.D.*, XXIV, 294 (25 July, 1869).

& faith as regards a variety of other truths or professed truths which encounter me, as the trustworthiness of the senses' (63).

Two main differences with Reid are apparent at this point. First, his distinction between intuition and faith, depending as it does on the inner/outer distinction, contrasts strongly with Reid's position. For Reid, whatever sanction the constitution of our nature provides cannot be divided up that way. Secondly, Newman seems to have a 'providential guarantee' of our faith in our faculties which Reid saw as illustrating the Cartesian circle which he was at great pains to avoid.[20]

Given this background about the position as expressed in the bulk of the paper, it is interesting to consider now a passage which, though not chronologically first (8 March 1860), is found opposite page one:

> If our consciousness ⟨perception⟩ of our existence is to be taken as true and to be trusted, then our consciousness ⟨perception⟩ of something external to us, answering both to phenomena & to typical principles or ideas is true and to be trusted. We must take ourselves for what we are—we cannot divide between the mind and its gifts—we only know the mind *through* its gifts & powers. (30)

This passage, which has a decidedly Reidian cast, appears ironically to use Newman's own argument (that mutual implication guarantees the equal status of the things implicated) to make the very point he argues against in the remainder of the paper—namely, that the reliability of the senses is on a par with the recognition of consciousness. It seems effectively to reject the distinction on which he had depended earlier.

What is clear, and intriguing, is that we begin in this passage to get language that sounds very much like his position as it is later found in the *Grammar*—not the language of trusting, to be sure, but the language of taking ourselves 'for what we are'. And it is this idea which seems to underlie his now very significant dissatisfaction with the notion, which others seem to use so easily, of 'trusting' our faculties.

In the *Grammar* he explicitly limits his consideration of the question of trust in our faculties to (1) reasoning and memory, and (2) the question of their 'telling truly' rather than of their exercise as such,[21] and in great part the themes are those found in his earlier

---

[20] See Chap. 6 above.

[21] Page 60. Further references in parentheses will be to the *Grammar*.

writings on the topic. But there is an important shift in the insights informing his response to scepticism.

He announces that shift dramatically by refusing to 'call the trustworthiness of the faculties of memory and reasoning one of our first principles' (61). The first argument he presents for that refusal is that we cannot trust either faculty as such because 'its acts are often inaccurate, nor do we invariably assent to them' (61). This theme that the faculties deceive us is found in his earliest writings up to and including the *Grammar* (261), in spite of Meynell's repeated criticism of the view. According to Meynell:

We are deceived in the *use* we make of what it [memory] presents to us, confusing and mistaking, and misreading: so likewise is it in the *use* of reason we err; reason itself is infallible. If Memory or reason really ever once *lied*, absolutely, how should we believe it another time.[22]

Such a position depends on Meynell's distinguishing between 'reason' and 'reasoning' or between 'the guide' and 'the guided subject'.[23] Newman, however, rather uncharacteristically, seems not to have made any qualification at all in the *Grammar* in response to Meynell on this matter.

The 'Proof of Theism' theme that we do not have 'faith' in the accuracy of particular exercises of the faculties, but rather have considered judgements as to their accuracy, is translated in the *Grammar* into having trust in such considered judgements. He writes:

At most we trust in particular acts of memory and reasoning ... we may be said to trust the mental act, by which the object of our assent is verified. (60)

But this does not mean that we 'trust' that our faculties are generally reliable.

His real 'ground' for his reluctance to use the language of 'trust', however—it is, he says, 'unphilosophical'—is that 'we are as little able to accept or reject our mental constitution, as our being' (61). This echoes the mutual implication argument elaborated in the 'Proof of Theism', and the claim that we cannot divide the mind from its gifts for we only know the mind through its gifts. But the main insight that informs the argument of this later discussion is the one adumbrated in the atypical fragment at the beginning of

---

[22] *L.D.*, XXIV, 307–8 (16 Aug. 1869).
[23] Ibid., 360 (23 Oct. 1869).

the 'Proof of Theism'—namely, that 'we must take ourselves for what we are'. He writes crisply:

We are what we are, and we use, not trust our faculties ... We act according to our nature, by means of ourselves, when we remember or reason. We are as little able to accept or reject our mental constitution, as our being. We have not the option ... We do not confront or bargain with ourselves. (61).

The paragraph contains in a nutshell the core of Newman's appeal to the sanction of 'the natural' underlying his response to scepticism. To *use* our faculties is not to *trust* them because to speak of 'trust' is to imply that we have a choice or option—and that, he admitted, was to open the way to scepticism. It is to speak as if there were a separate standpoint from which we could judge our performance—as if 'we' could be different from our faculties, as if we could 'confront' ourselves—and that is 'unreal'.

What lies behind each of these weighty claims? At the very least Newman is saying that 'we are what we are'—this is simply what we do. But that—the sceptic would respond—just shows that we have to trust, not that we are right or justified in trusting. Newman goes further by suggesting that there is something conceptually wrong and misleading about the category of 'trust'. To speak of 'trust' at all is to imply that both trusting and not-trusting are intelligible and coherent alternatives—that we can equally coherently choose either in principle, even if we cannot in fact. And that is what the sceptic claims—even if we cannot as a matter of contingent fact avoid trusting our faculties, to not trust them is a coherent notion and, moreover, the only 'justifiable' option. Necessity or unavoidability, the sceptic reminds us, says nothing about the truth or justification of our beliefs. We have to trust our faculties, he admits, but we are not justified in doing so because there is always the 'possibility' that we could be mistaken.

Newman is suggesting that the concept of 'trust' in our faculties is an idle one because it is not possible to frame a genuine question about it. He explains:

I am what I am, or I am nothing. I cannot think, reflect, or judge about my being, without starting from the very point which I aim at concluding. (347)

We cannot, that is, genuinely question the reliability of our faculties without using them and implicitly, therefore, deciding the question in their favour. Conceptually the concept of 'trust' is idle because it is impossible to *judge* our faculties as unreliable without using them and so declaring their reliability. Even the discovery that they err is an affirmation of their ultimate reliability since it is we, using them, who in principle can discover the error. Any attempt to answer the question of trustworthiness in general at all, or even to frame it, assumes a positive answer—the inquiry then is a pseudo-inquiry, because it is circular. He writes, for example, 'if nothing is to be assumed, what is our very method of reasoning but an assumption? and what our nature itself?' (377). Reid, as we saw earlier, argues for the idleness and circularity of the sceptic's challenge in the same way.

For Newman, the language of 'trust' is ruled out because the possiblity of distrust is ruled out—'If I do not use myself, I have no other self to use' (347), and if I use myself I cannot at the same time genuinely put myself in question. Without the possibility of genuine questioning there is no sense to be made of talk of rejecting our mental constitution; without the possibility of rejecting, there is no sense to be made of talk of accepting or trusting. Earlier, in the 'Proof of Theism' he had explicitly paralleled 'scepticism' and 'faith' or 'trust',[24] but he saw the problem then as simply one of rejecting the notion of 'trust' with respect to what is internal to us. Now he is repeating the parallelism, but extending it, untrammelled by the constraints of the inner/outer distinction. He thus brings himself into line with Reid's position—and, in so far as he refuses to use the word 'trust', he goes beyond Reid's position.

He makes another significant shift as well, which shows the similarity with Reid. Reid's response to scepticism criticized the need to depend on belief in God to justify trust in our faculties. Reid wrote:

He who is persuaded that he is the workmanship of God, and that it is a part of his constitution to believe his senses, may think that a good reason to confirm his belief. But he had the belief before he could give this or any other reason for it.[25]

Thus, as we saw in Chapter 6, belief in God is clearly not employed in a Cartesian manner in the battle against scepticism—Reid effec-

---

[24] *Philosophical Notebook* II, p. 37. [25] *Works*, 329: II, 20. See Chap. 6 above.

tively distinguishes between ontological dependence and epistemological dependence.

For Newman too belief in God ceases to be the *ground* of his
response to the sceptic. He claims, as we saw earlier, 'that the laws
of our mind are the expression ... of His will' *but* he adds, 'I should
be bound by them even were they not His laws'.[26] This crucial
qualification seems to confirm the claim in the earlier *Present Position of Catholics* that first principles come *either* 'from heaven, *or*
from the nature of things, *or* from the nature of man'.[27] There is
warrant then for the suggestion that Newman's appeal is ultimately
simply to the constitution of our nature—that nature is normative
even if it were not expressing God's will. The sanction lies within
human nature—there is no 'justification' for those laws of the mind
independent of our practices. The unintelligibility of the notion of
choice in such a case precludes our reliance being justified or unjustified. All we have is what is 'natural'.

This is why Newman can say: 'It is enough for the proof of the
value and authority of any function which I possess, to be able to
pronounce that it is natural.'[28] To repeat, what is 'natural' is determined by appeal to the 'common voice of mankind' because

That is to be accounted a normal operation of our nature, which men in
general do actually instance. That is a law of our minds, which is exemplified in action on a large scale, whether *a priori* it ought to be a law or
no.[29]

The 'natural' is found in the 'practice of mankind' which Locke
neglects (160). It is found, Newman says (and here we can as easily
hear Reid speaking as Newman), in the 'common sense and universal practice of man'.[30] The sanction of the 'natural', for Newman as for Reid, lies in universal agreement in 'what we do' as

---

[26] *Grammar*, p. 351.

[27] *P.P.C.*, p. 293, ital. mine. I am agreeing with Sillem (*Philosophical Notebook
I*, p. 66n.) that the appeal to God becomes 'secondary and corroborative', and with
Boekraad (*Argument From Conscience to the Existence of God*, p. 164) that one can
determine the value of the mind for Newman apart from considerations of Providence. These conclusions, however, are not unproblematical since Newman also
claims that 'we may securely take them as they are, and use them as we find them'
because 'He gave them to us, and *He can overrule them* for us' (*Grammar*, p. 351,
ital. mine). Perhaps Newman too can best be understood in terms here of the
distinction between epistemological and ontological dependence.

[28] *Grammar*, p. 347.

[29] Ibid., p. 344.

[30] *T.P.*, p. 129 (25 Sept. 1865).

evidenced in 'the tenor of human conduct' and the 'structure of language'.

Newman is attempting to offer the sceptic more than simple counter-description of the necessity of trusting our faculties. He is interpreting what the sceptic sees as merely the necessity of our nature, interpreting it in light of a philosophical position which argues for the unintelligibility of the notion of choice (and hence of 'trust') in such a case—because there is no standpoint from which we can judge the *general* status of our faculties, no place more sure to stand from which to challenge the validity of our natural responses in general.[31] So though doubt is 'possible', there is nothing on the basis of which it could be in this case 'reasonable'.[32] Just as his understanding of the relevance of 'trust' developed, so did his view of the sufficiency of the information we gain from our faculties. Both 'Religious Faith Rational' and 'The Theory of Developments in Religious Doctrine' emphasize practical sufficiency in a very Lockean manner. Such sufficiency is coupled with the notion of necessity in order to bypass the issue of whether we can rightly trust our faculties or whether they provide more than just 'the truth of things quite well enough to act upon'.[33] Newman's 1871 emendation of the University sermon, however, clarifies his position, for he claims there a speculative though imperfect grasp of truth possible to our faculties: 'The senses convey to the mind substantial truth, in so far as they bring home to us that certain things are, and *in confuso*, what they are'.[34] Thus, Newman's understanding of why it is 'unphilosophical to speak of trusting ourselves'[35] is formed by considerations which preclude the need to resign ourselves to less than the possibility of total and legitimate certainty.

[31] It is this which precludes the reasonableness of universal doubt. Newman is as insistent as Reid on this, emphasizing the role and relevance of credulity (*Grammar*, pp. 377, 54).

[32] It is interesting to note that Newman illustrates the unreasonableness of doubt, as Reid did, by reference to a man 'made of glass'; he writes that in some cases 'it is imperative, or it is a duty ⟨there is a call of common sense or of duty⟩ to be certain ... e.g. that we are not made of glass ...' (*T.P.*, p. 121 (1865)). Reid had used that same image in both the *Inquiry* and *Essays on the Intellectual Powers* (*Works*, 100: II,§3; 209: VII,§4; 259: II,5. It should be noted that Descartes (First Meditation) and Locke used the image as well.

[33] *P.P.S.*, p. 194.

[34] *U.S.*, p. 349n.

[35] *Grammar*, p. 60.

By way of conclusion to these chapters on Newman's thought, I want to address briefly an issue which is raised especially with respect to Newman, but which touches on another aspect of the relation of scepticism to the theological commitments of Reid and Newman. In the study I have tried to show that Newman's account is similar to Reid's in important ways—one additional way concerns the relation between scepticism and the legitimation of theistic belief.

Reid has always been represented quite unproblematically as an anti-sceptic. And although the complexity revealed in Hume's account has correspondingly revealed more subtlety in Reid's account, few would be tempted to label him a sceptic. And this is presumably just what one would expect given Reid's theological position. But the situation has been different with Newman, for, though a theist, he has by more than one commentator been placed in the sceptic's camp. Leslie Stephen and T. H. Huxley are classic examples and they have contemporary counterparts.[36] In his life of Newman, Wilfrid Ward gave the following reminder of Huxley's view:

Yet when Huxley said that he could compile a primer of infidelity from Newman's writings, those who knew them best saw at once the grounds for such a misreading. The sceptic's mind was vividly present to Newman's imagination.[37]

It was a 'misreading' for which Newman gave grounds,[38] but it was nevertheless a misreading, for Newman did not use scepticism as a way of defending religious beliefs as many others have done. Such a combination of religious conviction with scepticism about reason, aptly called 'sceptical fideism', has historically assumed a variety of forms,[39] but it has always been at heart a view which undermines the potential of reason in order to legitimate the acceptance of beliefs which are either against or above reason. Though Newman very explicitly attempts to show the importance

[36] Stephen touches on this in various essays, but he makes this particular charge against Newman in 'Newman's Theory of Belief', *An Agnostic's Apology* (London, 1903), pp. 168–241, esp. 180, 182, 238–9.

[37] *Life of J. H. Cardinal Newman* I (New York, 1912), p. 16.

[38] See the revised version of Newman's reply to A. M. Fairbairn's article (*Contemporary Review*, October and May 1885), printed in *Stray Essays on Controversial Points*, Essay III, esp. §§50–5. This is also found in *T.P.*, pp. 140–57.

[39] See Terence Penelhum, *God and Scepticism*, esp. Chaps. 1–5.

of context and the bearing of person-variance on rational believing, he—no less than Reid—was attempting to defend the potential of reason from an attack which narrowed it. Though both admitted that reason had limits,[40] neither Reid nor Newman denigrated reason in the interests of religious faith—what they did was to show the limits of a particular restrictive view of the achievements of reason. Newman's account, then, is just as anti-sceptical as Reid's.

Moreover, neither Reid nor Newman uses an argument common to sceptical fideists—namely, an argument which attempts to show the parity or analogy between belief in God and belief in common-sense matters. Such an argument, which has a modern form as well,[41] uses the sceptic's undermining of the rational justification of everyday beliefs (external world, other minds, etc.), coupled with an attempted analogy between such beliefs and belief in God, to put such theistic belief in the same category as the others—namely, rationally unjustified, but nevertheless acceptable. It is an attempt to put belief in God at the same level as indispensable everyday beliefs. But, whether it is successful or not, neither Reid nor Newman uses such a parity argument; they do not attempt to put belief in God at the level of the fundamental unreasoned-to principles which are their starting-points. Reid, for example, depends on a 'natural theology', emphasizing the importance for it of what he calls 'the argument from final causes'.[42] Such an argument for 'the existence and perfections of the Deity' has for its major premiss the first principle 'That design and intelligence in the cause, may, with certainty be inferred from marks or signs of it in the effect', and for its minor premiss the observation 'that there are in fact the clearest marks of design and wisdom in the works of nature'. The 'conclusion' which we derive is clearly an inference of a different status from first principles.

Newman too recognizes an obvious difference between theistic belief and the belief in conscience which is for him a starting-point. He writes:

[40] See Chap. 7, n. 46, above. Cf. also Reid's Preface to the *Essays* in the *Works*, p. 216.

[41] See Penelhum, *God and Skepticism*, Chap. 7; cf. my 'A Common Defense of Theistic Belief: Some Critical Considerations' for a critique of the parity or analogy argument in the work of Norman Malcolm, John Miller, and Alvin Plantinga (*International Journal for Philosophy of Religion* 14 (1983)).

[42] *Works*, 460-1: VI,6. Cf. his *Lectures on Natural Theology*.

Ward thinks I hold that moral obligation is, because there is a God. But I hold just the reverse, viz. there is a God, because there is moral obligation.[43]

He adds in the *Grammar* that to prove either the 'Being of a God' or His attributes or to gain a 'real' apprehension of Him, we 'must start from some first principle; and that first principle, which I assume and shall not attempt to prove, is ... that we have by nature a conscience'.[44] Elsewhere he says that from 'the witness of nature' we can gain a notional assent to the 'natural' truth that there is one God, though we need to appeal to conscience to gain a 'real' or imaginative apprehension.[45] Thus, neither Newman nor Reid put belief in God at the level of first principles—they fully admit significant differences in status.

[43] *Philosophical Notebook* II, p. 31 (7 Nov. 1859).
[44] *Grammar*, pp. 104–5.
[45] Ibid., pp. 98, 100, 102 ff.

Concluding Applications

THE aim of the preceding project has not been simply interpretation of these historical figures, but more importantly an attempt to see what they can tell us about the relationship between belief, action, and scepticism. The works of Wilkins, Hume, Reid, and Newman directly or indirectly suggest various forms scepticism can assume, and they illustrate various forms anti-sceptical responses based on appeal to human nature ('the natural', the instinctive, and the universal) can assume. My analyses have concentrated primarily on the determination of the character and status of their naturalist anti-sceptical responses, and in this concluding chapter I want to comment on those responses.

In Chapter 2 I argued that Wilkins's position is best read as proposing that certainty is constituted by the absence of reasonable doubt, and that such certainty is more than simply the assurance necessary for practical needs. His suggestion of a 'threshold' model of certainty paralleling that of truth supports a view of such certainty as equal in both assurance and legitimacy to demonstrative certainty. Such a view, I argued, differed from that explicitly offered by Locke (and by Chillingworth). I thus challenge a common reading of the relation between Locke and the tradition preceding him by highlighting his difference on this matter with Wilkins. But more importantly I introduce an understanding of the status of the certainty constituted by the absence of reasonable doubt, an understanding from which Locke diverted attention and which was taken up again by thinkers after him and significantly utilized in their responses to scepticism.

Chapter 3 considers Hume's critique of Locke's view of probability as a first, though not fully consistent or explicit, attempt to take up the earlier view of the relation between certainty and unreasonable doubt. I argue that Hume suggests, at least at times, an answer to the sceptic which incorporates both the notion of 'unreasonable' doubt and an appeal to the constitution of human nature in such a way as to offer to the sceptic more than merely counter-description of the irresistibility of natural beliefs. To repeat, if Hume was aware of and did not misunderstand Locke's claim that in cases of the highest probability we are put 'past doubting', he must have seen his category of 'proof' as implying more than Locke thought was true of the highest probability. If Hume only meant the certainty of proof to refer to a description of assurance with no implications concerning legitimacy, he would have been making no substantive change in Locke's position, for Locke already conceded that much. In criticizing the inadequacy of Locke's dichotomy, Hume had, whether consistently and knowingly or not, re-emphasized aspects of the earlier tradition in such a way as to imply, at least at times, the beginning of a response to scepticism which challenged the sceptic's philosophical thesis. And this response was progressively elaborated and defended by thinkers after him.

I have not suggested that there are no differences between Hume and the naturalist tradition which followed him. Rather, I have suggested what Reid himself seemed to suggest—namely, that there is in Hume's thought an implicit admission of many of the points he makes against Hume, and that his project can be seen in an important sense as rendering explicit, or drawing out the implications of, the 'naturalist' reserve in Hume's thought, while extracting it from a context in which other elements challenge its legitimacy.

The remaining chapters examine in detail that progressive elaboration and defence of a naturalist response to scepticism. I have argued there that, although Reid and Newman differ in significant ways, they share fundamental commitments which inform their responses to scepticism. In particular, both continue (Newman more explicitly than Reid) the development and defence of the model of non-demonstrative certainty which was initiated by Wilkins. Incidentally I suggested that their common criticisms of Locke make more sense if Locke is seen as departing from the position on certainty advocated by Wilkins, which was similar to their own proposals. Moreover, their understandings of the philosophical legitimacy of converging probabilities with a critical threshold share more with each other than with Butler's understanding of such certainty. In other words, although it is generally admitted that Wilkins was an influence on Butler, and that Butler was an influence on both Reid and Newman, I have suggested that a distinctive element in the proposals by Wilkins (in an incipient form) and Reid and Newman is not found in Butler.

It is important to distinguish this view of a threshold concept of certainty from a contemporary philosophical proposal which might, at first glance, seem similar. Peter Unger's defence of scepticism proposes the concept of certainty as an 'absolute term' (like 'flat')—one which only misleadingly admits of 'constructions of degree', but which actually has no degrees.[1] The 'threshold' concept which I have suggested is part of these naturalist responses to scepticism and Unger's 'absolute term' both deny that certainty is a matter of degrees, but Unger's proposal has the unfortunate and implausible consequence that 'As a matter of logical necessity, if someone is certain of something, then there never is anything of which he is more certain'.[2] In other words, 'if it is logically possible that there be something of which a person might be more certain than he is now of a given thing, then he is not really certain of that given thing'. His conclusion: we ought either to accept or suspend judgement about the proposition 'That, in the case of every human being, [since knowledge requires certainty] there is hardly anything at all, which the person knows to be so'.[3] For Unger, an absolute term (e.g. certainty) only applies correctly when what the correlative ('relative') term (e.g. doubt) denotes is not present 'at all',[4] and until doubt is ruled out absolutely it is still present in varying degrees. The degrees do not stop until doubt is impossible—the possibility of doubt equals the presence of doubt. Unger implies that despite an agent's claim to have no doubt (and hence be certain), there either *should* still be some or *must* still be some (his claims to the contrary notwithstanding) until the matter is absolutely indubitable. His concept of certainty equates unreasonable doubt with impossible doubt, and the result is that we cannot correctly say that anyone is certain of anything.[5] The threshold

---

[1] 'A Defense of Scepticism', in *Essays on Knowledge and Justification*, eds. George S. Pappas and Marshall Swain, pp. 317–36.

[2] Ibid., p. 332.

[3] Ibid., p. 336.   [4] Ibid., p. 326.

[5] James Cargile's general criticism of Unger's thesis is that he judges ordinary linguistic usage to be misguided, without offering reasons for his alternative prescriptions. The more specific objection, with which I agree totally, is that 'it is wrong to think that ruling out the logical possibility of error is always a case of leaving less "room" for error, or that not ruling out the logical possibility of error is automatically to leave "room" for error' ('In Reply to "A Defense of Scepticism"', *Essays on Knowledge and Justification*, p. 339).

concept of certainty, on the contrary, does not have such implications. It argues that certainty is achieved when all reasonable doubt is ruled out, and that there is no sense to the claim that there can be 'more' of an *absence* of all reasonable doubt—but it allows both that (1) one may be certain of many different things, and (2) it may take differing amounts and kinds of evidence to bring one to the critical threshold.

More importantly, informing Reid's and Newman's common view of certainty is a shared commitment to what I have called the sanction of 'the natural'. This appeal, present as well in Wilkins, and variously couched as an appeal to the laws of the mind (nature, our constitution) or the common voice of mankind, is an appeal to what is evident in what we in fact as human beings say and do. This, I suggested, was at the heart of their anti-sceptical responses and was a more significant element in those responses than any of their admitted differences. Once again their responses to Locke emphasize this. In Newman it is especially clear that his objection to Locke is directed against the methodology which precluded him from admitting more than the achievement of practical certainty in non-demonstrative cases, but both Reid and Newman share a criticism of Locke's methodological refusal to consider as philosophically relevant 'what all men call' knowledge or certainty. Moreover, Reid's anti-sceptical response contains an attack on the causal model of knowing which Locke exemplified—for example, Reid's general objection to a mind/body analogy constitutes an attack on a model of epistemic justification which requires spatial contiguity (ideas as 'impressions'), and this objection is made specific in his criticism of the epistemic ills inherent in the Aristotelian notion of phantasm or species which led to the vacillation he attributes to Locke and others between ideas as things in the brain and ideas as things in the mind.[6] The criticism of Locke is that his causal explanatory account, like his epistemological standards, is a priori speculation, the result of his failure to describe what counts for all men as knowledge or certainty. The question is how far from Locke's causal model of justification their criticisms of Locke take Reid and Newman. I have argued that they are not simply rejecting Locke's model for another more accurate model of the

---

[6] Richard Rorty makes these suggestions, *Philosophy and the Mirror of Nature*, pp. 142–6, though he does not make clear whether he thinks Reid, like Kant, gets half-way away from a causal model but falls back into one that is parasitical on it.

same kind (a better causal account), but rather moving toward a model in which the 'common practice of mankind' plays the central role.

A. DESCRIPTION, GRAMMAR, AND THE A PRIORI

Newman's *Grammar of Assent* has been termed a 'psychology of belief' and he has been praised as a psychologist.[7] But it has, on the other hand, been suggested that his choice of title is deliberate rather than a matter of fashion; what he offers can properly be described as a grammar. As one Newman scholar has insightfully concluded:

[Newman] tries to let the facts of the mind speak for themselves, and not assert anything *a priori*. Just as the grammarian confines his efforts to extracting from actual use the laws of language, so Newman aims at tracing out the structures of thought from his observations of mental life in its entirety, without any attempt at evaluation. His intention is expressed clearly in the title of his chief work, *The Grammar of Assent*.[8]

This is in line with how Friedrich Waismann characterizes grammar; grammar includes, he writes,

all the enormous number of conventions which, though nowhere expressly formulated, are presupposed in the understanding of everyday language. It is precisely the formulating and bringing to consciousness of these tacit conventions, the discovery of this complicated network of rules which constitutes the philosophical clarification of our ideas.[9]

Grammar is not simply description of practice, but description of the norms generated in practice. Genuine description cannot be a priori, and prescription cannot be arrived at without regard to description. Newman does not attempt to say a priori what should be practised; nor does he evaluate the norms he abstracts. In this sense there is no 'attempt at evaluation'. But the description he aims at is clearly meant to allow him to correct illegitimate usage,

---

[7] Aldous Huxley remarked that 'Among the psychologists who have been of assistance to me, I must give a high place to Cardinal Newman, whose analysis of the psychology of thought remains one of the most acute, as it is certainly the most elegant, which has ever been made' (*Proper Studies* (London, 1957), p. xix, Introduction).

[8] J. H. Walgrave, *Newman the Theologian*, trans. A. V. Littledale (New York, 1960), p. 73.

[9] *Principles of Linguistic Philosophy*, ed. R. Harré (London, 1965), pp. 13-14.

so it is description of norms (of what counts as certain, for example), rather than merely empirical generalization.

An attempt to formulate a grammar cannot, by definition, be a priori. But one might extract 'from actual use the laws of language' and yet not have a genuinely socio-linguistic model of justification, for part of what is crucial to such a model is the source of validation. And this possibility is pointed to by Leslie Stephen's nineteenth-century characterization of common-sense philosophy as an 'attempt at *a priori* philosophy'.[10] It is clear that the charge cannot rightly be that it is a priori in methodology, since we have seen over and over that Reid and Newman vehemently rejected the a priorism they saw in Locke. But perhaps Stephen is pointing to another way in which the enterprise in which Reid and Newman are engaged might be said to have an a priori character (a way equally incompatible with a socio-linguistic model of justification), and I suggest that consideration of that possibility can make clearer both the relevance of their appeal to description and their understanding of the sanction of the natural.

Stephen's suggestion that common-sense philosophy is an a priori philosophy can be read as the suggestion that the description to which Reid and Newman refer is of a priori principles or laws of the human constitution whose validity is independent of and prior to experience. Description in such a case would merely reveal conformity to norms which are given outside of and prior to experience. In this sense what everybody says or does reveals a constitutive principle—description reveals how we are providentially guided so as to conform to norms independent of human practice.[11] But I have argued that neither Reid nor Newman necessarily saw description as related to norms in this way. They are concerned, rather, with describing norms which are generated *by* the

[10] Stephen, *History of English Thought in the Eighteenth Century*, Vol. I (New York, 1962), p. 61.

[11] It has been suggested that Reid's constitutive principles are like the principles of Kant which transcendentally constitute experience. One early comparison between Reid and Kant, sympathetic yet critical, is by Andrew Seth (Pringle-Pattison), who suggests that, though in agreement on principles which 'are the source of a necessity which sense, as sense, cannot give', nevertheless, 'Reid and Kant part company entirely on the question of the reality of our knowledge, of what it is that we know' (*The Scottish Philosophy*, 3rd edn. (Edinburgh, 1889), pp. 115, 148. Baruch Brody has a relevant discussion in 'Hume, Reid and Kant on Causality', in *Thomas Reid: Critical Interpretations*. M. F. Sciacca's comparison between Reid and Kant is unsympathetic to Reid, in *La Filosofia di Tomaso Reid*.

'common practice of men'—whether they ought to be norms or not, as Newman would say. Newman's understanding of what constitutes the validity of those norms is made clear in Chapter 9—he sees the laws of our constitution as valid (1) whether they ought to be laws or not—i.e. it makes no sense to speak of an 'ought' in such a case, and (2) whether they are God's will or not. Newman thus rejects an a priori account both of methodology and of what constitutes conformity to appropriate norms. His rejection of a priorism is thus the obverse side of his attempt to give us a 'grammar' of assent.

Reid claims to be doing 'anatomy of the mind', but he speaks, in a Berkeleian mode, of the more general task of 'legitimate explanation' being 'to fashion a grammar of this language [of nature]'.[12] I suggest that his project in the *Inquiry* and *Essays on the Intellectual Powers* can be construed as a grammar on the above model. Reid rejects the causal explanatory model of justification, despite his reliance on the God-givenness of our constitution, when he does not require belief in God to warrant our trust in our faculties (*Works*, 329: II,20). But it should be emphasized again that in addition to rejecting the guarantee provided by God, he also rejects the guarantee provided by the irresistibility of our nature. To repeat, he writes concerning the constitution of our nature: 'If we are deceived in it, we are deceived by Him that made us, and there is no remedy' (130: V,§7). In the same vein, he writes in response to the sceptic's question why he believes that external objects exist:

The belief, sir, is none of my manufacture; it came from the mint of Nature; it bears her image and superscription; and, if it is not right, the fault is not mine. (183: VI,§20)

We have no guarantee—that something is natural does not mean that it is 'true'. The norms we describe are generated by practice; they do not get their validity by conforming to something outside and independent of such practice. The sanction of the natural derives, not from such conformity but from the fact that 'If these common notions were removed, human plans ... could have neither measure nor end and everything would of necessity be turned upside down'.[13] What legitimates is that it is unreasonable

[12] Philosophical Oration (1756), p. C-3.
[13] Ibid., p. C-5.

to doubt—and what makes something unreasonable to doubt is not that it is irresistible, but rather that there is nothing more sure on the basis of which to mount a challenge. It is irresistible because doubt of it is unreasonable, not vice versa. Even Reid's foundationalism is consistent with adoption of a socio-linguistic model of justification as long as the self-evidence of foundations is understood in terms of a particular kind of embeddedness in a socio-linguistic context—in terms of unreasonable doubt rather than a kind of Cartesian self-intimation.

B. NATURALISM—SCEPTICAL OR ANTI-SCEPTICAL

In the background of all the preceding discussions there has been an implicit distinction between at least three main types of naturalism. The first is what I call 'Sceptical Naturalism'; the others can be termed 'Reasonable Doubt Naturalism' and 'Justifying Naturalism.' That not all naturalism is anti-sceptical needs to be said here as a reminder of a point made several times in this work. One variety of naturalism, often attributed to Hume, offers merely the counter-description of unavoidability of natural beliefs with no challenge to the sceptic's requirements, and so remains distinctively sceptical. It accepts the sceptic's challenge to the legitimacy of natural beliefs, and responds with an emphasis on an alternative resource—the unavoidableness of instinct, the irresistibility of non-rational aspects of human nature.

Contrasted with such sceptical naturalism are two kinds of anti-sceptical naturalist responses—anti-sceptical because they offer a challenge to the sceptic's requirements for justification. The first, 'Reasonable Doubt Naturalism', centrally depends on a distinction between reasonable and unreasonable doubt, and argues that there is no reasonable ground for doubting fundamental beliefs of human nature. The level of things the sceptic challenges is somehow prior to the practice of justification which employs the forms of the things in question. We cannot 'justify' these sorts of things because at that level there is nothing to count for or against. This form of naturalism claims that justification and rationality are themselves 'practices'. What counts as justification has developed— there is no necessity built into these particular practices such that only they could have been generated. But there is no other appeal.

The undermining of the attempt to show unjustifiability of our basic beliefs is not in itself an attempt to 'justify' them, but rather to show that they are more basic than things that can be justified. Unless we believed those things we couldn't have justification at all. 'Reasonable Doubt Naturalism' sees description and norms tied closely together because description is *of* norms that have been established. We are concerned not simply with description of what is being done, but with description of the norms generated by practice. What links description and norms is that description reveals the norms that have been established in the practices we describe.

Such a response addresses directly the level of first principles and indirectly the level of conclusions of 'probable' reasoning. One might argue that this ought not to be called a philosophical response since it 'undermines' rationality by showing it to be a practice. Admittedly, it suggests that the sceptic's argument is philosophically nonsensical and renders contrary argument similarly nonsensical, but one can see it as a philosophical argument nevertheless, because it is an argument at the level of the sceptic's, rather than an uncritical attempt to evade the challenge.

'Justifying Naturalism' also appeals to what we do, and to natural human resources, but, not content simply to deflect the charge of 'unjustified', it positively attempts to *justify* in one of two ways. It can build on 'Reasonable Doubt Naturalism' and attempt to link together what is natural and what is justified (e.g. by providential creation, or other justification by origin). Or it can revert to the same level as the sceptical challenge and offer an alternative standard of justification. In either of these modes it is not, as 'Reasonable Doubt Naturalism' is, a rejection of the sceptic's demand for justification, but rather a rejection of a particular model of justification as alone legitimate.

In the preceding study of Reid and Newman it has sometimes been difficult to distinguish 'Reasonable Doubt Naturalism' from 'Justifying Naturalism', since both kinds of naturalism can assume the form of a rejection of an analytic paradigm of certainty and since for both thinkers such a rejection was a critical part of their anti-sceptical responses. But in the case of the rejection of an analytic paradigm in 'Justifying Naturalism', the defence of non-demonstrative certainty is not necessarily seen as grounded in practice. I have made the claim, however, that, although 'Justifying

Naturalism' can at times be found in both thinkers, there is strong warrant for attributing to them 'Reasonable Doubt Naturalism', with its validation in human practice.

C. CAN THE SCEPTIC LIVE HIS SCEPTICISM?

One way of assessing the naturalist responses of Reid and Newman is to review them from the perspective provided by a brief schematic presentation of a variety of contemporary responses to the question 'Can the sceptic live his scepticism?' The most extreme sceptical position would be that said to be ideally taken by Pyrrho himself—namely, having no beliefs at all and refraining from acting in ways appropriate to the beliefs held by others. In other words, it consists in absolute suspension of both judgement and action. But that obviously untenable position can be modified (as it was by Sextus Empiricus) so as to allow action in accordance with appearances, while requiring total suspension of judgement. Such action, however, according to this position implies no judgement whether something really is the case.

The standard objection to such a position, which as we saw in Chapter 6 was expressed even by Hume, is that the sceptic cannot live such a scepticism. But contemporary discussions of scepticism provide a variety of responses to the question whether it is possible, or to what degree it is possible. Myles Burnyeat argues a minimalist position, claiming that the sceptic cannot live with no belief at all, because he at least has meta-beliefs about the justificatory stalemate between p and not-p.[14] But he crucially concedes that the sceptic can *otherwise* live without belief because belief implies a claim that p is true (really the case).[15] Acting according to appearances is all that is necessary and such action is possible without believings of any kind, because acting according to appearances is simply assenting to being affected in particular ways. He argues that such assent to appearances is not and does not entail believings, because such impressions are passive affects which we are compelled to assent to, but which are not the sort of thing which can be true or false. They are things to be experienced, rather than

---

[14] 'Can the Skeptic Live His Skepticism?' in *The Skeptical Tradition*, ed. Myles Burnyeat (Berkeley, 1983).

[15] Ibid., pp. 121–2, 137.

believed.[16] For this reason, then, one need not read Sextus as proscribing only dogmatic beliefs; one need not read him as allowing appearances to be taken epistemically.

Burnyeat's position, then, is that assenting to and acting according to appearances is not (and does not entail) believing, because it is not claiming anything about what is really the case—with the exception of the belief that it is really the case that the arguments on opposing sides are equal and so warrant only suspense of judgement.[17] The scepticism he sees as livable is that in which one totally suspends judgement (except for the meta-belief about opposing justifications being equal) but acts in the same way non-sceptics do because one acts according to appearances. Such a mitigation of Pyrrhonism is clearly only a very limited pragmatic one. Even Hume, as we saw, goes beyond that.

Others, in line with Hume, deny that scepticism can be lived that fully; they argue that implicit in action 'according to appearances' are beliefs. Terence Penelhum, for example, argues that following appearances is not consistent with suspending judgement because acting according to appearances implies the belief that p seems to be true, or an inclination to believe p.[18] The suggestion that appearances can be taken non-epistemically is, for Penelhum, plausible at best only in the cases of sensory appearances. But not all appearances are of this kind,[19] and where they are not, following appearances implies inclinations to beliefs about them. Moreover, since belief is not voluntary, an 'inclination toward it is a mild or early stage of that condition itself'.[20]

But Penelhum goes further, introducing another part of the attack—namely, that appearances are motives for action.[21] He writes:

To permit activity, the appearances, or on our analysis the mild beliefs, have to be seen as sources of actions which would otherwise not get chosen

---

[16] Arne Naess supports such a view when he writes that '[t]o assert that something is true is one thing; to give one's impressions is quite another' (*Scepticism* (London, 1968)), p. 46; cf. also pp. 17-19.

[17] Naess denies even this, arguing that each sceptical phrase cancels itself out: 'Thus even "Not more this than that", which is said when comparing the force of argument with that of counterargument ... too cancels itself out ...' (*Scepticism*, p. 9).

[18] *God and Skepticism* (Dordrecht, 1983), p. 42.

[19] Burnyeat, 'Can the Skeptic Live His Skepticism?', p. 127.

[20] Penelhum, *God and Skepticism*, p. 42; cf. pp. 43-52.

[21] Ibid., p. 53.

and done; to offer the appearances in answer to the criticism that Skepticism does not allow action is to concede that otherwise action would not take place, which is to admit that suspense of judgement would otherwise freeze us into immobility.[22]

It is unclear whether Penelhum sees the appeal to action-guidance as a simple extension of the conclusion that the sceptic's action according to appearances implies beliefs, or whether he intends it to assume a more significant role—but it clearly assumes that more significant role for Reid. It is exactly this need of some action-guiding beliefs which I take Reid to be suggesting when he writes that the sceptic who 'keeps out of harm's way' is either hypocritical or deceived because

if the scale of his belief were so evenly poised as to lean no more to one side than to the contrary, it is impossible that his actions could be directed by any rules of common prudence. (184: VI,§20)

I would argue that even if the first part of Penelhum's argument is plausible for non-sensory appearances, it still seems reasonable to deny that acting according to sensory appearances implies a truth-claim (however mild), and it is here that Reid's appeal to action becomes necessary. The following argument can be used to support a claim that acting according to appearances implies taking the appearances epistemically.

The sceptic is, on a Pyrrhonist view, supposed simply to record the affects he experiences, with the recognition that contrary impressions had by others are equal in status to his. There is no reason for preferring one set to the other. Deference to custom, convention, etc. serves the same purpose as tossing a coin to see which of the two equally supported (or unsupported) positions to act in accord with. It is said that the sceptic acts in a particular way only because others do—not because he thinks the appearance he experiences has any more likelihood of being true (or of revealing what is the case) than its contrary. But I suggest that whatever motivates him to act in a given direction rather than another just is equal to believing that p appears to be the case. If the evidential considerations for and against p are equal, they cannot be what motivate him to act in one way rather than another. Since he acts according to custom or convention, he is responding to being

[22] *God and Skepticism.*

affected in *those* particular ways (rather than the possible contraries of custom and convention) and so grants his affects some peculiar privileged status—and *that* seems to be equivalent to believing them to be appearances.

Admittedly, that I am affected in a particular way does not warrant a claim that *p* is truly as it appears. Moreover, I can act as if *p* without believing *p*. But that I act in one way rather than another is not arbitrary, but directed by something—by my being affected in the related ways. The sceptic's claim is that the reasons for thinking that *p* rather than not-*p* is the case are equal—that I am affected in this way does not have any tie with reality (does not make it more likely that *p* is truly the case). But that I take a particular affect to direct my action rather than simply remain paralysed because of the equal likelihood of the opposing affect implies an epistemic preference for that affect, namely, for the belief supported by the affect.

Reid's point, then, would be that to say that what guides me is what others do, or what I have grown up doing, is to say none the less that I take those particular affects as having some weight over their possible contraries. That weight is an epistemic holding—one believes (it true) that that particular affect or appearance is and deserves to be action-guiding. Though the arguments on both sides are equal, a particular affect has a priority of sorts. We go by it because it is the one *we* have—we cannot live without that much attachment to self.

Penelhum concludes that the sceptic's conflict consists in a conflict between suspension of judgement and the inclination to belief (or mild belief) entailed by action in accord with appearance. In other words, the sceptic

cannot say that we are able to admit that things appear to be thus and so, yet be wholly without commitment on whether or not they are. To admit that they seem to be thus and so to him is to say that he has a mild degree of belief that they are.[23]

'The Skeptic cannot, therefore, *simultaneously* suspend judgment about *p* and follow the appearance of *p*'—though '[h]e can of course alternate these, between the study and the market-place'.[24] It is very important to an appreciation of what Reid and Newman are suggesting that we note here that Penelhum does not explicitly

[23] *God and Skepticism.*   [24] Ibid., p. 54.

take account of the distinction between first-order beliefs and meta-level beliefs—and this obscures the import of the sceptical conflict to which he points. Even if we grant Penelhum his entire case, the most it shows is that the sceptic must hold beliefs about *p* if his actions are to be guided by appearances, and that he cannot simultaneously suspend judgement about *p*. But the sceptic is still able, on this account, to believe that *p* and and also to believe that he is not justified in believing *p*. The sceptic, that is, can hold two conflicting beliefs in this way, and can live his scepticism in so far as he maintains the meta-belief which distinguishes him from the masses. Penelhum's argument does not show that a sceptic could not sustain his scepticism in this way. In fact Penelhum does not think it crucial that the sceptical meta-belief be maintained:

[S]omeone who follows a way of thought in which he regularly extinguishes his inclinations to commitment by the examination of arguments for and against each dogmatic position, can be said to live his Skepticism in spite of his occasional lapses into commitment in the marketplace.[25]

We need, he says, to go into the world to dispel sceptical doubts, and we can minimize doing that. He summarizes: 'suspense [of judgement] can properly be ascribed to someone, even in the face of temporary lapses'[26] because '[w]hat counts in judging any lapses is the fact that he is following a way of life which enables him to *contend* with them'.[27]

Reid's response to the question whether the sceptic can live his scepticism centres on this very point, however—namely, it argues that lapses from the meta-philosophical position are inevitable, and, moreover, that the inevitability says something of philosophical relevance. The previous position does not preclude the claim that Nature forces us to be irrational, to hold beliefs which we can see it is irrational to hold. Reid's position implies instead that Nature forces us to believe without rational justification, but not unreasonably. It argues that the inevitability of lapses from the

[25] *God and Skepticism*, p. 36.
[26] Ibid., p. 37.
[27] Ibid., p. 36. Arne Naess similarly argues that scepticism is a disposition: 'Psychologically, scepticism must be considered a stable disposition, even if a momentary state of mind may hide it and even be inconsistent with it' (*Scepticism*, p. 14). Cf. also pp. 26–8, but note that he makes the rather implausible suggestion that 'one must surely allow that the exercise of suspension of judgment as a mental act need not go so far as to colour the sceptic's private life' (p. 27).

meta-philosophical position (i.e. lapses from the theoretical commitment) indicates that we cannot sustain the view that the sceptical suspense is reasonable. It argues that it is not unreasonable to believe what we have no reasonable ground for doubting—no ground, that is, more sure than the belief to be doubted. Reid's view, to repeat, argues not only that we cannot entirely suspend first-order beliefs, but that we cannot sustain the theoretical commitment consistently—either because we cannot maintain the reasonableness of the doubt once we leave the study, or because *even* in the study we cannot maintain it.

As noted earlier, it is precisely this which Reid seems to have in mind when he writes not only of Hume that 'it was only in solitude and retirement that he could yield any assent to his own philosophy' (101-2: I,§5), but, taking the point even further, he continues:

It is probable the 'Treatise of Human Nature' was not written in company; yet it contains manifest indications that the author every now and then relapsed into the faith of the vulgar, and could hardly, for half a dozen pages, keep up the sceptical character. (102: I,§5)

Reid's point is that such lapses are inevitable, not merely that they occur. He therefore argues for a conflict within the realm of theory as well as for inconsistency between meta-level belief and action. He argues, *contra* Penelhum, that (1) though we can minimize our going out of the study, we cannot avoid it entirely, and (2) even inside the study we cannot maintain the sceptical belief. He argues, that is, that we cannot sustain the belief that the sceptical doubt is reasonable, and he explains why. Newman likewise challenges the coherence of the sceptical requirement, and goes further, making that incoherence more explicit by questioning the status of the opposite requirement of 'trust' in our faculties. Both Reid and Newman appeal to 'common sense' in terms of the distinction between reasonable doubt and unreasonable (though possible) doubt, and it should be clear by now that theirs was not a naïve, uncritical, or anti-philosophical appeal.[28] This should show how

---

[28] I am here taking issue with Penelhum's comment: 'One cannot throw away the skeptic's ladder without first climbing it. In this Skepticism resembles other anti-philosophical philosophies, like those of Hume and Wittgenstein, and differs fundamentally from those of Reid and Moore, who extol the philosophical wisdom they find among non-philosophers' (*God and Skepticism*, p. 10).

off the mark is Leslie Stephen's caricature of such an appeal, when he writes:

Our English sobriety and unwillingness ... to make fools of ourselves, has checked our philosophical ambition. We have, it may be, too much sense of humour not to be even pusillanimously afraid of the ridicule which awaits the daring adventurer when he falls back to earth from attempts to soar above the atmosphere. One consequence is that, in England, attempts at *a priori* philosophy have taken the form of an appeal to common sense. We cannot be exposed to ridicule when we are ostensibly endeavouring to confirm everybody's opinion.[29]

[29] *History*, Vol. I, p. 61. Stephen echoes Kant's critical comments on common-sense philosophy. Kant writes that Reid and the others 'were ever taking for granted that which he [Hume] doubted, and demonstrating with zeal and often with impudence that which he never thought of doubting' (*Prolegomena to Any Future Metaphysics* (Indianapolis, 1950), p. 6. He considered the appeal to common sense a 'convenient method of being defiant without any insight', but on the same page speaks of the legitimate rights of common sense with respect to 'judgements which apply immediately to experience'. Other references to common sense are equally double-edged (pp. 24, 25, 100, 118, 119, 120).

Select Bibliography

Books

Aristotle. *The Nicomachean Ethics*. Translated by Sir David Ross. London: Oxford University Press, 1954.
——. *Works*. Edited by W. D. Ross. Oxford: Clarendon Press, 1928. *Analytica Posteriora*, translated by G. R. G. Mure. *Topica De Sophisticis Elenchis*, translated by W. A. Pickard-Cambridge.
Barker, Stephen and Beauchamp, Thomas, eds., *Thomas Reid: Critical Interpretations*. Philadelphia: Philosophical Monographs, 1976.
Boekraad, A. J. and Tristram, H. *The Argument from Conscience to the Existence of God According to Newman*. Louvain: Editions Nauwelaerts, 1961.
Butler, Joseph. *Analogy of Religion, Natural and Revealed, to the Constitution and Course of Nature*. London: George Bell and Sons, 1889.
Chillingworth, William. *The Works of William Chillingworth*. 12th edn. Philadelphia: Reverend R. Davis, 1841.
French, D., *et al.*, eds. *Midwest Studies in Philosophy* V. Minneapolis: University of Minnesota Press, 1980.
Glanvill, Joseph. *Essays on Several Important Subjects in Philosophy and Religion*. London: J. D. for John Baker, 1676.
Grave, S. A. *The Scottish Philosophy of Common Sense*. Westport, Conn.: Greenwood Press, Publ., 1973. First published by the Clarendon Press, Oxford, 1960.
Hacking, Ian. *The Emergence of Probability*. Cambridge: Cambridge University Press, 1975.
Haecker, Theodor. *Vergil, Vater des Abendlandes*. Leipzig: Jakob Hegner, 1931.
Hick, John. *Faith and Knowledge*. Ithaca: Cornell University Press, 1957.
Howell, Wilbur Samuel. *Eighteenth Century British Logic and Rhetoric*. Princeton: Princeton University Press, 1971.
——. *Logic and Rhetoric in England, 1500-1700*. Princeton: Princeton University Press, 1956.
Hume, David. *Dialogues Concerning Natural Religion*. Edited by R. H. Popkin. Indianapolis: Hackett Publishing, 1980.
——. *Enquiries Concerning the Human Understanding and Concerning the Principles of Morals*. Edited by L. A. Selby-Bigge. Oxford: Clarendon Press, 1975.

Hume, David. *A Treatise of Human Nature*. Edited by L. A. Selby-Bigge. Oxford: Clarendon Press, 1978.

——. *Letters of David Hume*. Edited by J. Y. T. Grieg. Vol. I. Oxford: Oxford University Press, 1932.

Huxley, Aldous. *Proper Studies*. London: Chatto & Windus, 1957.

Kames [Kaims], Henry Home, Lord. *Sketches of the History of Man*. Dublin: United Company of Booksellers, 1775.

Kant, Immanuel. *Prolegomena to Any Future Metaphysics* (1783). Indianapolis: Bobbs-Merrill Company, Inc., 1950.

Locke, John. 'Of the Conduct of the Understanding.' In *Works*, Vol. III, 11th edn. London: W. Otridge and Son, *et al.*, 1812 (pp. 185–265).

——. *Essay Concerning Human Understanding*. Edited by Peter Nidditch. Oxford: Clarendon Press, 1975.

——. *Works*. Vol. IV. 11th edn. London: W. Otridge and Son, *et al.*, 1812.

Louth, Andrew. *Discerning the Mystery*. Oxford: Clarendon Press, 1983.

Marcil-Lacoste, Louise. *Claude Buffier and Thomas Reid: Two Common-Sense Philosophers*. Kingston: McGill-Queen's University Press, 1982.

Naess, Arne. *Scepticism*. London: Routledge & Kegan Paul, 1968.

Newman, John Henry. *Apologia Pro Vita Sua*. Edited by Martin J. Svaglic. Oxford: Clarendon Press, 1967.

——. *Discourses Addressed to Mixed Congregations*. London: Longmans, Green, and Co., 1892.

——. *An Essay in Aid of A Grammar of Assent*. London: Longmans, Green, and Co., 1901.

——. *An Essay on the Development of Christian Doctrine*. Edited by J. M. Cameron. Harmondsworth, Middlesex: Penguin Books, 1973.

——. *Fifteen Sermons Preached Before the University of Oxford—1826–43*. London: Longmans, Green, and Co., 1892.

——. *The Idea of a University*. Edited by Ian T. Ker. Oxford: Clarendon Press, 1976.

——. *Lectures on the Present Position of Catholics in England*. London: Longmans, Green, and Co., 1908.

——. *Letters and Diaries of John Henry Newman*. Edited by C. S. Dessain *et al*. Vols. I–VI (Oxford: Clarendon Press, 1978–84), Vols. XI–XXII (London: Thomas Nelson and Sons, Ltd., 1961–72), Vols. XXIII–XXXI (Oxford: Clarendon Press, 1973–7).

——. *Parochial and Plain Sermons*. Vol. I. London: Longmans, Green, and Co., 1894.

——. *Philosophical Notebook*. Vol. II. Louvain: Editions Nauwelaerts, 1970.

——. *Stray Essays on Controversial Points*. Birmingham: privately printed, 1890.

Newman, John Henry. *The Theological Papers of John Henry Newman on Faith and Certainty.* Edited by J. Derek Holmes and Hugo de Achaval, SJ. Oxford: Clarendon Press, 1976.

Newsome, David. *Two Classes of Men.* London: John Murray, 1974.

Norton, David Fate. *David Hume: Common Sense Moralist and Sceptical Metaphysician.* Princeton: Princeton University Press, 1982.

Pappas, George S. and Swain, Marshall, eds. *Essays on Knowledge and Justification.* Ithaca: Cornell University Press, 1978.

Peirce, C. S. *Charles S. Peirce: Selected Writings.* Edited by Philip P. Wiener. New York: Dover Publishing, 1958.

——. *Philosophical Writings of Peirce.* Edited by Justus Buchler. New York: Dover Publishing, 1955.

Penelhum, Terence. *God and Skepticism.* Dordrecht: Reidel Publishing, 1983.

——. *Hume.* New York: St Martin's Press, 1975.

Popkin, Richard H. *The High Road to Pyrrhonism.* San Diego: Austin Hill Press, 1980.

——. *The History of Skepticism from Erasmus to Spinoza.* Berkeley: University of California, 1979.

Price, Richard. *A Review of the Principal Questions of Morals* (1787) Edited by D. D. Raphael. Oxford: Clarendon Press, 1974.

Reid, Thomas. *The Collected Works of Thomas Reid, D.D.* Edited by William Hamilton. London: Maclachlan and Stewart, 1852.

——. *An Inquiry into the Human Mind.* Edited by Timothy Duggan. Chicago: University of Chicago Press, 1970.

——. *Essays on the Intellectual Powers of Man.* Edited by A. D. Woozley. London: Macmillan and Co., Ltd., 1941.

——. *Lectures on Natural Theology* (1780). Edited by Elmer Duncan. Washington, DC: University of America Press, 1981.

Rescher, Nicholas. *Scepticism: A Critical Appraisal.* Totowa, New Jersey: Rowman and Littlefield, 1980.

Rorty, Richard. *Philosophy and the Mirror of Nature.* Princeton: Princeton University Press, 1979.

Schulthess, Daniel. *Philosophie et sens commun chez Thomas Reid 1710–1796.* Berne: Peter Lang, 1983.

Sciacca, Michele Federico. *La Filosofia di Tommaso Reid.* 3rd edn. Milan: Carlo Marzorati, 1963.

Seth (Pringle-Pattison), Andrew. *The Scottish Philosophy: A Comparison of the Scottish and German Answers to Hume.* Balfour Lectures, 3rd edn. Edinburgh: Wm. Blackwood and Sons, 1889.

Shapiro, Barbara J. *Probability and Certainty in Seventeenth-Century England.* Princeton: Princeton University Press, 1983.

Sillem, Edward J. *Philosophical Notebook of John Henry Newman.* Vol. I. Louvain: Editions Nauwelaerts, 1969.

Stephen, Sir Leslie. *An Agnostic's Apology.* London: Smith, Elder, and Co., 1903.

——. *History of English Thought in the Eighteenth Century.* Vol. I. 3rd edn., 1902. Reprint New York: Harcourt, Brace & World, 1962.

Stove, D. C. *Probability and Hume's Inductive Scepticism.* Oxford: Clarendon Press, 1973.

Stroud, Barry. *Hume.* London: Routledge & Kegan Paul, 1977.

Tillotson, John. *Works.* Vol. III. 4th edn., by Ralph Barker. London: Printed for John Darby, 1728.

——. *Works.* 9th edn., 1 vol. London: Printed for J. Round, 1728.

Van Leeuwen, Henry G. *The Problem of Certainty in English Thought, 1630–1690.* The Hague: Martinus Nijhoff, 1963.

Waismann, Friedrich. *The Principles of Linguistic Philosophy.* Edited by R. Harré. London: Macmillan, 1965.

Walgrave, J. H. *Newman the Theologian.* Translated by A. V. Littledale. New York: Sheed & Ward, 1960.

Ward, Wilfrid. *Life of J. H. Cardinal Newman.* Vol. I. New York: Longmans, Green, and Co., 1912.

White, Alan R. *Modal Thinking.* Oxford: Basil Blackwell, 1975.

Wilkins, John. *Of The Principles and Duties of Natural Religion.* 7th edn. London: Printed for R. Bonwicke, 1715.

Willam, Franz W. *Aristotelische Erkenntnislehre bei Whately und Newman.* Freiburg: Herder, 1960.

Wittgenstein, Ludwig. *On Certainty.* Edited by G. E. M. Anscombe and G. H. von Wright. Translated by Denis Paul and G. E. M. Anscombe. New York: Harper and Row, 1969.

——. *Philosophical Investigations.* Translated by G. E. M. Anscombe. New York: Macmillan, 1958.

Woolhouse, R. S. *Locke.* Brighton, Sussex: Harvester Press, 1983.

Articles

Ardal, P. S. 'Some Implications of the Virtue of Reasonableness in Hume's Treatise.' In *Hume: A Re-evaluation*, edited by D. W. Livingston and J. T. King. New York: Fordham University Press, 1976.

Artz, Johannes. 'Newman's Philosophische Leistung.' In *International Newman Studien* X, edited by H. Fries and W. Becker. Heroldsberg bei Nürnberg: Glock und Lutz, 1978.

Barnes, Jonathan. 'Aristotle's Theory of Demonstration.' In *Articles on Aristotle: 1, Science*, edited by Jonathan Barnes, M. Schofield, and Richard Sorabji. London: Duckworth, 1975.

Beanblossom, Ronald E. 'Russell's Indebtedness to Reid.' *The Monist* 61 (1978), 192–204.

——. 'Introduction' to *Thomas Reid's Inquiry and Essays*. Edited by Keith Lehrer and Ronald E. Beanblossom. Indianapolis: Bobbs-Merrill, Inc., 1975.

Beauchamps, T. and Mappes, T. 'Is Hume Really a Sceptic About Induction?' *American Philosophical Quarterly* 12 (1975), 119–29.

Bellesheim, A. 'Newman'. In *Wetzer und Welt's Kirchenlexicon: Encyclopädie der Katholischen Theologie*. Freiberg: Herder, 1895.

Bernard, J. H. 'The Predecessors of Bishop Butler.' *Hermathena* IX (1894–6), 75–84.

Bonjour, Lawrence. 'Externalist Theories of Empirical Knowledge.' In *Midwest Studies in Philosophy* V, edited by D. French *et al.*

Brody, Baruch. 'Hume, Reid and Kant on Causality.' In *Thomas Reid: Critical Interpretations*, edited by Stephen Barker and Thomas Beauchamp.

Burnyeat, Myles. 'Aristotle on Understanding Knowledge.' In *Aristotle on Science, the Posterior Analytics*, edited by Enrico Berti. Padua: Editrice Antenore, 1981.

——. 'Can the Skeptic Live His Skepticism?' In *The Skeptical Tradition*, edited by Myles Burnyeat. Berkeley: University of California Press, 1983. First printed in *Doubt and Dogmatism: Studies in Hellenistic Epistemology*. Oxford: Clarendon Press, 1980.

Cargile, James. 'In Reply to "A Defense of Scepticism".' In *Essays on Knowledge and Justification*, edited by George S. Pappas and Marshall Swain. First printed in *The Philosophical Review* 81 (1972), 229–36.

Carnap, Rudolf. 'Empiricism, Semantics, Ontology.' In *Meaning and Necessity*. 2nd enlarged edn. Chicago: University of Chicago Press, 1956.

Connon, R. W. 'The Naturalism of Hume Revisited.' In *McGill Hume Studies*, edited by D. F. Norton *et al.* San Diego: Austin Hill Press, 1979.

Duchesneau, François. 'Locke et Le Savoir de Probabilité.' *Dialogue* XI (1972), 185–203.

Ferreira, M. Jamie. 'A Common Defense of Theistic Belief: Some Critical Considerations.' *International Journal for Philosophy of Religion* 14 (1983), 129–41.

——. 'Newman's Theory of Perception: Realism or Representationalism?' Forthcoming in *Philosophical Studies*.

Hacking, Ian. 'Hume's Species of Probability.' *Philosophical Studies* 33 (1978), 21–37.

Hanfling, Oswald. 'Hume and Wittgenstein.' In *Impressions of Empiricism*, edited by Godfrey Vesey. New York: St Martin's Press, 1976.

Huxley, T. H. 'Agnosticism.' *The Nineteenth Century* XXV (Feb. 1889), 169–94.

Huxley, T. H. 'Agnosticism and Christianity.' *The Nineteenth Century* XXV (June 1889), 937–64.

Imlay, Robert. 'Hume's *Of Scepticism with Regard to Reason*: A Study in Contrasting Themes.' *Hume Studies* 7 (Nov. 1981), 121–36.

Jessop, Thomas. 'Hume: Philosopher or Psychologist? A Problem of Exegesis.' *Rivista Critica di Storia Della Filosofia* (1967), 418–34.

Jones, Peter. 'Strains in Hume and Wittgenstein.' In *Hume: A Re-evaluation*, edited by D. W. Livingston and J. T. King. New York: Fordham University Press, 1976.

Laudan, L. L. 'Thomas Reid and the Newtonian Turn of British Methodological Thought.' In *The Methodological Heritage of Newton*, edited by Robert E. Butts and John W. Davis. Blackwell: Oxford, 1970.

Lehrer, Keith. 'Why Not Scepticism?' In *Essays on Knowledge and Justification*, edited by George S. Pappas and Marshall Swain. First printed in *The Philosophical Forum* 2.3 (1971), 283–98.

Marcil-Lacoste, Louise. 'Dieu garant de véracité ou Reid critique de Descartes.' *Dialogue* XIV (1975), 584–605.

Murphy, John L. 'The Influence of Bishop Butler on Religious Thought.' *Theological Studies* (1963), 361–401.

Pappas, George S. 'Some Forms of Epistemological Scepticism.' In *Essays on Knowledge and Justification*, edited by George S. Pappas and Marshall Swain.

Passmore, J. 'Hume and the Ethics of Belief.' In *David Hume: Bicentenary Papers*, edited by G. P. Morice. Edinburgh: Edinburgh University Press, 1977.

Popkin, Richard. 'David Hume: His Pyrrhonism and his Critique of Pyrrhonism.' In *Hume*, edited by V. C. Chapell. Notre Dame: Notre Dame University Press, 1968. First printed in *The Philosophical Quarterly* 1 (1951), 385–407.

——. 'David Hume and the Pyrrhonian Controversy.' In *The High Road to Pyrrhonism*, edited by Richard A. Watson and James E. Force. San Diego: Austin Hill Press, 1980. First printed in *The Review of Metaphysics* 6 (1952), 65–81.

Raynor, David, 'Hume's Mistake—Another Guess.' *Hume Studies* 7 (Nov. 1981), 164–6.

Raynor, Owen. 'Hume's Scepticism Regarding "Probable Reasoning" in the *Treatise*,' *Southern Journal of Philosophy*. (Fall, 1964), 103–6.

Robinson, J. 'Newman's Use of Butler's Arguments.' *Downside Review* (1958), 161–80.

Sosa, Ernest. 'The Raft and the Pyramid.' In *Midwest Studies in Philosophy* V, edited by D. French *et al.*

Stove, D. C. 'Part IX of the *Dialogues*.' *Philosophical Quarterly* 28 (1978), 300–9.

Stroud, Barry. 'The Significance of Skepticism.' In *Transcendental Arguments and Science*, edited by Peter Bieri. Dordrecht: Reidel Publishing, 1979.

——. 'Transcendental Arguments.' In *Kant on Pure Reason*, edited by Ralph Walker. Oxford: Oxford University Press, 1982.

Unger, Peter. 'A Defense of Skepticism.' In *Essays on Knowledge and Justification*, edited by George S. Pappas and Marshall Swain. First printed in *The Philosophical Review* 80 (1971), 198–218.

Verbeke, Gérard. 'Aristotelian Roots of Newman's Illative Sense.' In *Newman and Gladstone: Centennial Essays*, edited by James D. Bastable. Dublin: Veritas Publishers, 1978.

Vernier, Paul. 'Thomas Reid on the Foundations of Knowledge and His Answer to Skepticism.' In *Thomas Reid: Critical Interpretations*, edited by Stephen Barker and Thomas Beauchamp.

Wolterstorff, Nicholas. 'Can Belief In God Be Rational If It Has No Foundations.' In *Faith and Rationality: Reason and Belief in God*, edited by Alvin Plantinga and Nicholas Wolterstorff. Notre Dame: Notre Dame Press, 1983.

Unpublished Works

Lyons, James W. 'A Philosophical Critique of Certitude According to Newman.' Ph.D. dissertation, Loyola University, 1975.

Reid, Thomas. *The Philosophical Orations of Thomas Reid, 1753–62*. Edited by D. D. Todd. Translated by Shirley M. Darcus, 1977. From the Latin manuscript edited by W. R. Humphries, Aberdeen, 1937.

——. Aberdeen. King's College Library. Birkwood Manuscripts [Thomas Reid].

Walgrave, J. H. 'J. H. Newman, His Personality, His Principles, His Fundamental Doctrines.' Leuven: Katholieke Universiteit, 1975–7.

Wolterstorff, Nicholas. 'Thomas Reid on Rationality.'

Index

a priori methodology 2, 126-7, 207-11, 230-3

'a priori philosophy' 232, 242

acting-as-if 72-3, 183

agnosticism, in Reid and Newman 169-70, 170 n.

agreement *see* universal agreement

Analogy of Religion 66

anatomy 8, 57, 125-6, 128, 233

Apologia Pro Vita Sua 145

Ardal, Pall 53, 57

Aristotle: authority of general agreement 28; first principles 105-7, 167; influence of Reid's critique of 199; moral conditioning necessary for right reasoning 193; Newman's selective appropriation of 198-203, 206; notion of phantasm 230; phronesis 94, 175, 201; principle of suiting proof to subject-matter 19, 22, 34-6, 40; Reid's lack of appreciation of his agreement with 94; syllogistic paradigm 83, 86 n., 105, 145, 198

Artz, Johannes 146 n., 177 n.

assent: freedom of 21, 191, 193; in proportion to evidence 26, 36 n., 76-8; necessity of 17-20, 33, 37-8; to appearances 236; to first principles 156, 163-5; seventeenth-century position 13-14, 16-23, 36, 70; unconditional 179, 208

Bacon, Francis 127, 147, 211

Baconian/Newtonian methodology 93, 127

Barnes, Jonathan 93 n., 201 n.

Beauchamps, T. 52 n.

Berkeley, Bishop 87, 147, 193

Bernard, J. H. 28 n., 67 n.

Boekraad, A. J. 194 n., 213 n., 222 n.

Bonjour, Lawrence 110 n.

Boyle, Robert 65

'Brief Account of Aristotle's Logic' 73, 86 n., 92, 105, 199 n., 203 n.

Brody, Baruch 232 n.

Burnyeat, Myles 93 n., 236-7

Butler, Bishop Joseph 28 n., 66-9, 147, 182, 184-7, 196, 209, 228-9

cable, image of *see* certainty

Cargile, James 229 n.

Carnap, Rudolf 138 n.

Cartesian appeal to God, Reid's critique of 123

certainty: 'absolute term' 229; analytic paradigm of 44 n., 198, 235; and illative sense 174, 177; as equivalent to 'Truth' 24; as interchangeable with 'knowledge' 21; cable image of 182, 186-9, 199; conditionally infallible 13, 17-18, 25; contrasted with certitude 172 n.; demonstrative paradigm of 91, 94-5, 194; dependent on context 87; distinguished from infallibility 82-3, 189; does not require absolute indubitability 90, 195; indubitable 16-18; infallible 13, 16-18, 25; Locke's position on 11; mathematical-logical 13-14; moral 1-2, 10-14, 17-18, 21-2, 25, 27-8, 31-3, 36, 63, 65-8, 70-1, 179-80, 185, 194; non-demonstrative 3, 64, 67, 78, 91-2, 95-6, 148-9, 172, 178-80, 187, 199, 202, 206-7, 228, 235; only reasonable doubt precludes 3-4, 227; physical 13-14, 17; practical 72-3, 183-6, 230; rope image of 65, 67, 75-7, 82, 182, 187-8; speculative 21, 72, 98, 132, 183-4, 186, 201, 210, 223; syllogistic paradigm of 198; threshold concept of 25, 76, 187, 227

Chillingworth, William 1, 3, 16-17, 22, 32, 34, 94, 189 n., 198, 227

circularity: of sceptical challenge 142-3, 221; of syllogism 92, 200

common language: authority of 118-19, 195; limits of 119; Reid's departure from 64

common notions 30, 140, 233